PENGUIN BOOKS

THE CONTEST OF THE CENTURY

'As Geoff Dyer observes in his stellar book, China is adopting a more expansive vision of its national interests and modernizing its military to match that vision. The challenge is to distinguish between those policies of Beijing that any other rising power would develop and those that could fundamentally alter the post-war global order'
Ali Wyne, *The Wall Street Journal*

'Assessing China's growing rivalry with the U. S., the author, a former Beijing bureau chief for the *Financial Times*, does not subscribe to the idea of a "linear transfer" of power from the U. S. to China . . . he thinks that the contest with China will come to define U. S. foreign policy, and that America's interests are best served by fiscal and military restraint' *The New Yorker*

'Original ideas and illuminating insights . . . a simple but persuasive explanation for why a geopolitical contest between the United States and China will dominate the new century . . . a very timely book that has a clear and sophisticated argument. For the cottage industry of books on contemporary Chinese foreign relations, *The Contest of the Century* has definitely set a new and more demanding standard'
Minxin Pei, *San Francisco Gate*

'Provides a corrective to the lately fashionable gloom-and-doom analysis . . . Impressive' *The National Interest*

'A colourful and compelling read that offers three crucial insights. America's relationship with China will define the twenty-first century. Their relations will be far more subtle and dynamic than post-Cold War conventional wisdom suggests. There is nothing inevitable about either China's rise or the outcome of the two countries' competition. This is a fascinating story from an experienced journalist who knows how to tell it'
Ian Bremmer, author of *Every Nation for Itself*

'Illuminating . . . Dyer's lively prose, vivid reportage, and long experience reporting on the country really shine, making this one of the most lucid, readable, and insightful of the current rise-of-China studies' *Publishers Weekly*

Geoff Dyer is an award-winning journalist and the *FT*'s former Beijing bureau chief. Now in the Washington DC bureau, he writes about American foreign policy. A former Fulbright scholar, he studied at Emmanuel College, Cambridge and the Johns Hopkins School of Advanced International Studies.

GEOFF DYER

The Contest of the Century

The New Era of Competition with China

PENGUIN BOOKS

PENGUIN BOOKS

Published by the Penguin Group
Penguin Books Ltd, 80 Strand, London WC2R 0RL, England
Penguin Group (USA) Inc., 375 Hudson Street, New York, New York 10014, USA
Penguin Group (Canada), 90 Eglinton Avenue East, Suite 700, Toronto, Ontario, Canada M4P 2Y3
(a division of Pearson Penguin Canada Inc.)
Penguin Ireland, 25 St Stephen's Green, Dublin 2, Ireland (a division of Penguin Books Ltd)
Penguin Group (Australia), 707 Collins Street, Melbourne, Victoria 3008, Australia
(a division of Pearson Australia Group Pty Ltd)
Penguin Books India Pvt Ltd, 11 Community Centre, Panchsheel Park, New Delhi – 110 017, India
Penguin Group (NZ), 67 Apollo Drive, Rosedale, Auckland 0632, New Zealand
(a division of Pearson New Zealand Ltd)
Penguin Books (South Africa) (Pty) Ltd, Block D, Rosebank Office Park,
181 Jan Smuts Avenue, Parktown North, Gauteng 2193, South Africa

Penguin Books Ltd, Registered Offices: 80 Strand, London WC2R 0RL, England

www.penguin.com

First published in the United States of America by Alfred A. Knopf 2014
First published in Great Britain by Allen Lane 2014
Published in Penguin Books 2015
001

Printed in Great Britain by Clays Ltd, St Ives plc

ISBN: 978-0-718-19462-8

www.greenpenguin.co.uk

Penguin Books is committed to a sustainable
future for our business, our readers and our planet.
This book is made from Forest Stewardship
Council™ certified paper.

For Angelica and Jack

CONTENTS

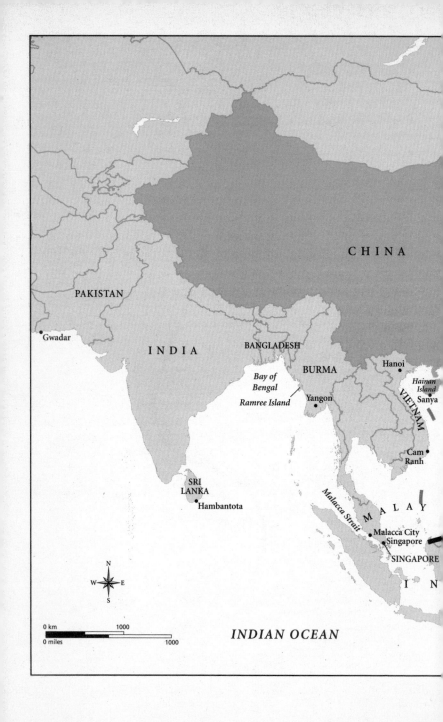

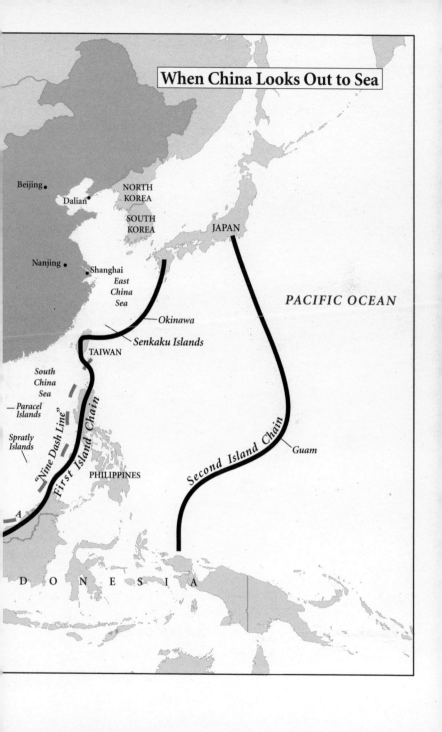

When China Looks Out to Sea

Beijing

Dalian

NORTH
KOREA

SOUTH
KOREA

JAPAN

Nanjing

Shanghai

*East
China
Sea*

PACIFIC OCEAN

—Okinawa

Senkaku Islands

TAIWAN

*South
China
Sea*

—*Paracel
Islands*

*Spratly
Islands*

"Nine Dash Line"

First Island Chain

Second Island Chain

—*Guam*

A

PHILIPPINES

D O N E S I A

THE
CONTEST
OF THE
CENTURY

Introduction

BEIJING WAS IN a state of heightened anxiety and had been for weeks. Each day in the run-up to the National Day parade, the security measures seemed to get a little bit tighter. Our apartment building had a distant view of Jianguomen, which is the main east-west avenue that runs through the center of Beijing, traversing Tiananmen Square along the way, and which was to be the main parade route. During rehearsal the Sunday before, we were told not to go onto our balconies. "What happens if we do? Will we be shot?" a neighbor jokingly asked. The building manager replied in a deadpan manner, "Maybe; who knows?" All the pigeons in the city were locked up and kite flying was banned, presumably to prevent undesirable threats to the safety of airspace. On the day itself, the two blocks on either side of the route were closed off to passersby. The 2009 event was to be the sixtieth anniversary of the foundation of the People's Republic of China, the first parade in a decade, and only the fifth time since the 1950s that such an event had been held. But, unlike in previous October 1 parades, no ordinary people were allowed to line the route and watch the festivities. The center of Beijing was hermetically sealed off from the city's residents. For everyone but the invited crowd of VIPs and journalists, this was a television-only spectacle. Despite the country's booming wealth, China's rulers can often seem insecure, looking anxiously over their shoulders at the people they govern. In the weeks leading up to the parade, they had conducted a crackdown on human-rights lawyers, and three months later they ordered an eleven-year jail sentence for Liu Xiaobo, the democracy activist who would later win the Nobel Peace Prize. The heavy-handed security was fruit of this nervy mindset.

A few hours before the parade was to start, I watched a stream of maybe fifty, maybe one hundred buses pass by, all with a regulation thirty meters in between them. The first group stood out because of the bright clothes of the excited young people inside—this bus orange, that one green, another blue. The next group were filled with soldiers in dress uniform, some trying to catch a last-minute nap, their heads pressed against the glass. With precision timing, they were being ferried to their starting places for a three-hour-long spectacle which was at times intimidating, at times impressive, and at times folksy, but never anything but meticulous. Like the morning mist, which lifted to make way for bright sunshine, the pre-parade paranoia quickly evaporated. By midday, two hundred thousand soldiers and civilians had taken part in the procession, and I did not see a single foot put wrong. It was a display that mixed North Korean mass choreography with the sort of swagger the Soviets used to muster for May Day. The kids in colored T-shirts that I had seen on the buses filled the vast expanse of Tiananmen Square to hold up cards that formed gigantic phrases: "Obey the Party's Command," "Be Loyal to the Party," and "Long Live the Motherland." For an hour, the military showed off the very latest of its hardware, the product of two decades of double-digit spending increases. There were the J-10 fighter jets, China's first homegrown jets, and a long line of DF-31A intercontinental ballistic missiles, which have the range to hit Los Angeles, and which the Xinhua News Agency later described as "remarkable symbols of China's defense muscle." A decade before, much of the weaponry on display had been bought from Russia; this time it was all developed at home.

Military parades have been a feature of Chinese statecraft for centuries. During the Qing dynasty (1644 to 1912), victory ceremonies were often organized for the emperor to demonstrate his authority, and under the Communists they have been revamped for television. Geremie Barmé, an Australian expert on Chinese culture, recalls that in 1984, which also happened to be the year of Deng Xiaoping's eightieth birthday, a group of students from Peking University held up an impromptu sign during the parade that said "Hello Xiaoping." As this was not in the script, the television cameras missed it. Once the event had finished, the spontaneous greeting was restaged and edited into the official broadcast. In 2009, the television highlight was the contingent from the Beijing Women's Militia, who marched in precise fashion past the podium in red miniskirts and knee-high white boots, and who, Chinese media later revealed, were all models specially chosen for their uniform height. The main audience for the parades was the domestic one, which was to be both entertained and cowed by the organizational capacity of the Chinese state. But China is too big and too important for such an event to go unnoticed overseas. China's leaders knew that images of its bristling military display would be beamed around the planet and seemed untroubled if the outside world was also a little intimidated. "It represents the realization of the great revival of the Chinese nation as a result of tireless struggle," as the army described the event.

Before the military parade reached Tiananmen Square, the soldiers stopped in a long column along the main avenue to be reviewed by then President Hu Jintao. He was standing in the back of a Red Flag, China's homegrown limousine, his head and upper body visible through the sunroof as it drove past the troops. Hu, a gray bureaucrat skilled at the inner workings of the party, went out of his way to cut a dour public profile, an almost deliberate anti–cult of personality. Dressed in a Mao tunic buttoned to the top, and with his dyed black hair immaculately coiffed, he seemed at first to have a slightly comic air, and I chuckled when a colleague quipped about his resembling an Austin Powers villain. Yet, as he boomed into the microphone in front of him *"Tongzhimen hao"* ("Greetings, comrades") and *"Tongzhimen xinku le"* ("Thanks for all the suffering, comrades"), his voice, echoing all around the vast square, was a little chilling. Stern-faced, he returned to the podium at the gate of the Forbidden City, right above the giant oil portrait of Mao Zedong, and stood on the same spot where sixty years earlier Mao had declared that the "Chinese people have stood up." Flanked on both sides by the other eight members of the Communist Party's Standing Committee, the body that really runs the country, all dressed in dark business suits with red ties, Hu addressed the crowd. "Today a socialist China, geared toward modernization, the world, and the future, stands rock-firm in the East," he declared. It was his biggest applause line.

Just over two decades before, the same square had been the scene of bloodshed. In the streets surrounding Tiananmen, Chinese soldiers massacred hundreds—maybe thousands—of Beijing residents as they tried to clear the student-led protests. Realizing their legitimacy had been called into question, Chinese leaders would sit somewhat meekly for years afterward as foreigners lectured them on the need to change their political system. Bill Clinton once told his counterpart, Jiang Zemin, that the Chinese Communist Party was "on the wrong side of history." The scars from those events contributed to a desire among China's leaders to maintain a low profile overseas and to focus on development at home. Shortly after the massacre, Deng Xiaoping devised his famous slogan to define Chinese foreign policy, advising his colleagues to *taoguang yanhui*—literally, "hide the brightness and nourish obscurity." Deng knew that the resurgence of China's economy would stir anxieties in the U.S. and across Asia, where many festering rivalries remain—even more so after the 1989 display of authoritarian muscle in Tiananmen. Deng realized that only by emphasizing humility and a willingness to cooperate could China develop its economy without provoking a regional and international backlash. For two decades, China looked inward and focused on rebuilding.

Yet, sitting under the baking sun in Tiananmen Square that morning, I felt Hu Jintao was delivering a very different message—the words of a risen China, not a rising China. He was telling the country and the world not only that the Communist Party was still very much in charge, but that it was also pursuing a path that was moral and right. China, he suggested, was now an important nation with legitimate interests, and it would not be afraid to defend them. Nations do not change tack overnight, of course, but the parade brought to the surface powerful forces that had been building for some time. It represented a symbolic turning point in modern Chinese history, when it became hard to ignore the way the Deng Xiaoping formula of self-restraint was crumbling and the new era of geopolitical competition with the United States that was emerging. The socialist rock in the East wanted to escape from the shadow of the West.

———

This is a book about the new age of rivalry. It is about why China now wants to start exerting influence around the world and about the growing competition with the U.S. that will be the single most important factor in world politics over the coming decades. If globalization has been the driving force over the last few decades—in fact, since China embarked on its economic reforms in the late 1970s, after the death of Mao—then there is now a powerful force pulling in the opposite direction, an old-fashioned struggle for influence and power between China and the U.S., the two most important nations in the world.

The Contest of the Century revolves around three central points.

The first is that China has started to make the crucial shift from a government that accepts the existing rules to one that seeks to shape the world according to its own national interests, from rule taker to rule maker. Beijing is starting to channel its inner great power. The book provides a portrait of the new Chinese mentality, the energies, ambitions, and tensions that are pushing China in this direction. Much of the discussion of modern China focuses on the nature of the Communist Party and its hold on power, and, indeed, it is impossible to detach ideology from the way China relates to the rest of the world. But China is also responding forcefully to the same sort of instincts that have animated new great powers in the past, with particularly strong echoes from both the U.S. and late-nineteenth-century Germany. "History does not repeat itself, but it does rhyme," as Mark Twain is often quoted as saying—even though it is not clear that he ever did.

Second, to pursue those goals, China is inevitably finding itself pulled into a geopolitical competition with the U.S., the country in whose image much of the global order is fashioned. China and the U.S. are starting to contest the high ground of international politics, from control of the oceans in Asia to the currency that is used in international business. Forget their bland rhetoric: China's leaders think very much in geopolitical terms and would like to gradually erode the bases of American power. Almost every important global issue will find itself colored by this rivalry. Yet it will not be the win-at-all-costs ideological struggle of the Cold War. Instead, this will be an older, more fluid form of rivalry that is based on balance of power and building coalitions of support.

Finally, I will argue that the U.S. is in a strong position to deflect this new Chinese challenge to its position in the world. Whether they have come to praise or to warn about China's rise, most authors on China subscribe to an almost linear transfer of wealth and influence from West to East, from a U.S. in decline to an irrepressible China. There is an air of inevitability in the way China is presented. Yet the roots of American power are deeper than they seem and hard to overturn. If the U.S. can clean its own financial house and avoid the temptations of either confrontation or isolation, it will still hold many of the best cards in the twenty-first century.

———

"Great power" is a phrase with an old-fashioned, dusty feel to it, something from the history textbooks to do with the Schleswig-Holstein Question or the assassination of Archduke Franz Ferdinand. The age of the great power seemed to have passed with the Cold War and America's unipolar dominance that followed the fall of the Berlin Wall. Yet the rise of China strikes many notes from a very different era. "No nation has ever experienced such an increase in its power without seeking to translate it into global influence," Henry Kissinger once wrote about the U.S. in the late nineteenth century. Today's China is animated by the same energies that stirred in the U.S. from the 1890s, when it announced itself to the world. At home, new great powers are possessed by an economic dynamism and a zeal for grand engineering, by the construction of modern cities and the laying of vast railway networks across continents. Before long, that energy takes them overseas, where their companies develop trading posts and factories across the globe. They feel the need to use their new economic power to strengthen their own security, to fend off potential rivals, and to protect their overseas interests—a mixture of pride and fear that leads them to build grand navies. As their standing grows, they try to mold the political, military, and economic rules that govern the international system. Rising wealth creates rising expectations among a new middle class that wants its rulers to stand up for their country. The material benefits of a growing economy are never enough for aspiring great powers—they also want respect, recognition, and influence. Power changes countries, just as it changes people.

When America started staking its claim in the world in the 1890s, it was propelled in part by a growing centralization of power in the presidency. The horrors of the Civil War had given way to a fragmented political environment in the 1870s and 1880s, with neither the executive nor Congress able to establish control of foreign policy. America's international role only started to be transformed when the White House began to exert more decisive influence in the 1890s. In China, something close to the opposite has happened. The last decade has seen what might be described as a fracturing of power in China in ways that have begun to have a decisive influence over the country's foreign policy. China's leaders have not abandoned Deng Xiaoping's advice to keep a low profile—on the contrary, they regularly insist that it remains their guiding principle. Instead, the Deng consensus is being gradually overwhelmed by the reality of modern-day China and its society. Deng's cautious strategy is slowly fraying. Fragmentation of power is not the same as political liberalization, of course, but, rather, a dispersal of influence within the elite. It means that China's senior leaders do not enjoy the almost untrammeled authority that Deng once enjoyed. They face powerful vested interests within the party-state, and an officer class that has its own hawkish take on global affairs. They also have to keep an anxious eye on the nationalist views of a rising middle class. On airport bookshelves in China these days, alongside the Jack Welch and Bill Gates biographies, you can now find titles such as Xue Yong's *How to Be a Great Power,* a sort of Cliff Notes for modern geopolitics. All these voices are pushing China to be more ambitious overseas. China remains resolutely authoritarian, but these days, it also has a lot more politics.

To think about China as a great power might seem obvious to readers who have watched the swagger and military buildup of recent years, but it goes against the two most dominant interpretations of what really drives modern China.

The first is what one might call the Davos view, after the home of the World Economic Forum, the contention that China's leaders are so obsessed with economic development at home that they have little time for or real interest in getting too involved in the affairs of the world. Even if they did want to push harder against the U.S., so the argument goes, they would soon be confronted with the reality of the enormous economic interdependence between the two countries. It is easy to see why such a view would take hold. Achieving high rates of growth has been the singular achievement of China's Communist leaders over the last two decades and their principal justification for maintaining an iron grip on power. And for Davos optimists, globalization has transformed international politics, creating a web of economic connections and dependencies that prevent any country from rocking the boat. Geopolitics, with its emphasis on competition and struggle between nations, has been rendered unnecessary by the multinational global economy. In China, there is a cottage industry of scribes developing slogans to impress the rest of the world with how unthreatening its rise really is—from the "Shanghai smile" and "win-win" economic cooperation to "peaceful development." ("Peaceful rise" was taken up at one stage, but then dropped when it was deemed to be too threatening.) In *The Post-American World,* which is in some ways the most influential international-relations book of recent years in the West, Fareed Zakaria writes that the Chinese are too pragmatic to let the vanities of power politics damage their economic interests. "The veneration of an abstract idea is somewhat alien to China's practical mind-set," he writes.

Yet, when even the most materialistic countries arrive at a certain scale and economic reach, they feel they have no choice but to try and influence events beyond their shores. China's epic urbanization push is being fueled by goods from the four corners of the earth—by oil from Saudi Arabia, by coal from Indonesia, by iron ore from Brazil, and by copper from the Congo. For the first time in its millennial history, China's economic interests are genuinely global, and it needs a foreign policy to match them. Deng Xiaoping's "hiding the brightness" is no longer sufficient. To keep its economy humming, China feels it needs to start molding the world it is operating in. China's economy relies on the continued safety of seaborne trade—something which has been guaranteed since the end of the Second World War by the navy of the United States, the country which the Chinese elite mistrusts the most (with the possible exception of Japan). Like other great powers before it, China is building a navy to take to the high seas because it does not want to outsource the security of its economic lifelines to someone else. The problem-solving China so heralded at Davos is being replaced by something with much harder edges. In short, geopolitics is back.

The second brand of conventional wisdom holds that the regime in Beijing is too insecure about its hold on power at home to think seriously about challenging the U.S. The brittleness is everywhere to be seen, from the heavy-handed security at the 2009 National Day parade to the periodic arrests of dissidents to the opacity of the political process. One of the most commonly cited factoids about modern China is that Beijing actually spends more money on internal security than it does on its defense budget, even though military spending has been rising sharply. But what this explanation misses is that domestic insecurity is feeding, not inhibiting, the desire to stand tall overseas. In one way or another, the Chinese Communist Party has been suffering a legitimacy crisis since it abandoned Marx and embraced the market in the late 1970s, and that crisis has been more acute since the Tiananmen Square Massacre in 1989. The party has tried to fill this gap in all sorts of ways. Economic growth and a reputation for competent governance have been the main props. But China's leaders have also buttressed their legitimacy with an appeal to a nationalism that is tinged with a sense of victimhood. Brittle politics at home are stimulating a more assertive voice abroad.

In the end, thinking of China as an aspiring great power is the best way to demystify the country, to resist the temptation to either demonize or exoticize. China is neither an anti-democratic hegemon launching a new Cold War, as its more conservative critics suggest, nor the postmodern, Confucian meritocracy that some supporters imagine. China is, instead, a state which is behaving in many of the same ways that other states have behaved when they started to become very powerful.

———

It is an indication of the influence of Deng Xiaoping's *taoguang yanhui* formula that it has simultaneously been attacked by hard-liners at home and inspired fear abroad. The advice was kept secret at first, and to this day, there are differing accounts of the full text that he wrote. In the 1990s, the phrase was heavily criticized by Chinese leftists who thought it a sop to the U.S. Yet for many foreign audiences, it had a different feel. The official translation in China is "hide the brightness and nourish obscurity"; however, in the U.S., the same words have often been translated as "bide one's time," a phrase that contains a certain menace about future intentions. For Deng, the ambiguity was a way of keeping different groups happy. He always knew that a powerful China would start competing for power and influence with the U.S. He just wanted to put off the rivalry for as long as possible.

Such self-restraint has become harder to sell since 2008. A year before Hu Jintao stood up to speak in Tiananmen at the parade, Lehman Brothers had collapsed. The psychological fallout from the global financial crisis was particularly important in China, where predictions about inevitable American decline have taken deep root. Within the Chinese elite, there has been a long-standing argument about how China should behave toward the U.S. when China became a powerful nation: the doves said that China would be best served by playing along with the U.S.-led international system, while the hawks said China would need to stand up to the U.S. Yet it was a debate held in suspended animation. Everyone knew that Beijing would have to answer this question one day, but the priority for the time being was to focus on the building up of what Chinese officials call "Comprehensive National Power." Just as 9/11 empowered American neoconservatives, the financial crisis ended the shadow boxing in Beijing and unleashed powerful demands within parts of the elite to begin taking on the U.S. The time to answer the question, the hawks demanded, was now.

To warn about growing competition, however, is not to predict conflict, especially in an era when nuclear deterrence provides a powerful brake on both nations. There are no Chinese plans for the sort of territorial expansion that scarred Europe in the late nineteenth century, or for a project of global domination. Instead, Beijing has more subtle, long-term instincts about gradually undermining the foundations of American power and influence, starting in Asia and moving outward. International-relations scholars like to ask whether new powers will rise within the existing order or try to overthrow it. But neither explanation captures China's behavior. Instead, Beijing is beginning a process of gradually trying to mold the system in its own direction, to shape rather than tear down. Chinese leaders understand the limitations that globalization places on them, and the benefits that thirty years of trading with the U.S. have brought, but they are also far more skeptical and resentful about American influence than most in Washington realize. There is nothing surprising about what China is now doing. If anything, the surprise is that it did not start sooner.

Competition between the U.S. and China is usually thought of in terms of the location of a factory or the value of exchange rates, but that is rivalry at the retail level. The real contest for power and influence is over the geopolitical high ground: the rules, institutions, and power dynamics which dictate how the world really works. The core of this book will be about the three different fronts on which the competition will take place—military, political, and economic.

The first section focuses on the military contest in Asia, where China's new navy is beginning to challenge the dominance of the U.S. in the western Pacific, setting up one of the defining stories of the coming decades. The tussle that is developing for control of the seas surrounding China is in some ways the central contest, because naval power can create the conditions to shape political and economic realities. Chapter 1 will look at the reasons behind China's naval modernization, the historical and geopolitical anxieties together with the changing role that the military occupies within the Chinese system. Chapter 2 looks at whether China will seek to strike out as a naval power into the Indian Ocean, and Chapter 3 examines the deep backlash that China has provoked in Asia. Chapter 4 analyzes America's response to China's Asian ambitions.

The second section examines the political challenge that China is now presenting. One chapter looks at China's huge investments in soft power; other explores the impact that China's rigid ideas about state sovereignty are having on the way human rights are treated by the international community. Before that, Chapter 5 provides a slight detour into the psychology of China's new assertiveness, looking at the particular form of nationalism which has sprung up over the last two decades and which is the emotional crutch for the desire to challenge the West.

The final section focuses on two different ways in which China is threatening to rewrite the rules of the global economy, first through its plans to challenge the U.S. dollar, and second through the coming boom in Chinese finance and investment, which has the potential to reshape globalization.

———

Of course, Beijing is not the only capital gripped by talk of American decline. Washington, too, is full of fin-de-siècle anxiety, the result of the global financial crisis which laid bare a wealth of much deeper, unresolved problems in the economy and a political system that seems allergic to addressing long-term problems. "The Desperate States of America," as the German magazine *Der Spiegel* calls the U.S.; or, as the former Morgan Stanley analyst David Roche puts it, "Wall Street's crack-up presages a global tectonic shift: the beginning of the decline of American power." America's huge budget deficits and debt levels mean that the risk of a much deeper crisis and a collapse in the credibility of the U.S. dollar is a very real one. And all this is taking place while Washington watches the seemingly unstoppable rise of China. It has become a favorite parlor game among economic pundits to predict the year when the Chinese economy will overtake the U.S. to become the biggest in the world. Some believe it could happen within a decade.

The declinists are correct about two things. America's ability to project power will depend on bringing its long-term debt under control and restoring its reputation as the most innovative large economy in the world. A decade of economic stagnation would derail many aspects of its foreign policy. It is also clearly true that the world has changed in important ways. China's rise is only the most visible example of a diffusion of economic power toward the developing world, which includes India, Brazil, Indonesia, and a host of other nations. The unipolar era that the U.S. enjoyed after the end of the Cold War was always an aberration, and it is quickly coming to an end. If the U.S. strives to maintain the kind of military dominance it has enjoyed for the last two decades, installing China as the new enemy to scare up budgets, it will be in big trouble. Yet the obsession with the *sorpasso* moment, when China's economy becomes the world's biggest, confuses the way power is wielded in international politics. There will be no new military parade in Beijing on the day when China's economy overtakes that of the U.S., no handover ceremony to usher in a new leader. Power and influence are not transferred, like a property title: they have to be earned.

When you start looking at the world through Chinese eyes, it is striking how deeply entrenched American influence begins to appear, and how difficult it will be for China to overturn it. America's alliances are solid and its core political values still widely shared. At the same time, with a political system that strangles creativity, China lacks the tools to project around the world its own ideas about good governance and the good life. The market for Chinese military and diplomatic power is also much smaller than many in Beijing realize, especially in Asia. The harder China pushes, the more likely it is that a coalition of neighbors will emerge, with the U.S. at the helm, to restrain its ambitions. China risks becoming a very lonely great power.

Instead of American decline, the bigger question is whether Washington can sustain broad international support for the system of free trade, freedom of navigation, and international rules it put in place after the Second World War. The rise of China and the other new powers means a return to a world where a balance of power is the natural state of affairs, with the U.S. still the most important nation but unable to dictate terms. Instead of rigid alliances, there will be fluid coalitions that shift depending on the issue. On occasion, China and the U.S. will be on the same side, but more often than not they will be opposed and Washington should have no illusions about China's willingness to push back against American leadership. The most influential state will be the one that is best at setting agendas, mobilizing support, and which comes across as the more reasonable. This should be an environment that suits the U.S., which for decades has shown a flair for the patient work of sustaining alliances and coalitions. But Washington will have to find new ways to work together with Europe, which will remain a natural partner, and to establish stronger ties with India, Brazil, and some of the other new swing voters of international politics. If the U.S. wants to retain its role at the center of international affairs, it will have to convince enough countries that its ideas still work. A quest for continued military dominance will not do the trick: Washington needs to enlist new partners. This is the real challenge that China laid down at its National Day parade in Tiananmen Square.

Section I

MILITARY IN ASIA

I

---·---

China Takes to the Near Seas

To THE LIST of industries now dominated by China, there is one surprising new entry: Miss World. Beauty contests were banned in China by Mao Zedong as one of the worst forms of Western decadence, but their bland internationalism appeals to modern China's desire to be included. Of the last nine Miss World pageants, five have been held in China, all at the seaside resort of Sanya, on subtropical Hainan Island, off China's south coast. Sensing a great way to boost tourism, the local government spent $30 million to build a special venue for the contest, the Beauty Crown Theater, a huge arena near a man-made beach which is shaped like, well, a crown. When it opened in 2003, the winner was Rosanna Davison, a nutritional therapist from Dublin whose father, Chris de Burgh, wrote the syrupy global smash hit "Lady in Red." Qi Guan, a Chinese model who wore a flowing red ball-gown for the evening's finale, was the second runner-up. Her compatriot Zhang Zilin went one better in 2007, winning China's first Miss World title.

When the Miss World show is in town, the swimsuit photo shoots take place across the road, at the Sanya Sheraton Hotel, which looks out onto the white sands of Yalong Bay, a crescent-shaped cove lined with palm trees. With a Ritz-Carlton on one side and a Marriott on the other, Yalong Bay is a transplant of multinational tourism on China's southernmost point. The resort has become hugely popular with prosperous

Chinese families, who escape the urban grind for a few days of sun that before would have required a trip to Thailand. On the beach, I met one couple from Jiangxi Province who were sporting his and hers Hawaiian shirts and shorts. On the winter day when I traveled, it was minus nine degrees Celsius (not quite sixteen degrees Fahrenheit) when the plane left Beijing, and a balmy twenty-three degrees Celsius when we arrived three hours later in Sanya, a reminder of the continental size of China. The Sheraton is also a popular escape for well-to-do Russians living in eastern Siberia. On the menu at the Lotus Café, which is surrounded by a landscaped Japanese-style koi pond, the Sheraton Club Sandwich is offered in English, Mandarin, and Russian.

That day, the hotel was hosting a corporate retreat for the Chinese subsidiary of Syngenta, a multinational based in Switzerland which sells genetically modified seeds. The hundred or so employees spent the afternoon playing games on the beach, including the confidence-building drills in which one person falls back into the arms of a colleague. "Trust your partner, trust your partner," the master of ceremonies shouted. Having fun on the beach, they barely looked up when a Chinese Type 054 frigate sailed casually across the bay, in plain view of the tourists. Yalong Bay, it turns out, has a double life. The brand-name hotels occupy only one half of the beach; at the other end lies China's newest and most sophisticated naval base.

Yalong Bay is where the two sides of China's rise now intersect, its deeply connected economy and its deep-seated instinct to challenge America—globalization China and great-power China vying for a spot on the beach. Celebrating their success in the China market, the Syngenta employees at the Sheraton all wore T-shirts emblazoned with the English-language slogan for their event: "Step Up Together." Yet right next door to their party was one of the most striking symbols of China's great-power ambitions. Ideally situated for quick access to the busy sea-lanes of the South China Sea, the base in Hainan is one of the principal platforms for an old-fashioned form of projecting national power, a navy that can operate well beyond a country's coastal waters. For the last couple of decades, such power politics seemed to have been made irrelevant by the frictionless, flat world of globalization. Yet Yalong Bay demonstrates a different reality. It is one of the launchpads for what will be one of the central geopolitical tussles of the twenty-first century—the new era of military competition in the Pacific between China and the U.S.

———

The Asia-Pacific region is now the most dynamic economy in the world and accounts for around half of all output, an intricate network that takes software and design from California, tiny microchips from Japan, and sophisticated screen technology from South Korea, and assembles them into iPads in a factory in southern China. Given that nearly 90 percent of intercontinental commerce travels by ship, Asia's seas have become the principal arteries of the global economy. If there is a symbol that defines the era of globalization, it is the container ship. Traveling the long sea-lanes west from Asia toward Europe and east toward the U.S., the biggest ships now carry as many as seven thousand containers, stacked eight rows high. The enormous economies of scale that container ships offer have made it possible to manufacture socks and televisions in Asia and then sell them at low cost in Walmart or Primark. The ease and safety with which these hulking ships, the length of four football fields, travel safely across the world's oceans is what makes the global economy tick. Freedom of navigation is the unwritten label on the modern consumer economy.

Two very different visions of Asia's future are now in play. Since the defeat of Japan in 1945—and especially since the end of the Cold War—the United States Navy has treated the Pacific Ocean as almost a private lake. It has used that power to implement an international system in its own image, a rules-based order of free trade, freedom of navigation, and, when possible, democratic government. That Pax Americana was cemented in June 1971, when Henry Kissinger pulled Richard Nixon away from a state dinner for the president of Nicaragua and showed him a secret cable from Chinese Premier Zhou Enlai in which Beijing agreed to a face-to-face meeting between the leaders of the two countries. "This is the most important communication that has come to an American president since the end of World War Two," Kissinger told Nixon, with his customary mixture of grandiloquence and flattery. The four decades since Nixon met Mao Zedong have been the most stable and prosperous in Asia's modern history. Under the agreement, the U.S. endorsed China's return to the family of nations, and China implicitly accepted American military dominance in Asia.

In many ways, China has been the biggest beneficiary of this system. History is full of examples of rising powers which have complained that the existing rules were rigged against them. In the first decades of the last century, Germany and Japan found themselves squeezed out of important aspects of the global economy as the major powers used their imperial networks to guarantee the essential raw-material supplies they needed for their economies. The roots of both world wars lay partly in this friction. However, since the late 1970s, China has been able to use the very openness of the U.S.-led order to promote its extraordinary growth. China has been allowed to insert itself into an international trading system which has clear and established rules, and it has been able to buy the oil, copper, and iron ore that it needs on global markets. Now the world's biggest exporter of manufactured goods, China has a vast seaborne trade that is underpinned by the calming influence of American naval dominance.

Never written down or officially announced, this understanding between Beijing and Washington on America's role in Asia is crumbling. China now wishes to recast the military and political dynamic in the region to reflect its own traditional centrality. Great powers are driven by a mixture of confidence and insecurity. China wants a return to the leadership position it has enjoyed so often in Asian history. It also frets about the security of its seaborne commerce, especially in the area it calls the "Near Seas"—the coastal waters that include the Yellow, East China, and South China Seas. The Yalong Bay naval base on Hainan Island is one part of the strategy that China is starting to put in place to exert control over the Near Seas, an effort to push the U.S. Navy ever farther out into the western Pacific. In the process, it is launching a profound challenge to the U.S.-led order that has been the backbone of the Asian economic miracle.

Although the Chinese navy's name—the People's Liberation Army Navy, or PLAN—betrays the fact that it was once the poor cousin of the army, for the last twenty years China has been undergoing a rapid military buildup, and the navy has been given pride of place. More important, China has been investing in its navy in a very specific way. China's naval planners have focused on the warships, silent submarines, and rapid small boats which form the basis of what the U.S. Navy calls "access denial." The clear implication of the investment plan is that China is trying to prevent the U.S. Navy from operating in large areas of the western Pacific. China's new navy is both an expression of power and a means to a diplomatic end. By weakening the U.S. naval presence in the western Pacific, China hopes to gradually undermine America's alliances with other Asian countries, notably South Korea, the Philippines, and maybe even Japan. As American influence declines, China would be in a position to quietly assume a leadership position in Asia, giving it much greater influence over the rules and practices in the principal arena of the global economy. Through its navy, China hopes to reshape the balance of power in Asia.

Countries compete for influence in all sorts of ways, over economic rules and political philosophies, but the military arena is the most important. If allowed to blossom, military rivalries have the capacity to calcify all other interactions between the countries. Compromise is hard for political leaders when senior generals are muttering dark warnings in their ears. That makes the emerging contest in the western Pacific one of the central global issues over the coming decades. It will be a crucial test for how the U.S. and China manage their emerging great-power rivalry. It will also be a laboratory for many of the questions about China's rise—how Beijing intends to pursue its leadership aspirations in the region, and whether, in an era of fiscal retrenchment and political polarization, U.S. global influence still has staying power. The naval competition in the western Pacific will set the tone for a large part of global politics.

———

Aspiring great powers have often taken to the high seas as a route to expanded influence. The U.S., U.K., Spain, Venice, and even ancient Athens all built powerful navies to defend their far-flung interests. In the late nineteenth century, Germany was gripped by the allure of constructing a grand navy, prompting Kaiser Wilhelm II to establish the special rank for himself of *Großadmiral* (great admiral). Sea power is not just about control of the seas; it is also a tool to influence other countries and to shape events. Superior sea power allowed the Europeans to begin asserting control over Asia in the fifteenth century, led first by the Portuguese, and it has enabled outside countries to dictate terms in the region ever since. It was through sea power that a small country like Britain, with only a modest army, could command an empire that covered a quarter of the globe. More recently, domination of the Pacific and Indian Oceans since the end of the Second World War has allowed America to be the preeminent power in Asia. American naval power, combined with the air superiority that comes from a large fleet of aircraft carriers, has been the backbone of its effort to spread free trade and democratic values throughout the region.

Navy building can explain a lot about a nation's intentions, its ambitions, and its anxieties. Long lead times mean that naval planners are not thinking about tomorrow; they are placing bets on how the world will look in one, two, or three decades' time. Navies can also provide a grandeur that beguiles some countries. Hu Jintao defined the development of Chinese naval power in 2006 as a "glorious task"; Rear Admiral Wu Shengli, commander of the Chinese navy, described the quest for a strong fleet as part of "the great revitalization of the Chinese nation." The same sentiments are echoed by popular military commentators. "When we look at history, we can see [that] whether a country is powerful or not is closely related with its naval forces," writes Major General Luo Yuan of the China Military Science Society. "When its naval forces are powerful, then the country is strong; when its naval forces are weak, then the country is also fragile." In 2009, the year when the Chinese Communist Party celebrated its sixtieth anniversary with the grand military parade in Beijing, the navy had their own parade earlier in the year. Fifty-two vessels took part in special review at the east-coast port of Qingdao, including previously unseen nuclear submarines. In many ways, it was a coming-out party for China's new navy.

For anyone who grew up during the Cold War, it can be tempting to see all this as an ideological contest. There is a deep chasm in political values between Washington and Beijing that heightens the sense of competition between the two governments. The U.S. believes the Chinese political system is in some sense illegitimate, while the Chinese insist—not without some justification—that the U.S. would like to see a form of regime change in China. Yet one of the striking aspects of China's turn to the seas is that it is rooted in history and geography in a manner that transcends its current political system. It was from the sea that China was harassed during its "century of humiliation" at the hands of the West. China was one of the most prominent victims of nineteenth-century gunboat diplomacy, when Britain, France, and other colonial powers used their naval supremacy to exercise control over Shanghai and a dozen other ports around the country. The Opium Wars were principally a naval exercise: During the first war, in 1840, the British navy was able to deploy the *Nemesis,* a steamship made of iron whose large guns bombarded Chinese defenses. China learned the hard way that having a weak navy leaves a country vulnerable to pressure and bullying by others. The instinct to control the surrounding seas is partly rooted in the widespread desire never to leave China so vulnerable again. "Ignoring the oceans is a historical error we committed," says Yang Yong, a Chinese historian. "And now even in the future we will pay a price for this error."

This sense that China is under siege is aggravated by looking at a map. Chinese talk about the "first island chain," a perimeter that stretches around the western Pacific from Japan in the northeast, through Taiwan, to the Philippines in the south, all allies or friends of the U.S. This is both a geographical barrier, in that it creates a series of channels that a superior opponent could block in order to bottle up the Chinese navy, and a political barrier controlled by governments close to Washington. For a country that wants to start flexing a few of its muscles, this map makes China deeply uncomfortable; it is almost hemmed in from the sea. Chinese strategists talk about "breaking through the thistles," the development of a naval capability that will allow it to operate outside the barrier of the first island chain they think the U.S. has constructed to keep China contained. *The Science of Military Strategy,* a 2005 statement of the PLA's military doctrine, says that if the navy is kept within the first island chain, "the essential strategic space for China's rejuvenation will be lost." Zhang Wenmu, a well-known and hawkish writer on naval issues, argues, "Restricting China to the shallow seas west of the first island chain is both unfair and impossible and China simply cannot accept it."

When China looks out to sea, it also quickly sees the U.S. According to Chu Shulong, an academic at Tsinghua University, this grudge with the U.S. has grown stronger in recent years, as the Chinese navy has expanded. In the decades when China had little more than a coast guard, it was largely unaware that the U.S. Navy was patrolling waters near its shores. But now that its capabilities are more advanced, it witnesses on a daily basis that the American navy is superior, and operating only a few miles from many of China's major cities. "For them, this is a major humiliation that they experience every single day," says Chu. "It is humiliating that another country can exercise so close to China's coasts, so close to the base in Hainan. That is the reason the navy wants to do something to challenge the U.S."

Anxieties about history and geography have meshed with broader concerns about economic security. One of the key turning points in China's push to the high seas took place when China became a net importer of oil for the first time, in 1993. By 2010, China had become the biggest consumer of energy in the world and the second-biggest consumer of oil, half of which is now imported. A Chinese company has built the largest oil tanker in the world, a 333-meter-long vessel called the *Xin Buyang*, which carries three hundred thousand tons of oil each time it travels from the Middle East. New great powers often fret that rivals could damage their economy with a blockade. Such warnings have become common in China over the last decade. For every ten barrels of oil that China imports, more than eight travel by ship through the Strait of Malacca, the narrow sea channel between Indonesia, Malaysia, and Singapore, which is patrolled by U.S. ships. Fifteenth-century Venetians used to warn, "Whoever is the Lord of Malacca has his hand on the throat of Venice." Hu Jintao echoed similar sentiments when he warned in a 2003 speech that "certain major powers" are bent on controlling this crucial sea-lane. Until now, China's maritime security has been guaranteed largely by the U.S. Navy. But, like aspiring great powers before it, China has been forced to confront a central geopolitical dilemma: can it rely on a rival to protect the country's economic lifeline?

———

China's naval buildup may be directed at the U.S., but in lots of ways it has also been modeled on the U.S. At the very least, it should come as no surprise to the U.S. that an aspiring great power should seek to exert greater control over its regional waters. From the early days of the American republic, strategists in Washington fretted about the presence of the old European powers in the Americas. In 1823, these anxieties were given an official stamp when President James Monroe declared that the American continents were "henceforth not to be considered as subjects for future colonization by any European powers." In effect, America put up a large "Stay Out" sign over the hemisphere. It is a natural instinct of rising powers to try and establish a buffer that prevents the more established powers from threatening their security. Like China today, America then worried about the risk of a blockade of its economy, or that a European power might organize a coalition among its neighbors to contain its rise. Like Chinese leaders today, American politicians in the nineteenth century took geopolitics very seriously while all the time professing disdain for the old European games of power politics. And, like China today, America was planning for the long term. The Monroe Doctrine was more bluff than fact for over half a century after it was announced. Britain continued to interfere in and occasionally colonize parts of the Americas for much of the nineteenth century. Even by the 1880s, Chile, Brazil, and Argentina all had larger navies than the U.S. It was not until the 1890s, when America started to establish a world-class navy, that it was able to genuinely enforce the Monroe Doctrine—a crucial point not lost on the Chinese today.

Indeed, China's naval push is drawing heavily on American influences. In 1890s America, one of the most important evangelists of naval power was Alfred Thayer Mahan, an undistinguished naval captain who had started to plot a maritime history while whiling away some days at the English Club in Lima, Peru. The book he eventually wrote, *The Influence of Sea Power upon History, 1680–1783,* turned out to be one of the most influential of his generation when it was published in 1890, with the aid of a $200 personal loan from J. P. Morgan, and helped convince Washington of the need for a big navy. Mahan had two major themes. The first was about the virtues of building a naval force that could fight "decisive battles" against prospective rivals, thereby ensuring the command of the seas that can guarantee national greatness. The second was a more nuanced geopolitical theory about the importance of controlling the sea-lanes that are vital to a nation's commercial life.

In the West, if Mahan is remembered at all today, it is largely for the first set of ideas, which have cast him as one of the warmongers of his age. The notion of applying "overbearing naval power" was taken seriously not only in the U.S. but also in Germany, where Kaiser Wilhelm was a big fan and ordered a copy of his great work placed in every battleship. ("I am . . . devouring Captain Mahan's book and am trying to learn it by heart," he once said.) When the Kaiser met with his naval officers for drinks, they would make toasts to "The Day," the chance they craved to show off their newfound naval strength in one do-or-die battle with the dominant maritime power of the age, the British navy. Mahan died just after the outbreak of the First World War, and his obituary in the *New York Times* said that his writings were "really responsible for the German Navy as it exists today." Sir Charles Webster, the British historian and wartime diplomat, once claimed, "Mahan was one of the causes of the First World War"—a charge from which his name has never completely recovered.

But in today's China, it is the geopolitical aspects of Mahan's writing that are greatly admired, the relationship between expanding commercial interests and naval power. Just as China worries about the Strait of Malacca and the first island chain, Mahan obsessed about building a canal across the Isthmus of Panama and about having naval capabilities in both the Caribbean and the Pacific to defend America's new commercial arteries. He pushed for the U.S. to acquire bases in the Caribbean, to allow U.S. ships to control access to the Panama Canal. For Mahan, sea power was a crucial aspect of economic development. The ability to secure sea-lanes and the critical geographical locations that facilitate commercial traffic "affects the very root of a nation's vigor." Mahan's ideas from the 1890s echo many of the challenges the Chinese see today, the mixture of a quest for national greatness and insecurity about economic lifelines at sea. The "Near Seas" is a formulation that has a strong Sinocentric ring to it, with its implication of a form of Chinese historical ownership, but it also embodies Mahan's vision for a country to secure its vital maritime frontiers.

Neglected at home, Mahan has become deeply fashionable over the last decade in Chinese intellectual circles, including translations of his books, academic articles on their importance, and conferences on his ideas. He has inspired a generation of Chinese navalists. "A big country that builds its prosperity on foreign trade cannot put the safety of its ocean fleet in the hands of other countries," writes Ye Hailin, of the Chinese Academy of Social Sciences. "Doing so would be the equivalent of putting its throat under another's dagger and marking its blood vessels in red ink."

One publisher released an edition of Mahan's *The Influence of Sea Power* with a fold-out map of the Asia-Pacific that included all the U.S. naval facilities in the region. James Holmes and Toshi Yoshihara, two American historians who have tracked Mahan's influence in China, write: "His sea power philosophy remains hypnotic. . . . The Mahanian conceit that national greatness derives from sea power beguiles many Chinese strategists." As a result, they conclude: "We should therefore expect China to attach extraordinary value to fighting and winning in the waters that fall within the near-seas."

The U.S. and China have already indulged in some potentially dangerous sparring in the Near Seas—the sort of thing that in the Cold War was known as "nautical chicken." In March 2009, the USNS *Impeccable*, a surveillance ship, was on an operation around seventy nautical miles from the new submarine base in Hainan when it was confronted by a flotilla of ten different Chinese ships. The Chinese crew dropped planks into the water to obstruct the American ship's movements. When it braked, the Chinese sailors then used long poles to smash the surveillance instruments it was towing behind the ship. As the American ship retreated from the area, it was shadowed and harassed for some time. When the Chinese ships decided to take their leave, the crew of one boat dropped their pants and waved their bare bottoms in the direction of the Americans.

The confrontation was significant not just because of the risk that it might have escalated, but because it amplified one of the big underlying political issues in the western Pacific. China's new naval capabilities are interlaced with a broader political strategy designed to exert more control over its maritime reaches. Beijing's most extravagant claim is in the South China Sea, where a series of islets, reefs, and rocks are disputed by a number of countries, including Vietnam, the Philippines, and China. Beijing argues it has a historical right to be the dominant power in the area, a claim expressed in China's now famous "nine-dash-line" map, which assumes ownership of 80 to 90 percent of the South China Sea. (Chapter 3 will have a more detailed discussion of some of these disputes.) At the same time, China is pushing a version of international law which would potentially give it the right to exclude foreign militaries from large sections of the seas that surround it. A United Nations convention called the Law of the Sea tries to codify rules for national ownership of the world's oceans. The law gives countries an "exclusive economic zone"—or EEZ—that runs two hundred nautical miles from their coastline, where they have the rights to resources in the water or under the seabed. According to the U.S.—and a majority of other governments—there is a right to freedom of navigation in this zone that includes military vessels. However, China is the leading member of a smaller but significant group of countries which think that foreign militaries should be excluded from their EEZ unless they have permission. In particular, China objects to surveillance vessels operating too near to its coast, just as the U.S.'s *Impeccable* was doing.

Taken together, the two claims have huge implications. China argues that many of the islands in the South China Sea qualify to have their own exclusive economic zones, even though some are no more than largely submerged rocks and many are administered by other countries. As a result, China argues that most of the South China Sea is part of its exclusive economic zone. If it takes control of all the islands, and if its legal interpretation of the Law of the Sea stands, China would be giving itself the political case to turn away the vessels of foreign navies from most of the South China Sea. Given the centrality of the sea to the global economy, this is a far-reaching claim that has enormous implications for everyone in the region—and especially for the United States. Although China's ultimate aims are still not entirely clear, the evidence of growing ambitions is unnerving the U.S. military. "China is knowingly, operationally and incrementally seizing maritime rights of its neighbors under the rubric of a maritime history that is not only contested in the international community but has largely been fabricated," Captain James Fanell, deputy chief of staff for intelligence for the U.S. Pacific Fleet told a conference in 2013. He described an intelligence briefing he attends every morning at 6 a.m. which brings together the U.S. military's leading Asia-Pacific analysts. "Every day it is about China," he said, adding: "They are taking control of maritime areas that have never before been administered or controlled in the last 5,000 years by any regime called 'China.' . . . China's conduct is destabilizing the Asian maritime environment."

Even with these claims, it might seem improbable that China would seek to tamper with the right to freedom of navigation. China has been an enormous beneficiary of open seas; its economy is based on the free flow of imported raw materials into the country and the export of manufactured products. The assumption among many governments in the region had always been that, even if China would defend its territorial claims fiercely, it would not let those political disputes contaminate its booming commercial links with the rest of the region. Few worried that China would use its growing power to act as a toll keeper of naval traffic in the western Pacific.

Yet confidence in such an assumption is gradually beginning to weaken. Over the last few years, China has shown a willingness to use a form of economic blackmail and bullying during political disputes that raises real questions about how it would behave if it were ever to control the sea-lanes through the South China Sea. During a standoff with Tokyo in 2010, after the Japanese coast guard arrested a Chinese fisherman who had rammed one of its vessels in disputed waters, China limited exports to Japan of rare earths—a group of commodities which China controls and which are central to the manufacture of many products, such as cell phones. When ships from China and the Philippines clashed in 2012 over control of a small island in the South China Sea, Beijing refused to accept imports of bananas from the Philippines, leaving large shipments to rot in a harbor. The local government on Hainan Island has declared it has the power to board vessels which "illegally enter" Chinese waters—one in a string of announcements that have added to the sense of uncertainty about how China will use its growing power. The expansive and ambiguous claims China has made in the South China Sea, combined with its willingness to hold trade hostage to political arguments, have, at the very least, raised questions about freedom of navigation in the region. As Peter Dutton, a U.S. expert on maritime law, argues, China's approach to the Near Seas has already created "hairline fractures in the global order."

———

Shortly before he retired as head of the U.S. Pacific Command in 2009, Admiral Timothy Keating revealed a conversation he had had with a senior Chinese naval officer, who effectively offered to split the Pacific with the U.S. "You, the US, take Hawaii East and we, China, will take Hawaii West and the Indian Ocean," Keating recalled the officer, whom he refused to name, as saying. "Then you will not need to come to the western Pacific and the Indian Ocean and we will not need to go to the eastern Pacific. If anything happens there, you can let us know and if something happens here, we will let you know." Keating admitted that the offer was perhaps made "tongue-in-cheek," but it was revealing. One reason that tensions in the region are rising is the substantial gap between U.S. and Chinese views of America's natural role in Asia. For many in China, a U.S. retreat from the region is an inevitable response to the revival of Asia. Yet the view is very different from Washington. Since the early years of the republic, the western Pacific has played a large role in America's sense of its own security.

America's first Pacific alliance was signed as far back as 1833, a full two decades before Commodore Matthew Perry more famously first set anchor in Japan. President Andrew Jackson sent a sloop-of-war called the USS *Peacock* on a mission around parts of the South China Sea, including a stop at the kingdom of Siam, modern-day Thailand. During the visit, his envoy, Edmund Roberts, signed the Siamese-American Treaty of Amity and Commerce with a representative of King Rama III. Jackson sent as a present a sword whose gold handle had an elephant and an eagle emblazoned on it. The pool of people at the time in either country who spoke both Siamese and English was almost nonexistent, so, in order to make sure the treaty would not be questioned, it was also translated into Chinese and Portuguese.

The prominence of the Pacific in the American mind accelerated sharply in the 1890s, in the era of Mahan and another of his disciples, Theodore Roosevelt, who a century before Barack Obama was really America's first Pacific president. Roosevelt was the first to predict that Asia would become a center of global power, initially as a result of the rise of Japan, but later as China and India caught up. And he placed the maintenance of a favorable balance of power in Asia at the center of America's priorities. "The commerce and command of the Pacific will be factors of incalculable moment in the world's history," Roosevelt predicted.

America's Pacific role did not fall temporarily into its lap at the end of the Second World War and the decline of the British Empire, nor is it a product of the Cold War. Instead, it is much more deeply rooted in the U.S.'s own history and vision of the world. Over the last century, America has defined its vital interest as preventing any one power from dominating the other main regions of the world and turning them into a private sphere of influence, whether in Europe or in Asia. The U.S. eventually fought the First and Second World Wars because it did not want Germany to dominate Europe—and, in the second war, also to stop Japan from controlling Asia. Washington's ultimate goal in the Cold War was to prevent the Soviet Union from exercising control across the whole of Eurasia.

It should come as no surprise that the rise of China is beginning to stir something deep in the American psyche. Relative decline or not, Washington will be determined to prevent any other country from dominating such a central part of the world. China's naval push strikes to the core of how America understands both its security and its prosperity. The Obama administration's desire to "pivot" toward Asia, as the wars in Iraq and Afghanistan end, might seem like a new departure to address the rise of China, but it is also a very traditional American response to a shifting balance of power in Asia. Unless America suffers a much deeper economic collapse, it is difficult to imagine the U.S.'s not wanting to play a significant role in Asia in the coming decades. Washington was never going to acquiesce in a proposal to split the Pacific. "If the U.S. does not hold its ground in the Pacific, it cannot be a world leader," as Lee Kuan Yew, the former Singaporean leader, puts it in a cold assessment of the political stakes. "The 21st century will be a contest for supremacy in the Pacific because that is where the growth will be."

WEAK PARTY, STRONG MILITARY

Robert Gates was about to go into a meeting with President Hu Jintao when one of his aides showed him some images that had just appeared on a Chinese Web site that specializes in military gossip. It was January 2011, and the U.S. defense secretary had traveled to Beijing to try and mend fences after China had suspended military contacts between the two countries' militaries in protest of U.S. arms sales to Taiwan. The photos purported to show a test flight for the J-20, China's attempt to develop a "fifth generation" stealth bomber that can evade conventional radar. "It's flying!" wrote an Internet user with the name Little Bird King in one of the chat rooms for military issues run by the *People's Daily* group, publisher of the party's mouthpiece newspaper. A large crowd of onlookers watched the test run from outside the fence at a military airfield in Chengdu, some standing on the back of a white pickup truck to get a better view. For Gates, the timing seemed a deliberate insult: the Chinese military were rubbing his nose in one of their new high-tech capabilities.

The photos were a particular embarrassment to Gates, who had publicly dismissed the idea of a Chinese stealth bomber only two years earlier. China would have "no fifth-generation aircraft by 2020," he had told an audience in Chicago. Most American observers thought that China's jets were mediocre copies of old Russian models. A month earlier some grainy photos had appeared on another Chinese military-fan Web site showing the J-20 being pulled out on the Chengdu airfield. Soon after, the photos reappeared on the Aviation Week Web site in the U.S., after blogger Bill Sweetman posted them at 7:30 a.m. on Christmas Day and talked about rumors of a test flight. Yet the Pentagon did not believe the new Chinese jet fighter was ready to fly.

Gates was so angry that he suggested canceling the meeting with Hu Jintao, only to be persuaded to attend by Jon Huntsman, then the U.S. ambassador to Beijing. When Gates asked Hu about the test flight, he was greeted with a nervous silence. The president appeared to know nothing about it. They were seated in one of those U-shaped Chinese meeting rooms, with the principals at the top and a line of their aides on either side. Hu asked his defense minister, Liang Guanglie, who in turn asked the PLA's deputy chief of staff, Ma Xiaotian. No one seemed to know what had actually happened. Eventually, an air-force officer explained that the test flight of the stealth bomber had taken place by coincidence on that day. "I take President Hu at his word that the test had nothing to do with my visit," Gates said rather curtly after the meeting.

Sometimes an uncomfortable silence can tell you as much about a political system as a library full of theses. At the very least, Hu's reticence showed a lack of day-to-day coordination between the PLA and its political masters. Whenever a major U.S. naval vessel passes into the Asia-Pacific Region, the Asia director at the National Security Council receives a written note, so that the White House is not blindsided by activities of the Pentagon. China lacks such a coordinating mechanism. Yet it is equally possible that elements of the PLA were intending to send Gates precisely the message that he had imagined, and that the test flight was held on that day as a deliberate provocation. The Chengdu airfield has two landing strips—one far away from view and one visible from a public road. The test flight used the second runway, and when it was completed, the aircraft was parked beside the road, so that local military enthusiasts could take more pictures. In the past, China's pervasive Internet censors have taken down images of new military technologies they do not want the world to see. This time, they let the photos remain. Andrew Scobell, an analyst with the Rand Corporation, later told a congressional hearing that the message from the test flight was: "America, take heed. The capabilities of our weaponry are ever improving, and we are not intimidated by your technologically superior military might." If sending such a signal to the U.S. also caused a moment of acute diplomatic embarrassment for the country's president, then so be it.

———

One of the ironies about Deng Xiaoping's advice to "hide the brightness and nourish obscurity" is that it requires a decisive figure like Deng to implement. Playing nice with the neighbors involves making the sorts of concessions that can gall nationalists. It needs a strong leader who has the credibility to take a few blows on the chin, and who can face down the more ambitious and nationalistic of his colleagues, especially from the military. Yet Deng also made sure that China would never have such a strongman again. After the quixotic disasters of the Mao era, the Communist Party has gone out of its way to reduce the space for another all-powerful leader. The party now has a fixed retirement age, and an entrenched process of leadership transitions that take place every decade (with some housecleaning every five years). The upside is that the party is much more predictable and professional. The downside is that it is now governed by committee, which can slow decision making and can make it much harder for the leadership to stand up to more strident voices. Over the last decade, China has seen a fracturing of power among the elite, with different vested interests from within the party-state starting to push their own foreign-policy agendas more openly and more aggressively. Cheng Li, a Chinese political scientist now at the Brookings Institution in Washington, uses three couplets to capture the new dynamic of power in China. "Weak leaders, strong factions; weak government, strong interest groups; weak party, strong country," as he puts it.

China's determined push to the seas is a product of its history and geography, to be sure, but it is also being driven by these shifts within the Chinese political system as more voices start to be heard. China's leaders no longer enjoy the unquestioned authority over foreign policy that Deng was able to command. The cautious elite consensus on how to manage the country's rise is gradually being undermined in favor of a more strident defense of national interests and a greater willingness to ruffle international feathers. The Foreign Ministry should be in charge of international relations but is actually the weakest ministry in Beijing, outgunned and out-politicked by other influential groups. Not one foreign-policy official is a member of the twenty-five-strong Communist Party Politburo. Like new great powers before it, China is finding that success creates its own expectations. China's leaders now have to deal with the often raucous Internet nationalism of the urban middle class, which has been reared on stories about the "hundred years of humiliation." The wealthier these urban professionals become, the more impatient they are for China's leaders to assert a bigger role. Local governments and powerful state-owned companies want to have a say on important foreign-policy issues. And the civilian leaders also have to deal with a more restless and powerful military.

If there is one subject that is the hardest for foreign China-watchers to get a handle on, it is the relationship between the Communist Party and the military. Despite the breathtaking changes in Chinese society over the last three decades, high-level politics are still a black box, and that is even more the case for the People's Liberation Army. The military is formally under control of the Communist Party rather than the state, which adds to its sense of mystery and autonomy. To most outside observers, and to many Chinese, the PLA seems like a separate world walled off from the rest of the party-state. The very brief glimpses into the PLA afforded to the foreign media confirm that sense of an institution following its own rules. In 2008, one of my colleagues managed to organize an interview with a senior PLA official. We were instructed to come to the PLA's foreign-affairs office, north of the city center, an airy, palatial building with marble floors and long, empty corridors. As a journalist in China, you can tell a lot about a government official by the way he or she conducts an interview. Most government departments insist that you send over half a dozen sample questions beforehand, and they will reject an interview request if the topics are too controversial. The less secure the cadre, the longer they spend on the initial softball questions. I have conducted interviews in which the official in question proceeded to read out a twenty-five-page prepared answer to these questions, leaving only a few minutes for a real interview at the end. Major General Qian Lihua, director of the defense ministry's foreign-affairs office, walked into the conference room where my colleagues and I were waiting and shook our hands. He picked up a paper that one of his aides had prepared and handed it to us. "This is a written response for the questions you sent over," he said. "Now, what do you really want to ask me?" He went on to give the strongest indication yet that China was building an aircraft carrier. "The navy of any great power . . . has the dream to have one or more aircraft carriers," he said.

Like many of the party leaders of his generation, Deng was himself a veteran of the Communist Party's war against the Nationalists and the Long March. Not only did he have strong personal relationships with the military top brass when he assumed power, but they also had a sense of shared sacrifice in defense of the party. Over the last couple of decades, however, the party and the military have taken different paths. The party has become dominated by trained bureaucrats who have worked their way up the system, spending decades in provincial jobs learning the ropes. The new military leaders are also cut from a different cloth. Rather than party ideologues well schooled in the texts of Marxism-Leninism, they are now professional soldiers who are focused on honing their new skills. The PLA has less influence over domestic politics than it used to enjoy but, at the same time, the party is much less directly involved in the PLA than it once was. The PLA political commissars, who once enforced political orthodoxy among the rank and file, are now much more focused on boosting morale—one Chinese observer likens them to the equivalent of chaplains in a Western army. As Marxism has withered as a guiding force, the military has also developed a stronger sense of its role as a defender of the national interest. China now has a professional officer class with a slightly Prussian air, which is proud of the new capabilities at its disposal and was reared on a worldview that sees China as a powerful and strong nation.

The most dangerous situation would be if a few "rogue generals" started to freelance, using the perceived weakness of civilian leaders to push their own agenda outside of the formal policy process. That would be a large red-flag warning about looming future instability in China's relations with the rest of the world. Most informed observers of China's military believe that this is far from the case, and that the Communist Party leadership still remains firmly in control of the military. But every now and then, there are tantalizing glimpses of a restless military that is occasionally willing to push the boundaries. The test flight of the J-20 on the day Robert Gates was in town was one such case. Another incident happened in 2007, when China used a land-based missile to blow a weather satellite out of space. The test was a wake-up call for foreign militaries, a warning shot about China's cyberwar capabilities. Just as illuminating was the way the test was discovered. With no word coming from the Chinese government, the story first appeared in a U.S. magazine, which was probably tipped off by U.S. or other Western intelligence agencies. And even when the news did break, the Foreign Ministry gave the impression that it had been left completely in the dark by the military.

These little glimpses of the interactions between the PLA and the party suggest an occasionally confrontational streak, but they do not indicate a stark split. The real influence that the PLA is starting to have is more subtle, the result not of open lobbying but from the drip-feed effect of a military worldview that is both intensely proud of China and deeply skeptical about the U.S. military. It is this tide of hawkish views that is helping to gradually chip away at Deng's call for self-restraint. By exposing big shifts in relative power that have taken place between the U.S. and China, the financial crisis encouraged some in China to believe that the time was theirs. Hu Jintao had few connections with the military before he became president in 2002, and Chinese academics and officials who attend regular foreign-policy gatherings with military officials would describe the openness with which Hu was criticized— something that would have been unthinkable only a few years earlier. One leading academic told me of a discussion with some of his military counterparts in which Hu had been attacked by name for being soft on Japan. "Arrogant people with a lot of ego," the academic described them.

I got the full force of this worldview when I went to visit Senior Colonel Liu Mingfu. I wanted to meet Liu because a few months earlier he had caused something of a sensation when he published his first book, *China Dream*, a nationalist tract that called for the country to build a military force to rival and compete with the U.S. In his book he argued that the U.S. and China were embarking on a "marathon contest" for global leadership. Having spared no efforts to contain the rise of the Soviet Union and Japan, Liu argued that the U.S. would "fight a third battle to retain its title" against China. His book became a best seller both on the mainland and in Hong Kong. One large Chinese newspaper ran serializations of *China Dream* for a whole month. Yanghe, a company which makes one of the country's best-known brands of liquor, ordered ten thousand copies to give to its clients. "The chairman described it as a textbook for patriotism," Liu told me, not a little immodestly.

Liu lives in a complex of residential buildings reserved for military personnel, just along the road from the Defense Ministry's huge building in central Beijing. Foreigners are not supposed to enter the compound, he said on the phone, so I should wear a woolly hat and keep my head down when passing through the gate. In the end, the car drove in without any problems at all, the guard airily waving us through. Inside the compound, there were few signs of insecurity, but plenty of esprit de corps. There was a well-tended running track, and a theater that put on shows of revolutionary songs at the weekends. It was midmorning, and the exercise area was full of pensioners doing stretches on a series of yellow machines. A lithe fifty-year-old with dyed black hair and the rank of a senior colonel, Liu now teaches at the National Defense University, where he gives lectures on Marxist theory and U.S.-China relations. Liu said that on the very day he launched his book, in 2010, Barack Obama gave a speech saying that the U.S. would never be number two in the world. "It was such a coincidence. As an ordinary military man, I argue loudly that China should try to be the number one, should race to be the champion country," Liu said.

A few months before we talked, a Chinese admiral called Guan Youfei had caused a good deal of consternation at a high-profile U.S.-China summit when he launched into a long diatribe attacking the "hegemonic" U.S. According to American officials present, Guan accused Washington of plotting to encircle China and treating Beijing as an enemy. Liu Mingfu said he agreed entirely with Guan's analysis. For Liu, the Chinese leadership faces a stark choice: either China develops the military capacity to challenge the U.S., or it will be forever bullied by its larger rival. "For China, a runner-up who does not want to be a champion is not a good runner-up," he told me. "But the U.S. wants a mini-NATO to contain China." As we talked in his flat, his wife sat next to him, eating sunflower seeds from a plastic bag and nodding vigorously every time he made a forceful point. A few weeks before, Bill Gates and Warren Buffett had visited Beijing to encourage Chinese entrepreneurs to do more for charity. "Chinese people enjoyed seeing the civilization of Gates and Buffett. America should send more cultural and peaceful ambassadors like that," Liu told me. "But, instead, the American aircraft carriers make 1.3 billion Chinese people see America's hegemony and barbarism." As I was leaving, he gripped my hand firmly. "You British are reasonable people; Germans are very reasonable," he said. "But the Americans?"

Since the first Gulf War, in the early nineties, America has developed a battalion of "TV generals," retired members of the military who provide expert commentary on military operations and, every now and then, slip in a hawkish criticism of the commander-in-chief. In the last few years, something similar has started to happen in China. A small group of media-friendly members of the armed forces have begun to talk openly about their views on military matters, including their mistrust of and distaste for the U.S. military and its policies in Asia. Dai Xu, a colonel in the air force, writes regular articles and appears on television to criticize U.S. efforts to contain China. "If the U.S. can light a fire in China's backyard, we can also light a fire in their backyard," he wrote in 2010. In some ways, Senior Colonel Liu Mingfu is the latest addition to their numbers. The question that remained unanswered during our conversation was whether Liu's brand of saber rattling was a minority position, or if he was reflecting broader views about the U.S. among the armed services that are starting to influence the politicians. Liu is not in active service and is not involved in developing Chinese military strategy. The sort of crude and hard-line views that he puts forward are, therefore, by no means official policy, although *China Dream* did have a foreword written by Lieutenant General Liu Yazhou, the son-in-law of a former Chinese president and a close adviser of Xi Jinping, China's new president.

Many experts on China's military warn against seeing the PLA as a unified bastion of anti-Americanism. They say that the PLA, like so many institutions in China these days, is full of people who have substantial direct experience of the U.S. Indeed, the children of a few senior military figures are believed to have attended university in the U.S. They also have huge admiration for the operational skills and technology of the U.S. military. Others are less sanguine. A few days after I met Liu, I asked Chu Shulong what to make of Liu Mingfu and the other hawkish, military pundits. Chu spent eight years in the PLA before becoming an academic at Tsinghua University, and so speaks from some experience. "These scholars at military institutions have little contact with the real military leaders. They are giving their personal opinions, but they in no way represent the Central Military Commission [the body that runs the armed forces]," he told me. "The real military are much more hard-line than these scholars. They are even more hostile and suspicious of the U.S."

Every now and again, that resentment toward the U.S. leaks out into the open. In 2010, recently retired admiral Hu Yanlin, who had been the navy's chief political commissar and a close adviser to the top commander Wu Shengli, described the U.S. as "the fundamental anti-Chinese force." Talking about the South China Sea, he added that the U.S. "may seek to precipitate a crisis, hoping the internal difficulties would facilitate foreign aggression or that foreign aggression could cause internal anxiety."

The PLA does not dictate policy to its civilian masters, but it does help shape the atmosphere in which policy is made. The nationalist rhetoric and skepticism of the U.S. that are central to the PLA's worldview are slowly leaking into the policy process. Over the last decade, a weaker civilian leadership has found it harder to push back against hawkish voices in the military. All of which makes the personality and background of China's new president so interesting and important. Unlike his predecessor, Xi Jinping is steeped in Chinese military tradition. His father, Xi Zhongxun, was a central figure in the Communist Party war with the Nationalists in the 1930s, organizing a guerrilla base in Yan'an, in northeast central China, that later provided refuge for Mao Zedong. When the younger Xi left university in the late 1970s, his first job was as *mishu*, a sort of personal assistant, to Defense Minister Geng Biao, who was a friend of his father's. Xi proudly wore a military uniform to the office every day. His wife, Peng Liyuan, is a popular folksinger who is attached to the army's song-and-dance troupe. She holds the rank of major general, and until her husband became a senior leader, she was a regular in the huge television spectacle that airs every year on the eve of the New Year holiday. More recently, a photo has reappeared showing her singing to soldiers in Tiananmen Square in the days following the bloody suppression of the 1989 democracy protests.

In some ways, the military is part of his political support base. In two decades as a provincial official, Xi was known as a "military hugger" for his efforts to help the troops stationed in his area, giving them privileged access to amusement parks and festivals, and appearing regularly at military parades. Such a background could give Xi more credibility to stand up to some of the more restive generals. He will have a personal authority in their company that Hu Jintao always lacked. But it could also make him more sympathetic to their nationalist worldview.

In the years during which he was preparing to take the top job, his most famous comments were a rant he gave at a 2009 dinner of Chinese expatriates in Mexico City, in which he warned, "There are a few foreigners, with full bellies, who have nothing better to do than try to point fingers at our country." One of the central questions in China over the next decade will be whether Xi's core instinct is to control the military, or to channel its views. A more natural leader than his predecessor, Xi could be less intimidated by hawkish voices. Yet his early statements have been full of nationalist echoes, and some analysts believe he is relying on the military to consolidate its position. In a speech he gave aboard the destroyer *Haikou*, which patrols the South China Sea, shortly after assuming power, he expanded on his new slogan about promoting a "Chinese dream." "The dream can be said to be the dream of a strong nation and for the military, it is the dream of a strong military," he said. "We must achieve the great revival of the Chinese nation and we must ensure there is unison between a prosperous country and a strong military."

ASSASSIN'S MACE

Long before *Diamonds Are Forever* started playing on my China Southern flight back to Beijing, it had been hard to shake the slightly James Bond feel about Yalong Bay. If you stand on the beach at the Sanya Sheraton and look out to sea, and if the light is not too hazy, you can just about make out a headland to the southeast of the bay. What the eye cannot detect is the large underground submarine base that lies on the other side of the headland. First revealed in satellite photos published in 2008 by U.S. scientists, the images showed the cavelike holes which are the entrances for the submarines. The tunnels give way to a large harbor carved deep into the rock to protect the subs from bombing raids. The underwater base has the Chinese navy's only demagnetizing facility, which makes it much harder for the submarines to be detected. The disclosures about the Sanya submarine base form part of a relentless trend over the last decade, during which observers have been continuously surprised by the technical sophistication of China's military modernization. China has managed to catch a lot of people by surprise.

After touring the U.S. in 1890, Oscar Wilde had one of his characters react with surprise at being told that the U.S. had no ruins or curiosities. "No ruins, no curiosities!" the Canterville Ghost replied. "You have your navy and your manners." For sophisticated subjects of the British Empire, the American navy was an obvious punch line at that time. Yet, by the end of the decade, one in which the U.S. invested heavily in its navy under the influence of Teddy Roosevelt and Captain Mahan, the U.S. had roundly defeated Spain in battles in Cuba and the Philippines, sending an unambiguous message to the world about its new maritime power. As recently as a decade ago, China's navy suffered the same sort of condescension. The 1990 edition of *Jane's Fighting Ships,* a sort of annual bible of the world's navies, described the PLAN as "technically backward and operationally immature." In 1996, three Chinese warships made a goodwill port call in San Diego. American officials who visited the ships noticed that the interior walls were made of plywood, which made them not only flimsy but also a fire risk. The Chinese military was considered so primitive that some American strategists joked that its battle plan for taking control of Taiwan was "a million-man swim."

No one in Washington or any other Asian capital is making the same jokes now. If China's newfound instinct to challenge the U.S. in the Near Seas is rooted in its history, its expanding economic interests, and the restlessness of some of its officer corps, there is also one final and equally important component—it now has the military capabilities to start making a difference. China is starting to push back against the U.S. in part because it can. After two decades of double-digit increases in military spending, China now has the second-largest defense budget in the world, after the U.S. While the U.S. has been fighting a losing battle in Afghanistan for over a decade and pouring more than a trillion dollars into the debacle in Iraq, China has been carefully conducting the biggest military expansion in the world. Of course, China's budget is still much smaller than that of the U.S., which spends almost as much as the rest of the world combined on defense, and which will remain the most sophisticated military power for some time. But China has no intention of challenging the U.S. around the globe over the coming decades. It has no interest in establishing a serious naval presence in the Caribbean, for instance, or posting soldiers in continental Europe. Instead, it is focused on Asia.

With these more limited aims, China is catching up quickly with the U.S. By some estimates, China will have a bigger fleet than the U.S. by the end of this decade, and it already has more submarines. Although it is always dangerous to make straight-line predictions based on existing reality, if China continues with its current rate of increase in military spending, it will have a bigger defense budget than the U.S. by 2025, according to the International Institute for Strategic Studies. Yet China does not need to match the U.S. dollar for dollar in order to achieve its goals: it only needs to spend enough to change the strategic balance in the western Pacific. Chinese strategists talk about "asymmetric" warfare, tactics and tools that can allow a weaker and smaller country to inflict huge damage on a bigger rival. China is not preparing for a war with the U.S. Indeed, the goal is to secure Beijing's political aims without ever firing in anger. Instead, its military buildup is designed to gradually change the calculations of American commanders, to dissuade them from considering military operations anywhere near China's coast, and to push them slowly farther out into the Pacific.

"We do not need to be in such a hurry," Deng Xiaoping told a Central Military Commission meeting in March 1979. Deng was responding to pressure from his military colleagues for a big increase in spending on new weapons. It was a message he found himself repeating for the next decade, at meeting after meeting. China's economic boom did not immediately lead to a rapid military buildup. Though the PLA wanted to invest, Deng insisted that building up the domestic economy would come first; the military would need to show some patience. During the 1980s, the Chinese government actually decreased the proportion of the budget that was destined for military spending. "Deng had to explain over and over again to disappointed officers why it was in the national interest first to develop the civilian economy and then to modernize the military," notes Ezra Vogel, author of an authoritative biography on the Chinese leader. "Deng was probably the only leader of his time with the authority, determination and political skill to keep these officers from launching serious protests against this policy."

But over time, patience wore thin, and the military has started to receive the sorts of resources that it had long been clamoring for. After Deng was forced to call up units of the PLA from outside of Beijing to fire on the Tiananmen protesters in 1989, spending on the military started to increase, including salaries and housing. If Tiananmen was a key turning point, another was the first Gulf War, in 1990–91. The campaign to push Iraq from Kuwait had a profound psychological impact among the Chinese leadership. Watching the images of destruction on their televisions, Chinese military officials were acutely aware of both their own limitations and the vast technological superiority of the U.S.

At the start of the naval buildup, Taiwan was the primary focus. China wanted to have sufficient forces to take control of the island if it ever tried to declare independence formally, and to prevent any other power from intervening in a conflict if it did break out. In the early days of the People's Republic, almost all the viable ships were given to the northern and eastern fleets, which operate near Taiwan, while the southern fleet was considered a poor cousin. Taiwan remains a priority, but over time, the scope of China's naval ambitions has expanded. One of the reasons the opening of the new naval base on Hainan Island was so significant was that it demonstrated the new priorities of China's naval push, the ability to project power not just east, toward Taiwan, but also down into the South China Sea and beyond.

"Since no nation threatens China, one wonders: Why this growing investment? Why these continuing large and expanding arms purchases? Why these continuing robust deployments?" The questions were raised by Donald Rumsfeld in 2005, when the then defense secretary was visiting Singapore for a conference. Iraq was still engulfed with violence at that time, and his comments seemed another exercise in neocon scaremongering. But nearly a decade later, the questions have not gone away. The uncomfortable truth is that China's military investments are focused largely on the United States' presence in the region. There should be little surprise that an aspiring great power would choose to invest more in its military as its interests and power expands. Yet China is not investing in the sort of navy that could be used for policing the world's sea-lanes for pirates and terrorists. Instead, its principal target is the U.S. Navy. According to Dennis Blair, the retired admiral who was head of the U.S. intelligence services early in the Obama administration: "Ninety percent of their time is spent on thinking about new and interesting ways to sink our ships and shoot down our planes."

American strategists sometimes talk about a Chinese "anti-navy"—a series of weapons, some based on land, some at sea, which are specifically designed to keep an opposing navy as far away as possible from the mainland. China has a large and growing fleet of submarines, including nuclear-powered vessels and a group of Russia-supplied diesel submarines which are quiet and hard to detect. It is developing two different versions of stealth fighter jets (including the airplane that was tested the day Robert Gates was in Beijing), as well as its own unmanned drones that can deploy missiles. The navy is developing a new type of destroyer battleship which will have some of the missile defense capabilities of American Aegis ships.

Pride of place in the anti-navy, however, goes to the Second Artillery Force, which operates most of the more than one thousand missiles that China has built up over the last two decades. There are missiles that can take out facilities on land, missiles for targeting satellites, and missiles for attacking ships. One technology in particular has attracted a lot of attention. China has invested heavily in a new generation of so-called carrier-killer missiles, designed to destroy aircraft carriers at sea. Larry Wortzel, a former American military attaché in Beijing, recalls a jocular warning he once received at a diplomatic reception. A Chinese officer put his arm around Wortzel's shoulder and said, "We are going to sink your carriers with ballistic missiles." The missiles, which supposedly cannot be detected by radar, have a range of fifteen hundred to two thousand kilometers. They are the modern equivalent of an "assassin's mace," the weapons used in Chinese historical novels that can undermine a technologically superior enemy. The implicit threat is that commanders of American aircraft carriers would have to think carefully about operating anywhere within that radius from the Chinese coast—a fundamental challenge to the way America projects military power in the region. It is the first weapons system since the end of the Cold War that both is potentially capable of stopping American naval-power projection and was specifically designed for that purpose. The strategy also represents good economics. Each of its carrier-killer missiles cost around $11 million; a new aircraft carrier now costs $13.5 billion.

With any new, untried weapons, there is always an open question as to whether it will actually work. The carrier-killer missile is no exception. Hitting a moving ship at long distance is an incredibly difficult task. The U.S. Navy would have plenty of options to defend its carriers, such as shooting the missile down with Aegis missile-defense cruisers, or trying to jam the "seeker" technology that missiles deploy when they get near a target. Yet American commanders cannot guarantee that their defenses will work. "We want to spoof them, preclude detection, jam them, shoot them down if possible, get them to termination, confuse them," Admiral Jonathan Greenert, chief of U.S. naval operations, once said on being asked about the Chinese carrier-killer missiles. Can they be jammed? "Yes, no, maybe so?" he said.

The carrier killer is a technology whose potency will become apparent over the next decade. A more immediate threat comes from another innovation that has started to attract a lot of attention in Washington—China's growing fleet of fast, mobile patrol craft that carry cruise missiles designed to attack ships. This is another technology that fits the pattern of fighting "asymmetric" warfare against U.S. carrier groups operating near the Chinese coast. These patrol craft use a catamaran hull that was initially designed in Australia for passenger ferries, but which allows the attack craft to skim across waves at high speed. The Houbei-class vessels, as they are called, also copy many of the same features as stealth fighter jets, such as windows with jagged edges and a sloped hull, which help it avoid detection by radar. The Chinese fleet now has around sixty of these catamaran craft, and each vessel carries eight anti-ship missiles. Chinese strategists describe them being used in "wolf pack" operations, in which they can swarm a target group of vessels, attacking in numbers from different directions. Their limited fuel tanks mean that they cannot operate at long distances from the mainland, but they could be very effective in any exchange nearer to the Chinese coast.

The other string of China's "asymmetric" fighting capabilities is cyber- and space warfare. Whereas Chinese hacking of commercial secrets has won a huge amount of attention in the U.S., the potential use of cyberattacks during a conflict is less discussed. This could include attacks on infrastructure in the U.S., designed to inflict damage on the economy, but it could also involve attacking the information systems that the U.S. Air Force and Navy rely on. By taking out U.S. satellites, China could hamper the ability of U.S. fighter jets to operate effectively.

China's navy still has many weaknesses, including the inexperience of its sailors in combat conditions. But the era of the "million-man swim" is long gone. China is quickly acquiring the capabilities to start challenging U.S. power projection in the western Pacific. In the process, the U.S. and China are embarking on an epic tussle for who will have the upper hand in the Near Seas. How that contest plays out will depend on three factors, which we will see in the next chapters. It will depend on how the rest of Asia reacts to China's new ambitions, and on how America responds to the challenge, too. But it will also be heavily influenced by what China tries to do with its new navy in areas far away from its coastal waters. The rivalry between the U.S. and China in the western Pacific will be shaped partly by how China decides to approach the Indian Ocean.

2

The Lure of the Indian Ocean

"YOU DID NOT BRING any hundred-dollar notes?" the Yangon bank teller asked. There are all sorts of signs of just how detached Burma has become from the modern world after decades of sanctions and military-led incompetence, but the simple things are the most striking. Burma is one of the few countries in the world where visitors need to take large wads of dollar bills if they want to buy local currency. Forget ATMs; even travelers' checks have passed it by. I handed the teller a collection of $20 notes I had withdrawn shortly before leaving the U.S. She scoured each note carefully, sometimes taking several seconds at a time, handing back any that were marked or even slightly frayed with a polite "tut," as if I had been trying to cheat her. A few days later, as we were driving along rickety back roads on Burma's Indian Ocean coast, the sense of stagnation was even harder to ignore. The poorer houses still had thatched roofs, and in some cases the walls were thatched, too. In many of the villages we passed through, the market consisted of a few piles of bananas and coconuts laid out on plastic sheets on the ground, alongside a few consumer basics. There were very few other cars and only a handful of motorbikes, the road being mostly occupied by bicycles and bike-rickshaws. The buzzing metropolis of Bangkok was just one hour's flight away, and within three hours you could be in Singapore, whose vapid but impressive modernity is an unforgiving benchmark for just how far Burma has fallen behind.

Such a powerful sense of being stuck in time can also have its own allure, of course. The main road threaded through dense forest, but after a while weaved back to the coast. We passed golden beaches backed by palm trees and bougainvillea, empty but for the driftwood left by the tide. The monsoon had already passed through this part of the country, and there was a cool breeze off the Bay of Bengal. A century earlier, Rudyard Kipling wrote part of *The Jungle Book* at a resort just a bit farther south. At the time, both India and Burma were part of the British Empire, and the coast was a popular vacation spot for the Calcutta imperial class, just across the other side of the Bay of Bengal. It probably had not changed much since then.

After several hours of driving north, we came to a vast clearing that had been cut out of undulating forest and vegetation. The sense of timelessness ended with an abrupt shock. An area of several square kilometers had been surrounded by high fences, but there were plenty of telltale signs about what lay behind the locked gates. In the distance were a series of large tubular metal tanks suitable for storing oil. I counted three large red cranes of the type that I had seen on countless construction sites in China. The real clincher was in one corner of the site, where there were several long lines of portable buildings, their white walls and blue roofs marking them out as the dormitories for construction workers, some of whom I could make out in the distance by their orange hard hats. For anyone who had spent time on mainland China, these were the unmistakable sights and sounds of industrial development with Chinese characteristics.

We had arrived at Ramree Island, an isolated peninsula on the north of Burma's Indian Ocean coast, which is quietly becoming one of the geopolitical hot spots of the twenty-first century. The fenced-off construction site I was able to glimpse is part of the single most ambitious overseas project that China has yet undertaken. Ramree boasts a natural deep-water port that looks onto the Bay of Bengal. It is also the starting point for a 2,806-kilometer oil-and-gas pipeline that stretches all the way across northern Burma, over mountain ranges and through tropical jungles, until it arrives at Kunming, one of the main cities in the southwest of China. The plans include a port, a railway line, and a major oil storage-and-treatment facility. A video presentation about the project adopts the kind of breezy management-speak that often accompanies Chinese investments, gushing about "a concept of one development zone, three clusters, and six bases." The presentation includes a designer's drawing for a high-rise housing project and a shopping mall, identical to the sort of development you can now find in the suburbs of a thousand Chinese cities.

Ramree was the site of an important battle in the later stages of World War II: the Allies battled for six weeks in early 1945 to defeat the Japanese forces stationed there, with Indian soldiers doing most of the fighting. The Battle of Ramree Island is better known for the fate of the retreating Japanese soldiers, who tried to escape at night across a mangrove swamp; many of them ended up eaten by saltwater crocodiles. The reported deaths of nearly a thousand soldiers is listed in the *Guinness Book of World Records* as the greatest-ever loss of human life to animals. Ramree was strategically important for the Allies, because it was easily accessible by sea and because it provided an ideal airbase to support the rest of the Burma campaign. In the early twenty-first century, Ramree has again become a crucial geographical node, a place where commercial ambition and geopolitical calculation are colliding. By building a pipeline all the way through Burma, China is attempting to subvert the realities of its geography and to gain direct access to the Indian Ocean.

The basic idea is simple: As a result of the pipeline, some of the oil and gas that China buys from the Middle East will no longer need to travel through the chokehold of the Strait of Malacca. Instead, it can be transported overland from Ramree to China's urban centers. The pipeline gives China a direct outlet to the Indian Ocean that it has never enjoyed before. It is a way of avoiding all that complicated geography at the mouth of the South China Sea, an engineering solution to the "Malacca Dilemma." Why worry about sending ships down those narrow sea-lanes to the South China Sea, which can be blocked by opponents, when China can use a pipeline that starts at the Bay of Bengal?

That, at least, was the strategic thinking that helped win approval for the $2.5-billion pipeline project. But the law of unintended consequences has a way of turning such plans on their heads. The project was sold as a way of reducing risks to China's supply routes. Yet, by avoiding the Strait of Malacca, China has created a new problem for itself in the

Indian Ocean. "If we are going to have a big port and a terminal and a pipeline all on the west coast of Burma, then we are going to need some military protection there," as one Chinese academic, who was deeply skeptical about the pipeline project, told me. "The result is the opposite of what people thought. It means that we are going to need a navy that can operate effectively in the Indian Ocean."

The contest with the U.S. over the Near Seas is already a reality. But as China's power and ambitions expand, it is only natural that its gaze will start to stretch farther afield, toward the Indian Ocean. Ramree Island is potentially the herald of a very different, long-term project to develop the sort of navy that can operate in the Indian Ocean and beyond. China is already the biggest consumer of oil in the Middle East and is tentatively starting to build political relationships in the region— just as the U.S. did a century before when Britain and France were the dominant outside powers. If China is really serious about securing the sea-lanes on which its economy depends, it will need the sort of "blue water" navy that can contest seas all the way from the Strait of Malacca up through the entire Indian Ocean and into the Persian Gulf, home of America's Fifth Fleet. If China decides to go that route over the next two decades, it has the potential to alter fundamentally the nature of competition with the U.S. The challenge that China currently presents to the U.S. is intense but localized, restricted to China's immediate maritime periphery. China's immediate ambitions are regional, not global. But as it casts its sights across the Indian Ocean, the stakes become much higher, raising the prospect that China could pursue a much more sustained and broader challenge to the U.S.

Yet it is far from inevitable that the U.S. and China will end up as competitors in the Indian Ocean. China's approach will depend in part on a number of key decisions that China's leaders will need to take over the next decade, which will involve massive investments and will be crucial barometers of their long-term intentions. Distance from home drastically changes the military calculation for China. In the Near Seas, the geography is on China's side: it has missile sites along its coast, which it can use to exert control over sea-lanes. But in the Indian Ocean, those advantages disappear. If China wants to have the ability to contest the seas well beyond its periphery, and to project power in the Indian

Ocean, it needs to invest heavily in two areas. It will need to have bases in and agreements with friendly countries that will allow it to use their ports and airfields to support its forces. And it will need the sorts of warships that can provide some form of air cover across wide expanses of ocean. In other words, it will need aircraft carriers. The bad news for China is that, although both projects are superficially attractive, they will be politically difficult and economically costly to implement.

THE "STARTER CARRIER"

"Without an aircraft carrier, I will die with my eyelids open," Liu Hua-qing, the former commander of the Chinese fleet, said in 1987—a Chinese phrase that implies a deep, unfulfilled desire. In the modern era, Liu was the first official to push the case for a bigger fleet; he is often referred to as "the father of the modern Chinese navy." It was Liu who introduced the concept of "Near Seas" and "Far Seas" into Chinese strategic thought, and also he who, in the 1980s, led the navy's transformation from a glorified coast guard into a modern fleet. China, he argued, needed to stake its claim as a great power, and an aircraft carrier was the vital platform for projecting naval power over long distances. When he outlined these ideas in the 1970s and 1980s, at a time when most Chinese were not able to eat meat regularly, his plans seemed quixotic. But by the time he died, in early 2011, they had become mainstream: a few weeks before his death, Chinese officials acknowledged for the first time that the country was building its own carrier. All nine members of the Communist Party Standing Committee turned out for Liu Huaqing's memorial service, the only time in recent memory that this has happened for a military leader. A distraught-looking Hu Jintao presented a bouquet of white carnations to his widow. Xi Jinping gave a speech saying that China had to step up the development of its naval capabilities to match its new position in the world.

China's route to a modern carrier has been a tortuous one. In 1998, an obscure Chinese travel agency, whose directors had connections with the navy, purchased the hull of a former Soviet carrier called the *Varyag* from Ukraine. They paid $20 million and said that the ship would be used as a casino. It took them three years to get the vessel back to China.

The *Varyag* was held up in Istanbul for eighteen months while a dispute with the Turkish authorities was resolved, and then it hit bad weather on its way around the Cape of Good Hope, before it was eventually tugged into Dalian, a port in the northeast of China. But by 2012, the newly rechristened *Liaoning* carrier was ready to enter formal service for the first time. The relaunch was accompanied with much fanfare and national pride. The commander of the carrier, Senior Captain Zhang Zheng, gave an interview on the ship's deck to CCTV, the Chinese state broadcaster. Zhang talked rather modestly about all the training the crew would need and the heavy responsibility they faced, but the interviewer could not contain himself. "Captain Zhang, you give me a very deep impression of being open-minded and energetic," he beamed. "The navy also has very high hopes for you."

The battle to build the *Liaoning* carrier tells a lot about the shifting political sands and rising ambitions in China over recent years. As far back as 1928, Chen Shaokuan, the British-trained head of the Chinese navy at the time, first put forward the idea of building a carrier. In the 1980s, when he was head of the navy, Liu Huaqing started to lobby openly for the idea of a Chinese carrier, yet his civilian masters were not convinced. Deng Xiaoping pushed back against the expensive idea. In the early 1990s, Jiang Zemin, who had taken power after Tiananmen, also rejected the proposal. He was afraid that it would unnerve the U.S. too much to see China investing in such a striking symbol of great-power ambition. The early years of naval modernization focused mostly on the submarines and missiles that could help China exert more control over the Near Seas. The quest for an aircraft carrier became yet another of those ideas that were put on hold in the interests of "hiding the brightness."

But from the early 1990s, the idea of a carrier was taken up by China's version of the military-industrial complex. The drumbeat started first in universities and think tanks and soon included mayors who wanted the carriers to be built in their towns, and the shipbuilders who were desperate for the contract. Supporters emphasized the unique place that aircraft carriers held for realizing China's national destiny. Li Jie, a senior captain at the Naval Research Institute, claimed, "No great power that has become a strong power has achieved this without developing carriers." Zhang Wenmu, one of the most vocal champions, argues that in the twenty-first century naval power will be a decisive factor in competition between states. Aircraft carriers are "a concentrated expression of a country's comprehensive national power," he writes.

Kaiser Wilhelm was so fascinated with the navy that he once wore a naval uniform to a performance of Wagner's *Flying Dutchman*, with his sons also decked out in sailor suits. Bismarck had invested only in smaller, less expensive vessels, fearing that the real threats to Germany would come by land. However, under Wilhelm's and Admiral Tirpitz's direction, Germany invested in a huge fleet of battleships, the aircraft carriers of their day. "The Greeks and Romans each had their time, the Spaniards had theirs, the French also," Wilhelm argued to justify the huge investments. The historian Robert Ross argues that China is witnessing the same sort of "naval nationalism" that has infected many aspiring great powers before, in which the natural desire to build up the military becomes distorted by a demand for prestige projects that have a strong nationalist appeal, even if their strategic worth is not so clear-cut. Unlike any other aspect of the country's military modernization, the idea of a Chinese aircraft carrier became part of the popular imagination. As Ross puts it, "Chinese nationalists maintain that the realization of China's historical destiny depends on the possession of a carrier-based navy." Around the same time that China bought the *Varyag*, it purchased another former Soviet carrier from Ukraine, the *Kiev*. In this case, the vessel really was destined for tourism. It is now the centerpiece of a popular aircraft-carrier theme park in Tianjin, the large coastal city near Beijing. San Diego has a museum in a disused aircraft carrier, so the idea is hardly novel, but whereas the USS *Midway* Museum celebrates achievements from the past, the Tianjin museum is aspirational, a bid to capture the public enthusiasm for future naval grandeur. When I visited a couple of years ago, the insides of the *Kiev* were lined with worthy exhibits about the history of aircraft carriers. More recently, it has gone upmarket—part of the vessel is now taken up by a luxury hotel, a response to constant requests from people wanting to spend a night on board. The hotel photos indicate a preference for gaudy baroque, the low-ceilinged suites boasting white leather sofas and opulent chandeliers. Overnight guests have been promised an additional treat: the park intends to put on a mock naval battle every evening.

The launch of the *Liaoning* was a moment full of symbolism, to be sure, but Senior Captain Zhang was right: there is still a lot of work to do. China's "starter carrier," as some analysts have dubbed it, still faces a host of difficult challenges. The television images gave away one of those problems: there were no aircraft on the deck. China bought some fighter jets that can be used on carriers from Ukraine and is believed to have got hold of a similar Russian jet. There is even speculation that one of the models of its new stealth fighter jet could eventually be equipped to land on carriers. But developing its own jets for use on carriers—and training a team of pilots to use them—is another project whose time frame can be measured in decades rather than years. In 1954, the U.S. Air Force lost 776 aircraft and 535 aviators as it tried to develop its fighter jets. Carrier groups need a whole host of supporting ships, including submarines and destroyers that can provide modern defenses against missiles, some of which are still under development. In addition, the Chinese navy will also have to learn how to actually operate a carrier group, which requires the sort of detailed coordination and training that the U.S. has perfected over a century and through several wars. Again, developing this sort of seamanship is another decades-long enterprise.

It may well be that China's leaders will decide over the next decade to go all in and order a sizable fleet of carriers, but before then, they will have to overcome some powerful opposition to such an ambitious spending spree. According to naval planners, you need three carriers to ensure that one group is always operating, because at any single time one carrier is undergoing repairs and the other is preparing for the next mission. Now that China has launched its first carrier, the question is how many it will build. The Pentagon believes that another couple of domestically built carriers will be in operation by 2015. Chinese state media have talked about plans for three carriers, but other Chinese officials have privately talked about building five. The eventual numbers will make all the difference. If China develops a fleet that allows it to have two carrier groups operating at any one time, that will focus the minds of a lot of other countries in the region. But one carrier on its own does little to change the military balance in Asia. And as the Pentagon can attest, operating carrier groups is an extremely expensive business.

Ever since Liu Huaqing first proposed building a Chinese carrier, the project has been tied up in budgetary battles, and the fight for resources is likely to get still more intense. Some estimates suggest that a new carrier in China would cost $10 billion, around 10 percent of the yearly official Chinese military budget. Even with a growing budget, China does not have the resources for everything. If China invests in a big carrier fleet, it will have fewer resources to invest in the "anti-navy" weapons designed to exert greater control over the Near Seas.

For all the prestige that might come from having several carrier groups, plenty of hardheaded Chinese strategists believe they are of little actual military use once they leave China's immediate maritime surrounds. If Chinese military officials hope that they can take out American carriers in the Near Seas, then the U.S., with its far superior air power, would have the same advantage if Chinese carrier groups started operating in the Indian Ocean. "We would be sitting ducks," as You Ji, a Chinese analyst based in Australia, puts it. The lure of a "blue water" navy is strong, and the vested interests behind a push to build more carriers will be hard to ignore. Yet it is not at all clear that China will have the skills or money over the next couple of decades to construct the sort of navy that would present a serious challenge to the U.S. in the Indian Ocean. And that is before China's leaders tackle the trickiest issue of all—how to supply and protect a new fleet of aircraft carriers operating far from home.

CHINA'S GUANTÁNAMO

In 2004, the Washington office of the consulting firm Booz Allen Hamilton produced a research paper for the Pentagon which put forward the idea that China was trying to establish a permanent military presence in the Indian Ocean. It analyzed a series of commercial ports across the region being built with Chinese help and money and concluded that they formed a "String of Pearls," facilities with potential military use that could help China project military power all the way across the Indian Ocean and into the Persian Gulf. Initially classified, the paper was leaked to the *Washington Times* in 2005. Before long, it started to capture the imagination of the more hawkish observers of China's military buildup, including in India, where there are persistent fears that a rising China will try to encircle it.

If there is one issue that will define what sort of military power China becomes over the next couple of decades, it will be the question of overseas military bases. To build a network of bases would be a decisive statement about Chinese ambitions to project power and to build its own coalition of supporters. China's navalists are gradually becoming more open about pushing the idea. The topic has long been discussed in military circles, but over the last few years it has also started to spill over into public debate about the country's long-term military strategy. It plays into the nationalist sense in China that now is their time. "It is our right" to have bases that can be used to defend the country's new economic interests, says Shen Dingli, a respected academic at Fudan University in Shanghai. "We should be able to conduct retaliatory attacks within other countries or at the neighboring area of our potential enemies."

Proponents of the "String of Pearls" theory argue that China is effectively creating a network of bases in the Indian Ocean by stealth. In Sri Lanka, the island nation with a strategic position at the meeting of the Bay of Bengal and the Arabian Sea, China Harbour Engineering Company is building a mega-port which will be able to house large oil tankers and will have a major refueling facility. The port is in Hambantota, the hometown of Sri Lankan President Mahinda Rajapaksa, allowing China to mix commerce with more personal diplomacy. Just down the road from the port, the same Chinese company also built the thirty-thousand-capacity cricket stadium which was one of the venues for the 2011 World Cup, another propaganda coup for the president. The relationship with Rajapaksa goes well beyond infrastructure, however. With the help of $1 billion in military aid from Beijing every year, and a Chinese veto against criticism at the United Nations, Rajapaksa ended the country's long-running civil war in 2009 after a brutal final showdown. Given such complicit ties, there are plenty of suggestions that, over time, Hambantota could become the sort of place where Chinese vessels regularly dock to refuel and get supplies.

Something similar has been happening in Gwadar, a deep-water Pakistani port on the Arabian Sea, close to the entrance to the Strait of Hormuz—the strategic chokehold for a large slice of the world's oil supply. China helped build a commercial port at Gwadar, which was initially leased to a Singapore company, PSA International. But after a series of problems, the Singapore group dropped out and a Chinese company took over management control of the port. More important, a senior Pakistani official told one of my colleagues in 2011 that the government had asked China to build a naval base next to the commercial port, and that China would have access to the base, potentially allowing Beijing to station some of its ships and submarines in Gwadar. The Chinese have played down the suggestion, but a clear marker has been laid down.

The "String of Pearls" is, of course, an idea straight from the Mahan playbook for aspiring great powers. Mahan urged the U.S. to find strategic locations in the Caribbean and the Pacific that could help the navy patrol the key maritime supply lines and the Panama Canal. A peacetime naval strategy "may gain its most decisive victories by occupying in a country, either by purchase or treaty, excellent positions which would perhaps hardly be got by war," he wrote. Around the same time that America embarked on a burst of navy building in the 1890s, it also launched a drive to acquire overseas bases for its new ships. In the Pacific, it was supporters of the new navy who made the strongest case for incorporating Hawaii into the union. Secretary of State Hamilton Fish described Hawaii as an attractive "resting spot in the mid-ocean, between the Pacific coast and the vast domains of Asia, which are now opening to commerce," as well as being a useful platform for curbing the rise of Japan. Earlier, the U.S. had taken control of the Midway archipelago, which was named because of its location directly midway between Los Angeles and Shanghai. Mahan was particularly obsessed with the Caribbean, where the British navy still had a large presence, and which he thought of in terms not dissimilar to the way the Chinese think today about the first island chain. In 1903, the U.S. Navy leased a new base in the Caribbean, which gave it the perfect launchpad to protect the eastern entrances to the Panama Canal, but which has become famous in modern times for very different reasons—Guantánamo Bay in Cuba.

The "String of Pearls" concept appeals to a certain conspiratorial view of how China works, the image of a small group of Communist Party officials calmly hatching plans for global domination. It suggests that China already has a coherent and thought-out long-term strategy, a series of five-year plans that will eventually afford China a broad network of bases across the region. Given how utterly opaque China's top-level politics remains, it is easy to imagine that the top leadership might have such a disciplined view of its future. But the reality of modern China is much more improvised and reactive than this cliché recognizes. It is certainly true that China's interests are drawing it into the Indian Ocean. Yet Ramree Island tells a very different story about China's overseas expansion, and one which corresponds more closely to how decisions really get made. In a system in which the authority of the leaders is fraying, the driving force is often pressure from below. The Burma pipeline is part of a dynamic whereby business moves first, to create a new reality of its own, and then foreign and military policies are forced to come from behind to fill in the gaps.

The idea for the pipeline was first put forward by a history professor at an unglamorous provincial university. Li Chenyang, an expert on Southeast Asia at Yunnan University, in the southwest of China, started writing newspaper articles in 2004 suggesting that a pipeline could allow China to avoid bringing oil through the Strait of Malacca. In the long corridors outside Li's office, there are large framed maps of the region, detailing Yunnan's long borders with Vietnam, Laos, and Burma. By driving a pipeline from Kunming, Yunnan's capital, down through Burma, Li proposed China could gain access to the Indian Ocean. "The reality is the Americans want to control the Strait of Malacca," as Professor Li put it. "For China to fall under American control is a very risky thing." The idea was immediately taken up by the local government in Yunnan. But whereas Li and his academic colleagues were worried about energy and geopolitics, the local officials had a more prosaic motivation: jobs. Each year, Chinese officials receive a formal performance evaluation, and no matter whether they are running a village of a hundred people or a province of a hundred million, they are judged primarily on their ability to generate growth in their part of the economy. Their careers depend on the local GDP numbers. As a result, local officials are on the constant lookout for new investment projects that will boost growth. Although it has a rich cultural heritage, Yunnan is one of the poorer provinces of China, and its leaders have often complained that the industrial boom in other parts of the country has passed it by. They saw the pipeline as a perfect way to kick-start an oil industry in the province. The construction would bring a lot of jobs and funds, and a refinery would be needed at the end of the pipeline. A lot of the dynamism in China's economy in recent decades is derived from this basic equation, the ceaseless drive at all levels of government for the latest new opportunity. For Yunnan officials, the pipeline is not about geopolitics, it is about GDP.

The proposal also won support from the politically powerful oil industry. China National Petroleum Corporation is the biggest oil company in the country, but in the southwest of the country, it was coming second to its main rival, Sinopec. The new pipeline was a way into that market. Before long, CNPC was on board with the idea. Together with CNPC, the Yunnan authorities started lobbying Beijing hard to win approval. Initially, there was a good deal of resistance. But after several years of pressure by big-oil and provincial government officials, Beijing finally agreed to promote the idea. As Zha Daojiong, a Chinese academic who has followed these sorts of internal debates closely, told me: "From the outside, it can look like China has a coherent energy strategy, but in reality it often comes down to who shouts the loudest."

Europe's empires were not created overnight by grand design. Instead, they evolved through a gradual creeping process that started with trade and investment and ended with the use of military power to protect those business interests. The British Raj had its roots in the perceived need to protect the operations of the East India Company, and it was to defend those very same interests that the British invaded Burma in 1824. After defeating the Burmese forces—and ending Burmese independence for much of the next century—the British briefly moved the country's capital to Sittwe, on the northwest coast, just north of Ramree Island. It is facile to suggest, as some do, that China is trying to re-create an old-fashioned empire, but it is fair to say that China's overseas investments are repeating elements of the same imperial dynamic, the old story of the flag following the trade. In a political system in which some of the lines of control have eroded, ambitious local governments and connected state-owned corporations are pushing projects that involve substantial international commitments, the local economic tail wagging the Beijing diplomatic dog. In the case of the Burma pipeline, the project won the backing of Beijing even though its strategic benefits are really something of a mirage. If there ever were some form of conflict between the U.S. and China, then the pipeline would be much more vulnerable than the sea-lanes through the Strait of Malacca. It would take the permanent presence of a significant fleet to enforce a blockade of the strait, but only one bombing run to destroy the pipeline. The Ramree Island investment brings no actual security for China.

On Ramree Island itself, there is widespread suspicion about China's eventual plans for the area. Common among locals I talked to was the assumption that China would eventually want to have a naval base there, to help secure its interests and protect the commercial traffic to the port. In Yangon, I heard the same story, a constant refrain that the pipeline is some sort of Trojan Horse that will justify a Chinese military presence. There is no evidence that this is happening—and such an idea would likely spark considerable resistance in Burma, including from the new civilian government. But the reality is that China is now building a huge oil facility looking onto the Bay of Bengal, which it needs to protect. Its commercial interests are pulling it into the Indian Ocean in ways that were not originally anticipated.

———

Whether by secret design or by the inertia of its advancing business interests, China is likely to push for a much stronger presence in the Indian Ocean. But just as there are enormous operational challenges ahead if China wants to construct a navy that can contend in the Indian Ocean, so there are huge political obstacles if it tries to establish the sort of military basing rights that would allow it to project power far from its home base. If China really aspires to a stealth "String of Pearls" strategy, it will be very difficult to turn this into reality, because few countries will want to be seen taking sides. Every government in the region knows that, even with the huge investments China is making in its navy, the U.S. will have a superior fighting ability in the Indian Ocean for sev-

eral decades to come. This means that a Chinese base on their territory would turn them into a highly vulnerable target in the first days
of a conflict. Burma's new government has tilted away from China in
a way that makes it very hard to imagine its accepting a Chinese base,
despite the incessant rumor mill in the country. Sri Lanka, too, knows
how vulnerable it would be if Chinese vessels were permanently based at
Hambantota. "There may or may not be a Chinese string in the region,
but we will not be one of their pearls," as one Sri Lankan official puts it.

Pakistan is the one country that has expressed some interest in hosting a Chinese base. But the idea is a lot less attractive than it seems.
Gwadar is occasionally referred to in the press as "the most important
place you have never heard of," given its closeness to the Persian Gulf.
But on closer inspection, it is of much less strategic use than it seems.
Gwadar is an isolated city in the southwestern province of Baluchistan,
squeezed in between Iran and Afghanistan, where an insurgency against
the state has been running for decades, becoming particularly ugly in
recent years. The roads and rail links to the more prosperous parts of
Pakistan, around Karachi and Lahore, are, at best, precarious. The port
itself is also vulnerable, as it is on a small island, connected to the mainland by one bridge. In the event of a conflict, a single bomb could take
it out of action.

Just as the U.S. did in an earlier era, China has long shunned the idea
of foreign "entanglements." Beijing has persistently denounced alliance
building as a destabilizing form of power politics. We are not that sort
of government, Chinese leaders insist. As a result, the establishment of
an overseas base would be a Rubicon moment for China, one that cuts
to the core of the question about how China really interprets its future
role. Foreign bases are not just an exercise in logistics; they are sovereign territory within another nation. A base is the bridgehead to a very
different relationship, the sort of defense alliance whereby the bigger
nation offers to provide security in return for access and support. In
other words, China would need formal allies. But the question every
government would ask Beijing is, whom are we defending ourselves
from? If China moves down this path, it could start a process of dividing
the region between countries that rely on the U.S. for their security, and
those that lean toward China. Asian governments would increasingly

find themselves asked to take sides, the outcome they fear the most. For that very reason, some in China view it as an extremely dangerous step, one that would lead to greater isolation for China. "It is a self-fulfilling, delusionary idea to build our own bases and our own alliances," Zhu Feng, an international-relations professor at Peking University, told me. "I totally disagree with the idea. We would create a geographic split in the region. It really would be the start of a new Cold War."

———

Of course, the Indian Ocean already has a billion-person-plus rising power, with a growing navy and a strong sense of its own role in the modern world. India is another important reason why China will have to tread very carefully in the Indian Ocean. Washington is by no means the only capital where the rapid expansion in China's navy has provoked anxiety; New Delhi has also been watching the developments with some alarm. India and China share a tradition of fraternal ties rooted in the language of anti-colonialism and the Non-Aligned Movement. In 1927, two decades before he became the leader of a newly independent India, Jawaharlal Nehru signed a joint manifesto with delegates from the Chinese Communist Party at an anti-imperialist congress in Brussels. In 1962, however, the two countries fought a brief but fierce war over a border in the Himalayas that is still under dispute, and since then have viewed each other warily. Now that sense of competition is shifting to the Indian Ocean. "Rivalry has been a defining element of India's relations with China for 60 years," says Raja Mohan, one of India's leading foreign-policy analysts. "But it is now beginning to move from the Himalayas to the waters of the Indo-Pacific."

Just like China, India is also turning to the seas, and for many of the same reasons. As India has morphed since the early 1990s from an inward-looking and highly regulated economy to a more open, trading nation, it, too, has begun to fret about the safety of the sea-lanes that its new wealth depends upon. (Alfred Thayer Mahan is now the subject of great interest in India, too.) Having acquired its first aircraft carrier as far back as the 1950s, India now has three, and another which is a museum in Mumbai. Yet India's naval buildup has had a different quality. Although New Delhi considers the Indian Ocean to be its natural backyard, it does not have the same sort of sweeping ownership claim that China presents. India is neither as suspicious of the U.S. as is China, nor is it building a navy specifically designed to challenge the U.S. The Indian navy has also been much more willing to take part in joint exercises with the U.S., signaling its willingness to carry some of the security burdens in the existing U.S.-led system.

In 2005, the U.S. and India signed a nuclear deal which, at first sight, appeared to herald an exciting era of close relations. In return for Washington's turning a blind eye to India's new nuclear weapons, the U.S. hoped that New Delhi would become an important partner in its regional diplomacy. Commentators in the U.S. gushed about the meeting of minds between the two biggest democracies in the world, multicultural U.S. and opinionated, querulous India. Since then, those high hopes have been dashed. Washington has become frustrated at India's willingness to trade with Iran and to side with China at the Copenhagen climate-change conference. The more enthusiastic U.S. supporters of the deal were surprised to find that India still wants to conduct an independent foreign policy. India remains intensely proud of its hard-won autonomy and history of neutrality. The last thing it wants to be is a full-fledged American ally, to play the sort of loyal lieutenant role that Britain does. Nevertheless, New Delhi remains deeply suspicious about the nature of a rising China, and its relationship with Beijing will be shaped by how China decides to pursue its interests in its Indian Ocean backyard. The "String of Pearls" has had more resonance in India than in the U.S., because the idea anticipates India's fear that China will attempt to encircle it. The prospect of a Chinese naval base on its eastern flank (Burma) or its southern tip (Sri Lanka) plays into those fears. And nothing could exacerbate India's anxieties more than a permanent Chinese presence in Pakistan, which would be interpreted in New Delhi as a deliberate move against India. If China makes a concerted push to establish a permanent presence in the Indian Ocean, India will be pushed closer to the U.S.

AMERICAN PARTNERS?

As China's interests and ambitions expand, it is only natural that it will start to think about how to project naval power in the Indian Ocean, yet at every stage it finds itself facing obstacles that will not be easily over-come. It is years away from a naval fleet that could genuinely challenge the U.S., and it will be very hard to establish the sort of permanent naval bases that would undergird a real military presence. And if it does make a big push into the Indian Ocean, it is likely to pour oil on the slow-burning rivalry with India. Given such formidable obstacles, it is pos-sible to imagine that China will take a very different path in the Indian Ocean, and that it will look to collaborate more with the U.S. Navy. Washington has an opportunity to build a different sort of relationship with Beijing in the Indian Ocean, one that is much less inherently con-frontational. Admiral Michael Mullen, the former chairman of the Joint Chiefs of Staff, used to talk about a thousand-ship navy, a global mari-time network that would share the tasks of policing the oceans and of responding to disasters like the 2004 Asian tsunami. There is a chance China could be gradually drawn into the framework of burden shar-ing in the Indian Ocean that already exists. These exercises would be naval confidence-building measures, a way for the two navies to get to know each other and to learn how to rub up against each other. The rivalry in the Near Seas will not disappear, of course, but it is possible that collaboration in the Indian Ocean could take some of the edge off that competition. Or, as retired U.S. Admiral Eric McVadon once put it: "One can readily imagine a scenario in which U.S. Navy F-18s from car-riers are in air-to-air combat with Chinese planes over Taiwan. One can just as readily imagine those same planes . . . protecting sea-lanes from pirates and terrorists."

In small ways, this is already happening. For the last two decades, the most dangerous place in the world for commercial shipping has been the coast off Somalia, including the Gulf of Aden, where pirates have been able to operate freely. Chinese ships have been among those kidnapped. As a result, since 2009, China has been taking part in the international anti-piracy operations in the region. With the U.S. Fifth Fleet based in Bahrain often in the lead, the operations are an organized show of force by more than twenty of the world's largest navies, which escort commercial vessels through the most vulnerable waters. The contribut-ing countries include Denmark, the U.K., Netherlands, Pakistan, and South Korea—in other words, a broad cross-section of the international community. Chinese naval officials now attend the meetings in Bahrain of the international anti-piracy coalition, which goes by the name Shared Awareness and Deconfliction Group (SHADE), a ghoulish acronym that bears the fingerprints of Pentagon bureaucrats. From 2009 to 2012, Chinese warships escorted more than five thousand commercial ships, most of them not Chinese, through the Gulf of Aden. In the larger anti-piracy operations, a convoy of ships from various countries travels up and down the East African coast in a carefully organized pattern, usually with a U.S. destroyer at the helm. The Chinese ships have never operated under U.S. command, but on occasion they have tagged along on these larger drills. The Chinese captains sail five nautical miles to the north or south of the convoy, maintaining a discreet and wary distance—a powerful metaphor for a country that is still not quite sure whether it wants to collaborate with, or challenge, the U.S. maritime order.

3

The Asian Backlash

Tone-Deaf in Hanoi

W HEN YANG JIECHI STOOD to speak, he was almost shaking with anger. China's foreign minister launched into a twenty-five-minute diatribe aimed at most of the other governments at the 2010 Asia-Pacific Summit. "China is a big country," he fumed. "And you are all small countries. And that is a fact." The other ministers were arranged in a square at the Hanoi Convention Center and seated in large leather armchairs, which made it look as if they were slouching, even recoiling. But their mood was very different. A group of Asian ministers had just demonstrated a rare and powerful act of solidarity in defiance of Beijing. U.S. Secretary of State Hillary Clinton had declared that the U.S. viewed the stability of the South China Sea as a fundamental U.S. interest—a pointed rebuke to China, which argues that the disputes in the area have nothing to do with Washington. After she sat down, representatives of twelve other nations, including the host, Vietnam, stood to issue similar statements, some of them with even more direct criticisms of China.

Yang, who started out as an English translator, built his career in part on strong personal connections with the U.S. Back in the late 1970s, he translated for George H. W. Bush and James Baker on a trip to Tibet and became close enough to the Bush family to earn the nickname "Tiger" Yang. After Tiananmen, when Beijing wanted to mend fences with Washington, it was Yang who was dispatched to talk to then president Bush. It is an indication of how far the mood has changed in Beijing that by 2010 Yang felt the need to deliver such a public smack-down; to make sure he got the message right, he was overheard by some diplomats in the corridor beforehand rehearsing lines. Looking directly at Hillary Clinton, Yang told her that "outside powers" should not get involved in the South China Sea. He lectured the nations from Southeast Asia not to become a cabal organized by an outside power. And then he turned to his Vietnamese hosts, the only other government present run by a Communist party. Yang told them they were behaving like a "capitalist sinner." "As a fellow socialist country, you should be fraternal. Don't let yourself be used by an ideological enemy," he said. In the words of one of the diplomats present, it was a "bullying, eloquent, intimidating" speech. But the effect was disastrous. In less than half an hour, Yang managed to tear up more than a decade of subtle, diligent, and highly effective Chinese diplomacy.

More often than not, ministerial summits are all about the smiling photo, especially in Asia, where great emphasis is placed on presenting a unified front. The July 2010 ASEAN Regional Forum in Hanoi has often been cited as the start of the Obama administration's "pivot" to Asia, a broader shift in strategic priorities away from the Middle East and toward addressing the rise of China. But the real significance was elsewhere, in the mini–Asian revolt that prompted Yang's outburst. The summit lifted the lid on the profound anxieties that China's rise has started to prompt across Asia. From Vietnam to Mongolia, from Japan to Australia, China's expanding military might and political confidence are now producing an existential crisis, the perennial angst of "small countries" living alongside a "big country" they do not quite trust.

The central geopolitical assumption about China's rise is that economic heft will bring with it political influence, starting in Asia. During the last ten years, China has become the biggest trading partner of almost every Asian economy, in lots of cases pushing the U.S. out of that position. Yet Asian leaders have started to turn that logic on its head. The dozen governments which lined up behind Hillary Clinton in Hanoi were setting out a new dynamic of Asian diplomacy. Rather than acquiesce to China, most Asian governments will look to counter its influence if it tries to throw its weight around, enlisting the help of the U.S. There is no natural Chinese sphere of influence in Asia. The defining story in Asia in recent years is not the U.S. "pivot"; it is the Asian backlash.

During the Mao period, China supported Communist insurrections across the region in a bid to destabilize unfriendly governments, and during his first few years in power, Deng Xiaoping was equally careless of the opinions of his neighbors. In 1979, he ordered an invasion of Vietnam, and China fought a short skirmish with Vietnam in the South China Sea in 1988. Over time, however, Deng started to take the advice of Lee Kuan Yew, the Singaporean leader, who has at times been an unofficial mentor to China's leaders, and who warned him of the need to mend fences with the rest of the region. Deng's "hiding the brightness" strategy came to have as one of its central priorities establishing good relations with the rest of Asia; if China was going to be accepted as a participant in the global economy, diplomacy in Asia would be an essential task. In particular, Deng wanted Chinese exporters to be plugged into the network of Asian manufacturing that had sprung up since the 1960s in Japan, Taiwan, and South Korea. As China's economy started to take off, Deng instructed his colleagues to be careful about antagonizing their neighbors. For much of the 1990s and 2000s, China went out of its way to ease the concerns of the rest of Asia about its expanding power and wealth, a strategy that came to be known as its "charm offensive." It settled the outstanding land-border disputes with almost all of its neighbors, including Russia, Mongolia, Vietnam, and Burma, often with significant concessions (Burma, for instance, got 82 percent of the disputed land).

The Asian financial crisis in 1997 provided a huge tactical opening. From Bangkok to Seoul, Asian capitals were incensed at the high-handed and dogmatic way they were treated by the U.S. Treasury Department and the International Monetary Fund. Leaders complained loudly that Washington paid no attention to the particular conditions of their countries, opting instead to push the same cookie-cutter solution for everyone's problems. At the same time, China won respect for resisting the urge to devalue its currency and for its calm stewardship during the crisis. China also started to offer cheap loans and aid packages across the region. Anyone traveling through Southeast Asia these days can hardly miss the Chinese-made schools, government buildings, or football stadiums. The mood toward China shifted dramatically. Asian students started to come in large numbers to Chinese universities. Anti-Chinese sentiment had been so intense in Indonesia in the 1970s that Suharto banned the use of Chinese characters in newspapers for the country's large ethnic Chinese population. Yet, when my wife, Angelica, enrolled at a Chinese-language course in 2005 at Shanghai Jiao Tong University, almost half her classmates were Indonesians.

Chinese diplomats even had a poetic phrase to frame the policy—"*mulin, fulin, anlin,*" "establish good neighbors, make them feel prosperous, and make them feel secure." Diplomats from other countries would marvel at the patience and long-term strategy they witnessed in their Chinese counterparts. After 9/11, when the U.S. became obsessed with the threat from terrorism and embroiled in wars in Afghanistan and Iraq, the Chinese stepped up their efforts to present themselves to the rest of Asia as a reliable and trustworthy regional leader. Beijing also promoted regional organizations that excluded the U.S.—with some success, given that senior Bush-administration officials did not even bother to attend a handful of the regional summits. (President George W. Bush annoyed some of his colleagues by pushing to have Islamist terrorism on the agenda at Asia-Pacific summits.) Across the region, America's friends and allies started to doubt its commitment, providing an opening for China to cultivate its own supporters. During much of the 2000s, it was easy to imagine that Asia was gradually slipping into a Chinese sphere of influence, and it became fashionable to write obituaries for American influence in the region. "We are happy to have China as our big brother," Gloria Arroyo, the president of the Philippines—once a U.S. colony and still a treaty ally—said in 2007.

In many ways, Deng's strategy mimicked Bismarck's approach for managing the rise of a unified Germany in the nineteenth century. Bismarck also knew that the country's economy could be stifled if its neighbors formed a coalition to oppose it, and he set about trying to smooth historical enmities, forging strong ties with any country that might potentially become an adversary. As the American writer Walter Russell Mead once put it, this intricate and exhausting policy "sometimes looked like a French bedroom farce as Bismarck hid Austria in the closet when Russia stormed into the bedroom." But Bismarck's diplomacy worked, and Germany's economy overtook Britain's amid relative geopolitical calm. Adopting a similar approach, China has also boomed amid regional stability, its economy overtaking third-place Germany in 2007 and then Japan in 2010 to become the second-largest in the world.

Yet Bismarck's conciliatory approach did not outlast his own downfall from power. When Germany started trying to throw its weight around more in the 1890s, building up its navy and grumbling about territorial disputes, it soon found that republican France and conservative Russia had developed a firm alliance to oppose it. In one symbolic gesture, the Russian tsar stood for "The Marseillaise," the blood-curdling anthem of French republicanism, whose ideas his predecessors had spent much of the previous century fighting. The Hanoi summit in 2010 was also a symbolic turning point, one of those moments when the ground in Asian politics started to shift. As China has become more powerful, it has shown itself to be remarkably tone-deaf about its neighbors. For all the focus on the rivalry between China and the U.S., the most important shift in the region in recent years has been the rise in Asian anxiety about China. For many of the Asian governments in the room, Yang's diatribe lifted away the veil on how China would really behave when it decided that the period of "nourishing obscurity" was over. "It was a revelatory moment," one Asian diplomat present told me.

For two decades, academics have speculated whether the rest of Asia would "balance" or "bandwagon" with China. The Hanoi summit demonstrated that the new dynamic in Asia will involve a form of balancing, a sign that many of the other Asian powers will come together to block China if it pushes hard to assume a dominant role in the region. This will not be the sort of brittle balance-of-power dynamic that plagued Europe in the late nineteenth century, when countries made rigid military commitments to defend one another. Instead, it will be a more fluid and looser arrangement which seeks to marry greater emphasis on security with continued economic integration. Asia has its own built-in balance of power, which will be used to restrain Beijing's worst instincts.

Of course, the backlash did not occur in a vacuum. It is important to understand some of the historical baggage that Asian governments bring to the current situation. Yang Jiechi's implicit threat about big countries and small countries was so powerful because it carried deep memories of a historical relationship many Asian nations once had with China, one they do not want to return to. China may be the new great power of today's global politics, but in Asia it is also very much the traditional power.

THE ORIGINAL MALACCA DILEMMA

The observation tower in Malacca is not for the squeamish. Visitors enter into a circular glass booth, which is then pulled up a white pole to the top, like one of those hotel elevators with glass walls on three sides, but much, much higher. The top is 110 meters into the sky and gives tourists a spectacular 360-degree view of the Malaysian city. The real interest, however, is the extraordinary vista of the narrow sea channel that shares its name with the city. Look southeast and the Strait of Malacca stretches all the way down to Singapore and the entrance to the South China Sea, where, at its narrowest point, it is 2.8 miles wide. To the northwest, the channel eventually gives way to the Indian Ocean. On a clear day, the Indonesian island of Sumatra is visible on the other side, around thirty miles away. It was a Saturday when I visited, but global commerce has no respect for weekends, and, despite the haze, I could make out a large tanker as it was gliding slowly past the city. On any given week, four times more oil tankers pass along this narrow strip of water than go through the Suez Canal, making it perhaps the single most important conduit of globalization. This is the same Strait of Malacca that Hu Jintao fears could be shut down by "certain major powers" in order to asphyxiate the Chinese economy slowly.

Hu's warning, it turns out, is not an entirely new Chinese preoccupation. Not too far from Malacca's observation tower, past the replica of a Portuguese battleship, past the churches painted in red with large white crosses, and next to the old Dutch town hall, there is a small park which almost has a view of the strait. The park boasts a large, imposing statue of Zheng He, the commander of a Chinese fleet that made several visits to Malacca in the early fifteenth century—the last time China had an impressive navy. Nearby is the newly opened museum about Zheng He, which celebrates his presence in the city and tells the story of an earlier era of Chinese naval expeditions.

In the long arc of Chinese history, Zheng He is one of the most intriguing figures. A Muslim with the surname Ma, he was captured during a Ming dynasty army's invasion of what is now China's Yunnan Province. Castrated by his captors, he was sent to serve in Beijing as a palace eunuch; here he became a close confidant of Zhu Di, son of the Ming founder. (It was Zhu Di who gave him the name Zheng He.) Overlooked in the imperial succession by his father, Zhu Di staged a coup and imposed himself as the new emperor, assuming the name Yongle, meaning "perpetual happiness." One of Yongle's most important initiatives was to order a massive expansion in shipbuilding, and when he needed a commander to take charge of the new fleet, he turned to his loyal confidant Zheng He. Between 1405 and 1433, Zheng He led seven different voyages that explored the littorals of Southeast Asia and the Indian Ocean, even making it as far as Kenya, from where he brought back a giraffe to an astonished Chinese court.

His ships were known as "treasure boats." The biggest of them boasted nine masts and were four hundred feet long—making them four times the size of the Portuguese vessels of the age. When Zheng He's fleet set out on one of its voyages, there could be as many as a hundred other ships alongside, some carrying the porcelain, silks, and lacquerware that the Chinese commanders took with them to dazzle their hosts. There were boats to carry cavalry horses, and others that were essentially gunships, with gunpowder catapults. Including the traveling soldiers, the total crew on each trip numbered nearly thirty thousand. Zheng He and his vast fleets traveled freely around the South China Sea and the Indian Ocean, all this almost a century before Vasco da Gama's much smaller fleet arrived in the region.

The city of Malacca became a crucial staging post on his voyages, a place where goods could be stored while the fleet continued its travels around the region. Zheng He built a stockade with towers and four gates near the harbor, and inside it there were granaries and warehouses. As Louise Levathes, author of the excellent history on the voyages *When*

China Ruled the Seas, puts it, Zheng He's fifteenth-century armadas were so vast that they were "not to be surpassed until the invasion fleets of the First World War sailed the seas." Such was their scope and power that they threatened to reshape the map of the region completely. "China extended its sphere of political power and influence throughout the Indian Ocean," she writes. "Half the world was in China's grasp."

And then they stopped. Yongle's successor had no interest in the expensive voyages. Some of the ships rotted away in the harbor; others were burned. Many of the records were destroyed, and laws were passed banning future adventures. For a long time, the voyages of Zheng He's treasure fleet attracted more attention for why they were canceled than for what they actually did. Some historians put it down to new security threats from Mongol invaders in the north, others to the overwhelming cost of running such a large fleet. Confucian scholars resented the influence at court of the eunuchs, many of whom were involved in the naval adventures. Whatever the reason, it was a crucial turning point. China looked inward—just as Europe was catapulting to global dominance, led by its own naval adventurers. The burning of the "treasure fleet" became a symbol for the introspection and stagnation that eventually brought down imperial China in the early twentieth century.

———

Over the last decade, there has been a dramatic revival of interest in the story of Zheng He. A new museum has opened in Nanjing, and the six hundredth anniversary of his first voyage was celebrated with great fanfare in 2005, including a flurry of books and lavish television shows. The museum in Malacca is another example of the burgeoning interest. It is no coincidence that the revival of the Zheng He legend came at the very moment when China's naval modernization was beginning to take shape. The travels of the "eunuch commander" have been recast to provide a compelling and coherent story that knits together China's past maritime adventures with its new age of naval expansion. After an era when naval power was almost a taboo in China, the Zheng He story is a way of legitimizing the topic.

The legend has different messages for different audiences. For the domestic audience, Zheng He is a figure whom Chinese can take pride in, helping to build support for the new tilt toward the oceans. For China's neighbors, the messages Beijing hopes to send are equally important. The magnanimous nature of Zheng He's treasure voyages is a sign that China can be trusted as a benevolent guarantor of the regional order, and that the region need not fear China's new navy. It is also an appeal to a certain spirit of Asian pride. The arrival of Vasco da Gama to the region in the late fifteenth century ushered in an era of five hundred years of colonialism and outside control. After the Portuguese came fleets from the Netherlands, then the British and the French, followed eventually by America and its hulking aircraft carriers. The Zheng He story is a way of saying that Asia can reclaim control over its own destiny, with China's new navy at the helm.

"During the overall course of the seven voyages to the Western Ocean, Zheng He did not occupy a single piece of land, establish any fortress, or seize any wealth from other countries," as Xu Zuyuan, a vice minister of communications, put it in 2004. "He adopted the practice of giving more than he received, and thus he was welcomed and lauded by the people of the various countries along his routes." He added: "The essence of Zheng He's voyages does not lie in how strong the Chinese navy once was, but that China adhered to peaceful diplomacy."

China's most senior leaders have tried to promote the message of Zheng He. During a visit to the U.S., Premier Wen Jiabao used the Zheng He legend to launch a quiet dig at American interventionism in the Bush years. Zheng He "brought silk, tea, and the Chinese culture" to foreign peoples, he said, "but not one inch of land was occupied." Hu Jintao was even more audacious. In a 2003 speech in Australia, he told a Zheng He–inspired story about Chinese links to Australia that well predate Britain, a tale that historians consider far-fetched, but which is rich in symbolism. "The Chinese people have all along cherished amicable feelings about the Australian people," Hu said. "Back in the 1420s, the expeditionary fleets of China's Ming dynasty reached Australian shores. For centuries, the Chinese sailed across vast seas and settled down in what they called Southern Land, or today's Australia. They brought Chinese culture to this land and lived harmoniously with the local people, contributing their proud share to Australia's economy, society, and its thriving pluralistic culture." Why would anyone in Asia seek to balance against a nation, Hu suggested, that only wants such "harmonious" ties with its neighbors? And after five hundred years of outside domination and colonialism, why would Asia need foreigners interfering in its affairs?

At the same time that Beijing was reviving the Zheng He legend, some of the main themes behind the story were beginning to gain currency in Western academic circles. A number of scholars started to suggest that East Asia had sustained a much more stable system of interstate relations in the era before Western colonialists arrived, with China at the helm. Wars and territorial conflicts were much less common than in Europe, the argument went, and diplomatic interactions were more sophisticated. At the heart of this arrangement was a broad acceptance of Chinese leadership, in the form of the "tributary" system. Rulers who paid a level of tribute to China, both political and symbolic, were left to govern their own affairs, untroubled by too much interference from China, which was the principal cultural and intellectual influence in the region.

Such views permeated both the academia and journalism. The American scholar David Kang wrote a well-received 2007 book called *China Rising*, which essentially argued that East Asia was quite content to return to a similar pattern of relations, whereby most countries in the region accepted a degree of Chinese leadership as a natural and stabilizing influence. "China's neighbors recognized the preponderance of Chinese power and accepted it, rather than trying to balance against it," he said of the old regional system. Turning to the present, he added: "Most East Asian states view China's return to being the gravitational center of East Asia as inevitable." In *The Second World*, writer Parag Khanna argued in 2008 that while the U.S. was invading Iraq, China had been binding Asia together into a Greater East Asian Co-Prosperity Sphere, a reference to Japan's 1930s project for an Asian economic bloc, through the force of its economy and the attraction of its culture. He quoted a Malaysian diplomat who claimed, "Creating a community is easy among the yellow and the brown—but not the white."

One of the problems of the Zheng He story is that so few records exist to explain what really happened on his voyages, and the fragments that do remain are open to lots of different interpretations. It may well be that Chinese power and the tributary system acted as a soothing balm over the region long before the West arrived, and that Zheng He organized "voyages of friendship." But there are lots of other ways that his story can be told, many of which cast a very different light on Chinese power and the way it is remembered across the rest of the region. By some accounts, the Zheng He voyages were less about mutual respect and more about inspiring fear in China's neighbors through naval superiority.

The treasure fleet was an impressive sight, to be sure, but there is also some evidence that the voyages were accompanied by substantial violence. Geoffrey Wade, an Australian historian of the Ming period, describes the fleets as an exercise in "shock and awe," an "early form of maritime colonialism," or, more provocatively, as "gunboat diplomacy." Christopher Columbus set out across the oceans with three ships, Vasco da Gama with four, and Magellan with five; Zheng He's fleets had two to three hundred different boats. These huge armadas enjoyed "the best and most advanced firearms in the world," as Wade puts it. Zheng He projected political influence across Southeast Asia not through the inventiveness of Chinese products or the benevolence of Chinese rule, but through a show of naval power that could not be matched. His forces became involved in a civil war in northern Sumatra and in another conflict in Java. In one incident, Zheng He intervened in a conflict in Ceylon (modern-day Sri Lanka), destroying its military before capturing the king and his family members and bringing them back to Nanjing. The military nature of his voyages also left its mark on Malacca. The Chinese used Malacca not just as a place to store goods, Wade argues, but as the site of a semi-permanent military garrison, which Zheng He used to control the traffic along the Strait of Malacca. Even then, policing the strait was an important way of imposing the will of the Ming Empire on the states in the region that relied on maritime commerce. If Wade is correct, that would make Malacca China's first overseas naval base.

One of the problems with the official Chinese story about Zheng He is that it contrasts so dramatically with how China treated other parts of the region in the same era. In 1406, at the same time that Zheng He was on one of his seven voyages, supposedly bringing the marvels of Chinese culture to Southeast Asia, Ming China launched an invasion of what is today northern Vietnam. The Chinese forces disguised their horses with images of lions in order to frighten the elephants that led the Vietnamese forces. A year later, they declared victory after a conflict which by some accounts had killed several hundred thousand Vietnamese. It was a full-blown colonial occupation: China levied taxes on gold and salt, as well as lacquer, sappan wood, kingfisher feathers, fans, and aromatics. In this broader context, Zheng He's voyages seem less like an exercise in benevolent exploration than a crude expression of Ming power. As Zheng He has been quoted as saying, "When we reached foreign countries, we captured barbarian kings who were disrespectful and resisted Chinese civilization."

The competing myths about Zheng He are more than just historical curiosity; they are also hugely important for present-day discussions of Asia. They lay bare some of the fault lines in the region's politics, which are becoming ever more apparent. Behind Beijing's revival of Zheng He, there is a curious disconnect between how China views itself and the way others in the region often view it. Chinese elite and popular views are laced with the sort of sentiments contained in the official Zheng He story, that China's imperial record was benevolent and that it was widely appreciated across the region. Chinese accounts stress that the country was a benign great power, which never sought hegemony, and which attracted others only through the sophistication of its culture and the innovation of its economy. A sense of entitlement lies behind Chinese descriptions of its past "greatness," a feeling that China's centrality and superiority are preordained. "The rise of China is granted by nature," as the Tsinghua University scholar Yan Xuetong once put it. With such a narrow view of the past, there is little understanding of the violence and interference that sometimes accompanied the dominant role China historically played in East Asian affairs. Beijing had hoped the new interest in Zheng He would help make the case for revived Chinese leadership in the region. Yet the same events also serve as a reminder of the subservient position in which other Asian nations were once placed.

Whether the legend is accurate or not, China's revival of it misses the broader point about modern Asia. Countries such as Indonesia, South Korea, and Vietnam do not see themselves as "small nations" alongside a naturally dominant bigger power. They are proud, modern nation-states, which believe that they should be treated on the international stage as equals. In many cases, they have emerged from their own experiences of colonialism to construct resilient states with a strong taste for their own independence. They are not looking for a new era of Chinese protection, benevolent or otherwise. Zheng He is a figure from a world of hierarchy and deference that they do not wish to return to.

THE YEAR IT ALL WENT WRONG

"If Bismarck were in Beijing today, he would say this was our worst nightmare," Shi Yinhong, a scholar at Renmin University in Beijing, once told me. We were talking toward the end of 2010, the year when Beijing managed to alienate pretty much every one of its neighbors in ways that will be very hard to repair over the next decade. Every step China took to pursue its interests or to push back against American influence caused Asian anxieties to rise further. In 2010, Asia's fear of creeping Chinese domination became one of the dominant driving forces in regional politics. Shi Yinhong is one of the cooler-headed realist voices among the foreign-policy community in Beijing, a keen observer of the balance-of-power dynamics that were at the heart of Deng's strategy. He believes China should be doing everything it can to avoid encouraging a coalition of neighboring states that will club together against it. But as he looked around the region in 2010, he could sense that the tide might be starting to turn against China. "Bismarck's advice was always that, if you have five neighbors, you need to be on good terms with at least three," Shi said. "That is not our case."

The Bismarck playbook for China in Asia is pretty straightforward: chip away at America's alliances in the region. The U.S. overcomes the huge distances that separate San Diego and Hawaii from the western Pacific by maintaining a substantial presence in Northeast Asia. That presence is anchored in its decades-old alliances with Japan, where around fifty thousand U.S. soldiers are based, and South Korea, where there are around twenty-eight thousand. For China to assume quietly a much stronger role in the region, one of the quickest routes would be to engineer the gradual erosion of support for America in Japan and South Korea. Throughout the 2000s, there were plenty of warning signs that these alliances were coming under pressure, in part because of the allure of the growing Chinese economy, and in part because of American missteps. Beijing had a game-changing opening to weaken American standing in the region. But, rather than driving a wedge between the U.S. and its most important allies, China has managed to push them much closer together. In its effort to start throwing its weight around, China has reinforced the balance of power in the region in America's direction.

In Japan, the immediate bone of contention was the relocation of the U.S. base Futenma in Okinawa, a long-running and poisonous political argument that has been raging ever since three U.S. servicemen raped a twelve-year-old Japanese girl in Okinawa in 1995. But the Futenma issue reflected a broader unease about the alliance with the U.S. In 2009, voters threw out the Liberal Democratic Party, which had been in power for fifty years, and installed the Democratic Party of Japan, many of whose leaders had grown up in the era of anti–Vietnam War campaigns. The new prime minister, Yukio Hatoyama, openly flirted with the idea of a new East Asian cooperation forum that would bring Japan much closer to China and would cut out the U.S. The U.S.-Japan alliance had never looked so rocky, even during the intense economic disputes of the 1980s. In early 2010, Ichiro Ozawa, the power-behind-the-throne of the new government, took a group of 143 lawmakers to Beijing on a visit that had a deferential air. A smiling Hu Jintao posed for photos and shook the hands of every single member of the Japanese delegation.

Yet Japan was jolted out of its drift away from the U.S. by Beijing's behavior. In August, the two governments found themselves at loggerheads after the Japanese coast guard arrested a Chinese fishing-boat captain who had barged their vessels close to a group of disputed islands, which the Japanese call the Senkaku and in China are called the Diaoyu. (Japan has had administrative control of the islands since the end of the Second World War, though the actual land title was owned by private citizens.) The Chinese response stunned Japan. While the government launched an aggressive diplomatic campaign to get the captain released, large anti-Japanese demonstrations broke out across China. At one stage, the Japanese ambassador was hauled in to receive a formal complaint in what the Xinhua News Agency gleefully described as "the wee hours"—the fourth such dressing-down he had received.

At the same time, China also started to block some exports to Japan of rare earths, metals which are widely used in high-tech manufacturing; this was one of the first times Beijing had so blatantly used economic coercion in a dispute.

China insisted that Japan was using the legal process of the arrest to advance its claim over the islands. But the aggressiveness of the Chinese reaction sent a deep chill through Japanese politics. Support in Tokyo for the idea that Japan should seek greater rapprochement with China and should start to distance itself from the U.S. has withered. Yoichi Funabashi, the editor-in-chief of the *Asahi Shimbun,* one of Japan's leading newspapers, likened the Chinese reaction to a "shock-and-awe campaign." Funabashi had once worked actively to encourage student exchanges between the two countries and had been one of the more liberal voices calling on Japan to make amends with China for its wartime crimes. But in a letter shortly after the dispute, he revealed the sense of disillusionment. "Japan and China now stand at ground zero, and the landscape is a bleak, vast nothingness," he wrote. In an interview shortly afterward, he warned that Asia risked regressing to a "rule of the jungle."

The situation deteriorated further in 2012 over a new argument about the Senkaku/Diaoyu Islands. Japan opened the new dispute. When the nationalist firebrand governor of Tokyo, Shintaro Ishihara, suggested he would buy the islands, the national government intervened and purchased some of the land. Japan thought this less provocative than Ishihara's acquiring the islands, but China's reaction was even more furious than two years before. Beijing accused Tokyo of trying to change the informal status quo surrounding the islands and has maintained a constant stream of patrol vessels around the islands to reinforce its sovereignty claim. At the time of writing, tensions have escalated to such an extent that there is a genuine risk that a mistake or miscalculation between vessels or aircraft of either country could start a broader conflict.

Whatever the rights and wrongs of the immediate dispute, Beijing's reaction has helped consolidate the anti-Chinese shift in Japanese politics. At the end of 2012, the LDP was returned to power, with longtime China skeptic Shinzo Abe as prime minister. Prime ministers may come and go in Japan, but public opinion is now deeply suspicious of China. There is a broad consensus in Japan to shift its military from the north, which was its Cold War focus, to its maritime reaches in the southwest, a direct response to China. Tokyo is now pushing the limits of its espoused pacifism, talking about "dynamic defense cooperation." China's chance to slowly dislodge Japan from its U.S. alliance has been lost.

————

In South Korea, Beijing was presented a similar opening to peel the country away from the U.S. In 2002, riots broke out in Seoul after two middle-school-aged girls were run over by a U.S. armored vehicle, a signal of long-festering resentments about the heavy U.S. military presence in the country. Popular campaigns sprouted over the next decade calling for an end to the American bases. Among younger South Koreans, who had no memory of the war, it became common to suggest that the U.S. soldiers were a greater threat to the country than the North Koreans, whose vast armory of missiles is aimed directly at Seoul. Psy, the South Korean rapper, had the most-watched-ever YouTube video in 2012 with "Gangnam Style." But a decade earlier, his music captured the anti-American mood of his generation of South Koreans. The lyrics to his song "Dear American" included the lines "Kill those fucking Yankees who have been torturing Iraqi captives, Kill those fucking Yankees who ordered them to torture." In one 2002 performance, he smashed a model U.S. tank on the stage.

This popular sentiment found political expression in the "sunshine" policy, introduced in 1998 by President Kim Dae-jung, who had been a dissident while South Korea was a dictatorship. He sought to engage North Korea and to coax it toward Chinese-style reforms. For nearly a decade, Seoul played down human-rights abuses and did everything it could to assuage the hypersensitivity of the North Korean dictator Kim Jong-il. At the same time that George W. Bush was including North Korea in his "axis of evil," the South Korean government was sending Pyongyang hundreds of millions of dollars in bribes—delivered, it was later revealed, by the Hyundai Corporation.

Yet, through its close support of North Korea, China has lost its chance to weaken South Korea's ties to Washington. Beijing's indulgence of Pyongyang has become self-defeating, a triumph of ideology and anti-American paranoia over the country's long-term strategic interests. One of the key turning points was in March 2010, when a South Korean warship called the *Cheonan* was sunk by a torpedo, killing forty-six sailors. An investigation team, which included experts from Sweden and Australia, concluded that the *Cheonan* had been attacked by North Korea. International condemnation quickly followed, yet China demurred. While diplomats from the countries involved in the inquiry toured the world to show other governments their findings, Beijing declined a chance to survey the evidence. The cause of the *Cheonan*'s sinking was unclear, it said. The Chinese government also took five weeks to express condolences to South Korea for the loss of so many soldiers, causing deep offense in Seoul. Nuclear-armed and miserably poor, the Stalinist regime in North Korea relies on Chinese aid to fend off complete collapse. It is also the one country in the region that might plausibly be called an ally of China. The implication seemed clear: Beijing was simply unwilling to criticize its North Korean ally, no matter how dangerous that ally's behavior.

To outsiders, the Chinese position appeared rigid and dogmatic. On the inside, however, China's links with North Korea had been the subject of intense discussion, with many senior officials calling for the government to distance itself from Pyongyang. The alliance had been forged during the Korean War, when China fought alongside Kim Il-sung's army to push back the Americans. Several hundred thousand Chinese died in brutal fighting, including one of Mao Zedong's sons, who was buried there. From that day, Chinese propagandists described the relationship with Pyongyang as being as close as "lips and teeth."

By the early 2000s, however, the sense of comradeship had been replaced by a gnawing embarrassment. Millions were starving in North Korea while cronies of the vulgar, despotic regime of Kim Jong-il nipped across the Chinese border to buy Louis Vuitton goods at the new luxury malls in Shenyang, in the northeast of China. For many Chinese, it was an uncomfortable reminder of the worst days of China under Mao— the mixture of power worship and public misery from which modern China had escaped under Deng. The few scholars I knew who had been allowed contact with North Korea would quietly hint at a sort of shame that China was propping up such a regime. Popular views ran in a similar direction. The Internet in China almost never misses a chance to denounce American policy in the region, but in the case of North Korea, comments would often sympathize with the U.S. and openly mock China's ally.

The booming economic relationship with South Korea also pushed China to question its ties with Pyongyang. Tens of thousands of South Korean companies have invested in China, many of them around the east-coast city of Qingdao, and the flows of goods and people between the two countries have become one of the brightest constellations in the Asian manufacturing network. Two decades ago, there was one flight a week between South Korea and mainland China: by 2010, there were 642. In economic terms, South Korea will be a big part of China's future, not the sclerotic North. Courtesy of WikiLeaks, we know that this frustration occasionally spilled over into the conversations Chinese officials had with other governments. In 2009, Chinese Vice Foreign Minister He Yafei told an American diplomat that North Korea behaves like a "spoiled child." In another cable, a South Korean minister described two conversations with senior Chinese officials who said that they supported the idea of a unified Korea, rather than continuing to prop up Pyongyang. Of course, the Chinese diplomats were doing what good diplomats are supposed to do, presenting a version of events that the South Koreans wanted to hear. But the comments also seem to have reflected the view of significant parts of the foreign-policy establishment. According to Peking University Professor Zhu Feng, no question in Chinese foreign policy has been more hotly debated than the ties with North Korea.

Yet, by the time the *Cheonan* was sunk in early 2010, the party leadership had already ended the debate. China's leaders were given a mortal scare by two developments in North Korea. Kim Jong-il's stroke in 2008 reminded them of the political frailties of the regime. At the same time, a failed currency revaluation in late 2009 underlined the ever-present potential for economic implosion. Faced with the actual prospect of the regime's collapsing, China decided this was something it could not tolerate. Ever since Mao ordered his troops to fight in the Korean War,

China has seen North Korea as a sort of buffer, a placeholder that keeps the U.S. military presence at a distance from its borders. The passage of time and the decrepitude of the Pyongyang regime have not changed that fundamental reality. During a period when China was looking to try and push back against U.S. influence in the region, the last thing Beijing wanted was the end of the North Korean regime and its replacement by an America-friendly, united Korea. Beijing decided to double down on its support for the Kim family regime. Xi Jinping, then China's vice president, gave an extraordinary speech in October 2010, six months after the *Cheonan* sinking, describing the Korean War as "great and just"—a retreat to the 1950s orthodoxy that the U.S. had started the war, and a signal that the fraternal Communist links with the North would trump the economic pull of the modern South. When Kim Jong-il eventually died in 2011, Beijing had already given its support for the dynastic succession plan to hand over North Korea's nuclear keys to his twenty-something son, Kim Jong-un. China, in effect, has pledged to underwrite the North Korean regime for another generation.

The sinking of the *Cheonan* was the moment when South Korea's worst suspicions about China were confirmed. By then, South Korea had a different government, which was much more skeptical about the North and more supportive of Washington. Not only was Seoul outraged at the length of time it took for Beijing to send condolences, but China's continued tolerance for Pyongyang's truculence seemed to suggest to many in the South that it could not be trusted to uphold basic rules of international behavior if they conflicted with its interests. Beijing managed to make things worse with some ham-fisted diplomacy. In November 2010, North Korea shelled the small island of Yeonpyeong, near the sea frontier between the two countries, killing four South Koreans and causing an even more anguished reaction in Seoul. Under pressure to rein in its ally, Beijing decided to call for a meeting of the so-called six-party talks—the diplomatic forum that had been operating for the previous decade to resolve the North Korean nuclear issue. The Chinese government knew that Seoul would not accept talks until it received a public apology from North Korea, but it calculated that the gesture might help deflect some of the blame for the standoff onto South Korea. With no formal warning, Dai Bingguo, the senior Chinese foreign-policy official, turned up in Seoul to discuss the proposal. He did not have a visa, so South Korean Foreign Ministry officials had to rush out to the airport to get him into the country. Dai insisted on meeting with President Lee Myung-bak that evening, even though he did not have an appointment. And even though he asked that the meeting be off the record, he brought a group of Chinese journalists along with him. Lee told him that Seoul would not agree to a meeting involving the North Koreans, but Dai went out and announced the proposed summit anyway. The ill-feeling that Dai generated in Seoul summed up the broader setback to China's long-term interests. By giving so much support to Pyongyang, Beijing was actually doing some of Washington's own diplomatic work. South Korea's unease about the American military presence has not ended, but the alliance between the two countries has been reinforced.

A LINE WITH NINE DASHES

If it was the sinking of the *Cheonan* that prompted a lot of soul-searching in Northeast Asia about China, then the moment of clarity in Southeast Asia came from a more mundane source: the United Nations Commission on the Limits of the Continental Shelf.

In 2009, this largely obscure UN body set a deadline for countries in the region to deliver submissions of their claims in the South China Sea and its myriad of disputed rocks, islets, and coral reefs. The South China Sea has a large and complicated list of claimants. China, Taiwan, and Vietnam claim most of the area and its islands, but the Philippines, Brunei, and Malaysia also claim part. The UN Law of the Sea Treaty provides a framework of international legislation to adjudicate such disputes, a process of case law and precise legal language which is designed to take the heat out of emotionally charged arguments. In the case of the South China Sea, however, the result was the exact opposite. After Vietnam and Malaysia submitted a joint written claim to the panel, China was incensed. Beijing released its own note, which stated: "China has indisputable sovereignty over the islands of the South China Sea and the adjacent waters." Alongside this diplomatic *note verbale*, Beijing attached a map of the area, in which China's claims are demarcated by a line made up of nine dashes.

The "nine-dash line" map was not new: it was first drawn by Chinese cartographers in the 1920s and was adopted as a semi-official map in 1947 under the Nationalist leader Chiang Kai-shek, before the Communists had even taken power. But this was the first time it had been used as part of an official Chinese claim in an international forum. And for many in Southeast Asia, it was a symbol of a certain kind of new Chinese arrogance. Shaped like a large U, the "nine-dash line" starts from China's southwest coast, snakes down adjacent to Vietnam's coastline, curves round along the littorals of Malaysia and Brunei, and then returns to the Chinese mainland after skirting close to the Philippines' coastline. In effect, it marks out almost the entire area of the South China Sea, except a narrow strip beside the coast of the other countries in the region. China says the map is a reflection of its "historical rights" that come from having controlled the different islands for centuries. The Chinese sometimes say the map's U-shape resembles a "cow's tongue"; one acquaintance describes it, slightly less flatteringly, as "a distended testicle."

"We will never seek hegemony," declares China's latest defense White Paper—a stock phrase that is one of the mottoes of official Chinese policy. But in many other Asian capitals, where claims to such "historical rights" inevitably remind them of the subservient position that they were placed in during previous eras of Chinese power, the sheer, jaw-dropping breadth of the Chinese map felt a lot like a push for hegemony. "We maybe should not have been so surprised," a Thai diplomat confided about the introduction of the Chinese map with the "nine-dash line." "But to see with your own eyes that they were actually trying to claim pretty much everything—well, it was quite a jolt."

One legacy of five hundred years of Western naval ascendancy in Asia is the names that are commonly used for many of the island features in the South China Sea—there is Mischief Reef, Macclesfield Bank, Woody Island, and Scarborough Shoal. The sixty or so rocks in the South China Sea are mostly divided into two groups: the Paracel Islands in the northern section of the sea and the Spratlys farther to the south. For decades, the disputes over who owns the land features were a somewhat obscure sideshow, even if China and South Vietnam did briefly fight over some of the islands in 1974, when China took control of the Paracels, and again in 1988. But over the last five years, they have rapidly become a perfect storm of modern geopolitics. The South China Sea has been the place where American and Southeast Asian concerns about China's military buildup have started to overlap. For the U.S., China's claims set off alarm bells about the long-term threat to the U.S. maritime order. But for the Asian claimants, the dispute also brings together oil, fish, and potent nationalism.

For what might appear a few insignificant specks of land, the economic stakes over the disputed South China Sea islands are enormous. In China, the South China Sea is sometimes referred to as a "maritime Daqing"—the oilfield in the northeast of China which was discovered in the 1950s, a lifeline to the Maoist economy in an era of economic isolation, as well as a staple of Communist propaganda about hardworking self-reliance. Chinese estimates suggest there could be as much as 213 billion barrels of oil in the South China Sea, not far short of Saudi Arabia's reserves. Another Chinese estimate suggests there is enough natural gas to meet demand for four hundred years, at current levels of consumption. (Some private estimates are much less optimistic, partly because much of the oil is incredibly hard to recover, indicating reserves closer to 2.5 billion barrels.) If a potential oil boom were not enough, the seas are also rich in fish, making them increasingly attractive to fleets in China and Vietnam, which have seen the stocks in their more traditional catchment areas near the coasts decline through overfishing, pushing them ever farther afield, into contested waters. China is the biggest consumer (and exporter) of seafood in the world, and seafood provides half of the protein intake in the average Vietnamese diet. For both countries, fishing is an industry whose importance is hugely underappreciated.

As tensions have escalated in recent years, China has insisted that the other countries are principally to blame, and it has plenty of evidence to support this claim. Beijing was outraged that Malaysia and Vietnam put forward a joint submission to the UN panel, which the Chinese saw as evidence of other countries' ganging up against them. Chinese officials complain loudly that China is the only country not to have exploited oil resources in the South China Sea. "There are seven hundred wells already in areas that we believe are ours," a Chinese official told me. "And yet people accuse us of being assertive." They point to the buildup of infrastructure on island features controlled by other countries, notably Vietnam in the Spratlys, where it controls twenty-nine of the land features. Beijing is also adamant that Washington's attempt to involve itself in the dispute has emboldened Vietnam and the Philippines to take a more confrontational stance toward China. Many in China are convinced that the U.S. is conspiring against it in the South China Sea. "China is not the maker of these problems and still less the perpetrator of harm," says Cui Tiankai, a former vice foreign minister who became ambassador to the U.S. in 2013. "Rather, China is a victim on which harm has been imposed."

The other claimants tell a very different story. They describe a gradual but decisive increase in China's naval presence in the region over the last decade, as well as a deliberate buildup of military installations on some of the islands that it controls, part of a creeping process in asserting sovereignty. Satellite images from Woody Island (Yongxing in Chinese) in the Paracels bear this out. The small island is around two hundred miles south of the submarine base on Hainan. It has no indigenous population or natural water supply, but over the last few years it has become a fortified military stronghold. A major port has been built from an area that was dredged. At the same time, the landmass has been extended to build a runway for military planes: the satellite images show a thin strip of land almost twice the length of the island. Another thin strip denotes a mile-long road between the island and a small islet, which is now used as a monitoring center for naval activity in the region. In 2012, Beijing declared the island's main town, Sansha, to be a formal municipality. There is a local government building, which, with its painted white walls, long neoclassical columns, and a large dome, looks like a small version of the U.S. Capitol. On the day it was declared a municipality, a local agriculture official from Hainan called Xiao Jie was dispatched on a twenty-hour boat trip to become the mayor. "There is no arable land here," he said of his new job. "The main objective is to protect our nation's maritime sovereignty."

———

Southeast Asian governments accuse Beijing of adopting a strategy of "talk and take." Given the chance, Vietnam and the Philippines can reel off long lists of behaviors by the Chinese they consider to be bullying. The Vietnamese point out that two of the nine lines on the famous Chinese map are in territory which under international law is considered Vietnam's exclusive economic zone, the two-hundred-mile area beyond a country's coast that is recognized by international law. In 2007, Beijing pressured Exxon Mobil and several other foreign oil and gas companies into abandoning drilling operations off the Vietnamese coast—an event that some cite as the start in the current period of tensions. In 2011, Chinese government vessels cut the cables of two ships that were conducting oil and gas surveillance for PetroVietnam. Two months earlier, a Philippine vessel doing a seismological study in a disputed area was forced to leave by two Chinese government ships. Every year, the Chinese authorities enforce a fishing moratorium in parts of the South China Sea, which they say is to preserve stocks, but the decision is not taken with other governments. And each year, they arrest dozens of fishermen who break the moratorium.

It is tempting to think of this activity as a calculated, long-term plan to gradually assert control over the region. Yet, like so many incidents in which China's inner great power has started to be unleashed, there is another side to China's new assertiveness in the South China Sea, a simmering pressure from below to take more action. China's approach to the South China Sea has been one of the clearest examples of how competing vested interests are helping to drive parts of foreign policy—the fracturing in power that the Chinese establishment has witnessed. A whole series of different government bureaucracies have overlapping responsibility for elements of the government's presence in the South China Sea, and sometimes they tussle with one another to make their presence felt. The Chinese are acutely aware of this, labeling the different groups as "the nine dragons," a reference to the ancient legend of a dragon king whose nine sons can be seen in countless murals "stirring up the sea."

Some of that pressure has come from local governments. The government of Hainan Island, where the new naval base is, has administrative responsibility for the Spratlys and Paracels, and for the last two decades has been trying to launch high-end tourism on the islands as part of its own development plan. In recent years, it has gradually worn down the resistance of the central authorities to these initiatives. Travel agencies on Hainan offer luxury diving trips to customers in the Paracels, and there is now a sailing contest between Hainan and the Paracels. The big oil companies, which are among the most connected and powerful sections of state-owned industry, have also lobbied hard for the government to push its claims in the region more aggressively. In 2012, CNOOC, one of the big three oil companies, invited foreign oil groups to exploit jointly nine blocks in disputed areas—several of which are in Vietnam's exclusive economic zone.

Even among the Chinese government departments which enforce activities in the region, there are competing interests. The Bureau of Fisheries Administration is responsible for policing fishing in Chinese waters, but China Marine Surveillance also conducts law-enforcement activities in the region. Like any good bureaucracy, they are both keen to show their worth in order to boost their budgets, which have grown rapidly in recent years. They even have a phrase to justify their sometimes vague and overlapping roles: "Grab what you can on the sea and then afterwards divide responsibility between the agencies." The Agriculture Ministry, which is responsible for the fisheries bureau, operates a reward system for individuals who have been "tough and brave in defending China's sovereignty": officials get a bonus for evicting a large number of foreign boats from waters that China claims as its own. With dozens of armed vessels and aircraft at their disposal, these agencies have also played a role in pushing the boundaries of China's sovereignty claims. While sending the navy could be seen as a highly provocative move, these law-enforcement vessels can stake China's claim in a less confrontational fashion.

There are two other factors behind the deep sense of unease in Southeast Asia. It is not only the extent of China's claim that has rattled the region, but also the ambiguity of it. No one quite knows what they are dealing with. Even though the "nine-dash line" map has been in circulation for several decades, China has never actually defined the territory that is included in its map. At times, Foreign Ministry officials have attempted to calm nerves by indicating that China claims only the islands and land features within the line. Such a claim would still involve a series of difficult disputes but is much less expansive than claiming the entire area on the map. Yet, at other times, Chinese officials and analysts have indicated that their historic "title" to the South China Sea gives them exclusive rights to everything inside the line. Others have suggested that the area is part of China's "sovereign waters." Peng Guangqian, a hawkish major general in the PLA, has described the waters inside the "nine-dash line" as "China's . . . 'blue-colored land'" and as a region "owned" by China. CNOOC's attempt to sell oil leases within disputed waters and the fishing bans imposed by China indicate an official position that is very different from the one outlined by the Foreign Ministry. Such ambiguity could mean several things. It could suggest that there is flexibility in China's position, which could be exploited in negotiations. But it could also mean that China is trying to have it both ways, its diplomats sticking to a narrower claim while its actual behavior pushes for a much more expansive version.

There is also a question of size. In dealing with China, the other countries feel less like sovereign equals and more as if they are trapped next to a large elephant that could swat them aside. That very size difference makes Chinese moves seem much more threatening to its neighbors than Beijing realizes. The Southeast Asian claimants want a multilateral discussion of the different claims, believing that only this will allow them to talk as equals. Fearing the others will gang up on it, China insists that each country should deal with it on a one-on-one basis. For the smaller countries, Beijing's insistence on bilateral negotiations feels like a form of bullying. "China's attitude," says a senior politician from one Southeast Asian nation, "is, 'It does not matter what the precise nature of our ultimate claim is; if we say it is ours, then that means it is ours.'"

———

To be fair to the Chinese, the regional backlash against its behavior in the South China Sea appears to have been given a gentle push by some clever American spin. If there is one area where Washington still holds a decisive advantage over Beijing, it is in the dark arts of the background media briefing. In March 2009, Jeff Bader, the Asia director at the National Security Council, and James Steinberg, the deputy secretary of state, traveled to Beijing for a series of meetings with their Chinese counterparts. The South China Sea was one of the topics that featured heavily in the meetings. A few weeks later, the *New York Times* ran a story saying that China now referred to the South China Sea as a "core interest."

In diplomacy, small phrases can carry immense power. In the code language of Chinese diplomacy, these two words are enormously important. The other "core interests" are Taiwan and Tibet, issues on which the party will move mountains to prevail. To describe the South China Sea in such terms would indeed represent a substantial escalation, a sign that China saw absolutely no room for compromise or negotiation. The Chinese officials had in fact been in an uncompromising mood during the meetings, delivering several lectures on their rights in the South China Sea. Yet Bader and Steinberg insist that the explosive "core interests" formula was never actually used in their meetings. Hillary Clinton later said that Dai Bingguo, the leading Chinese foreign-policy official, used the phrase with her at a U.S.-China summit two months after Bader and Steinberg's meetings, although this, too, is disputed, both by Dai's underlings and by some of the American delegation. ("Hillary appears to have refreshed her memory," as one American official acidly puts it.) Whatever the origin of the phrase, however, China had been snookered. The government could not confirm the statement without provoking outrage in Southeast Asia. But neither could it officially deny the story, for fear that it would be accused by nationalists at home of being weak. Instead, Beijing suffered in silence.

If the "core interest" story was spin, it was the sort of exaggeration that was instantly believed around the region, because it seemed to tally with the reality of Chinese behavior. Washington's rhetoric since 2010 has sometimes leaned on clumsy slogans along the lines of "America is back" in Asia, but the real story was the open door that was waiting for Washington in a region where anxiety about China was soaring. In the Philippines, for instance, there had been popular rejoicing when the U.S. Navy was forced out of its base in Subic Bay in 1992, and leaders like Gloria Arroyo welcomed China as a "big brother." But U.S. warships are now returning with ever-greater frequency, and the country's new president, Benito Aquino, declared in 2012: "We need to take a united stand against the recent aggressive actions from China."

In essence, China has started to suffer from the fundamental contradiction of its strategy. For the best part of two decades, Beijing had been pursuing two separate goals. It has a military strategy of trying to gradually push the U.S. back into the Pacific Ocean and exerting greater control over the Near Seas. At the same time, it has a diplomatic imperative of preventing its neighbors from forming a coalition to block it. Yet it turns out the two goals are not compatible. The harder it pushes back against the U.S. and in favor of its territorial claims, the more it rallies the region to embrace Washington. China has suffered one strategic setback after another. It has ended up strengthening the cornerstone U.S. alliances in Northeast Asia. At the same time, China's behavior in the South China Sea has allowed the U.S. to become much more engaged with the nations of Southeast Asia. As Shi Yinhong, the Chinese academic and Bismarck fan, put it rather mournfully: "We have achieved the very opposite of what we had hoped for."

America's own experience in the nineteenth century demonstrates the extent to which China's strategy has misfired. For almost two centuries, the U.S. has claimed a form of regional ownership and has worked to exclude other great powers from exercising decisive influence in the Western Hemisphere. "Why should we not have our own Monroe Doctrine?" a Chinese diplomat once quietly suggested. He quickly checked himself, because China denies it has any such pretensions, but it is not hard to understand the sense of frustration behind the question. To some Chinese ears, the U.S. operates a double standard by working so hard to prevent China from exerting the same sort of influence that it enjoys in its own backyard. It used to be considered somewhat glib to compare China's attitude toward the Near Seas to the Monroe Doctrine. But as China's claims have hardened, the comparison has started to seem more valid. What are the "nine-dash line" and claims to "historical rights" if not an assertion of a certain sense of ownership and entitlement to regional dominance? Yet the very different history behind the Monroe Doctrine underlines the substantial disconnect between how China sees itself and the way much of Asia experiences China. American naval power from the 1890s was certainly one factor in allowing Washington to expand its writ, but it was not the only one. Just as important was the generous reception that the U.S. received in large parts of Latin America at the time. The Monroe Doctrine was not imposed on an unwilling hemisphere: in much of the region, it was welcomed.

When Brazil hosted the Third Pan-American Conference in 1906, the star turn was Elihu Root, Teddy Roosevelt's secretary of state, who was touring the region to explain the implications of the Monroe Doctrine. Root was given a rapturous reception, because many South American governments saw the Monroe Doctrine not as the imposition of American power but as a guarantee of their independence from European colonial rule. Confidence in Washington was so high that the Brazilians renamed the building that hosted the conference the Palacio Monroe— a name it retained when it became the permanent home for the Senate. Joaquim Nabuco, one of the most influential Brazilians of the era for his role in the abolition of slavery, was happy to publicly declare himself a "Monroista." "For me the Monroe Doctrine means that we have separated ourselves from Europe as completely and definitively as the earth from the moon," he said. Of course, in the decades after the Second World War, during which the U.S. helped overturn elected governments in Guatemala in the 1950s, Brazil in the 1960s, and Chile in the 1970s, the region's view of U.S. primacy shifted dramatically. Anti-Americanism quickly became part of the Latin American political DNA. Since then, many governments have tried to push back against Washington in just the same way that Asians are doing today against China. But the fact that the Brazilian Senate building was named after Monroe underlines the way his doctrine was understood in the region at the time.

The Asian backlash that started to take shape in 2010 will not be easily reversed by China, even if it tries to return to another bout of "smile diplomacy." The year was not a flash in the pan, but instead represented a long-term realignment in Asian politics, one in which many governments concluded that their interests overlapped with those of Washington. One way to demonstrate that this is no temporary setback for China is to look more closely at two pivotal countries in the Asia-Pacific Region, which could not be more different in terms of politics, culture, and history, but which are exhibiting similar instincts about a rising China: Australia and Vietnam.

THE WEATHER VANE

"You could not get much closer to China than we are," Geoff Raby, the former Australian ambassador in Beijing, likes to joke. "But we will." Australia figures in very few accounts of international politics, an isolated if enormous island perched on the bottom edge of the Asia-Pacific with a modest population of twenty-two million. But such neglect is misplaced. For the last three decades, Australia has been an important weather vane for China's rise, a sort of early-warning center for the opportunities and risks. If you want to find out how the world will react to a more powerful China, Australia is a good place to start.

Australia was one of the first countries to wake up to the economic potential of the Chinese boom. The signature breakthrough came in 1985, when the then Chinese leader Hu Yaobang decided to visit Australia. Bob Hawke, Australia's prime minister, threw out the protocol of a formal visit and instead took him on a tour of the Pilbara, a distant region of Western Australia more than three thousand kilometers from Canberra that is rich in minerals. There is a famous photo of the two of them, both in white shirts without ties, standing on top of a mountain and looking across acres of red earth that have since become one of the biggest iron-ore mines in the world. In many ways, the photo was the start of the current commodities boom.

Fast-forward more than two decades, and one-quarter of Australia's exports now go to China, its biggest market. Chinese demand not only soaks up Australian resources, but has caused the prices of those commodities to soar, too. Australia has been one of the biggest beneficiaries of China's growth. The economy has grown every year for the last two decades, even during the financial crisis—the first time this has happened in the country's history, and a record that no other developed economy has matched over the same period. The China market has also created pockets of huge wealth. The average price of a home in Peppermint Grove, the smart suburb of Perth in Western Australia, the heart of the mining boom, is now $5.1 million. With the possible exception of South Korea, no country is now more dependent on the Chinese economy. In Kevin Rudd—or Lu Kewen, as he is known in China—Australia became the first Western country in 2007 to have a prime minister who speaks Chinese. Immigration has also forged a powerful personal link with China, of the sort that can start to mold self-perceptions. Mandarin Chinese has now overtaken Italian as the second-most-spoken language in Australia. Chinese tourists spend more money in Australia than do visitors from any other country.

The extent and velocity of these economic links with China are prompting some profound questions for Australia. Australia has been a loyal ally of the U.S. since the end of the Second World War, and, more than any other country in the Asia-Pacific, Australia is extremely comfortable with U.S. military dominance in the region. The last few decades have been the best in Australia's history. It is free to trade with anyone it wants in Asia, while enjoying the political and military protection of a country with very similar political and cultural traditions. Australians, however, are starting to wonder if they can afford to remain so close to America when they do so much business with China. "Australia is having to ask itself how to reconcile its two core interests," says Michael Wesley, former head of the Lowy Institute, the Sydney-based think tank that is one of the best sources of analysis on China. "Its security, which is tied to the United States, and its prosperity, which is ever more closely tied to China."

Politics will follow economics—that is the core insight behind the predictions of inevitable Chinese leadership in Asia, the idea that the countries which depend on Chinese economic dynamism for their livelihood will start to bend to the political prerogatives of Beijing. If that idea is true, then one might expect to see Australia looking for some sort of middle ground. Indeed, if the Asia-Pacific region was comfortable with the prospect of China's assuming a central leadership role, one of the early signs would be a decision by Australia to drift gradually away from its close defense relationship with the U.S.

Through one of the quirks of presidential scheduling, Presidents George W. Bush and Hu Jintao happened to visit Canberra on consecutive days in 2005, and both leaders were invited to give speeches to Parliament. These were during some of the darkest days of the Iraq War, which Australian troops were helping to fight. Bush, who lectured the audience on the fight against terror, received a reception that might be described as cordial. Hu came to Parliament the next day and gave a very different speech, about respecting differences. "Our world is a diverse place, like a rainbow of many colors," he said. "Civilizations, social systems, and development models, different as they may be, should respect one another, should learn from each other's strong points." The *Australian Financial Review* summed up the visit with the headline "Bush Came, Hu Conquered."

The reaction to the visits was one of the signals of a deeper bout of uncertainty in Australia. At one stage, Australia's foreign minister, Alexander Downer, referred to the alliance treaty with the U.S. as "symbolic." The reality was very different—a treaty imposes legal obligations on both parties—but his comments caused consternation in Washington. The Chinese sought to apply subtle pressure. According to Chen Yonglin, a Chinese defector who had worked at the consulate in Sydney, senior officials in Beijing were openly suggesting that Australia could come to play a role somewhat similar to France's—still part of the Western alliance, but detached from America and willing to take its own path on important issues.

Yet, in the end, the very opposite has happened. Trade with China has boomed, investment from China has boomed, the Australian economy has boomed, yet Australia has not only decided to maintain its ties with the U.S., it has actually strengthened them. In late 2011, Barack Obama visited Australia to announce that up to twenty-five hundred U.S. marines would be deployed to the country, part of an expanded defense alliance between the two countries. "Our enduring interests in the region demand our enduring presence in this region. The United States is a Pacific power, and we are here to stay," he said in a speech to the Australian Parliament, which received a standing ovation.

Of course, a couple of thousand marines will not alter the strategic balance in Asia, but the politics are very important. Australia is defying the apparent logic that China's economic size will give it political influence. Canberra sees that China's military buildup could undermine the stability of the region's economy and believes a robust American military presence is the best way to fend off that prospect, a bulwark against the worst instincts of a more powerful China. As Kevin Rudd told Hillary Clinton, the goal should be to integrate China into the international community "while also preparing to deploy force if everything goes wrong." The U.S. marines are an insurance policy for an uncertain future.

Australia has also been one of the first Western countries to start thinking long and hard about what it means for a democracy to be so economically close to the authoritarian Chinese state. In 2009, Stern Hu, a China-born Australian citizen working for the mining multinational Rio Tinto in Shanghai, was arrested on charges of stealing state secrets. At the time, Rio Tinto was also involved in a tense commercial dispute with Beijing over iron prices, lending a heavy political hue to the arrests. The charges were later reduced to stealing commercial secrets, and Hu received a ten-year jail sentence. Hu admitted to taking bribes, but few in Australia believed he would have been prosecuted had his company not been involved in a difficult argument with the government. A month later, Beijing launched a fierce lobbying campaign to change the program of the Melbourne Film Festival to exclude a film about Rebiya Kadeer, an exiled activist from the heavily Muslim province of Xinjiang in northwestern China whom Beijing accuses of sowing ethnic unrest. When that pressure was ignored, four Chinese films were withdrawn from the festival. The dispute sent a chill through parts of Australia about the implications of growing Chinese influence. "The Chinese embassy told me I had to justify my actions including the [Xinjiang] film in our programme," Richard Moore, the head of the festival, complained. "But, hey, we are just an independent arts organisation and it is our programme!"

Australia will continue to be an important weather vane. Although the beefed-up alliance with the U.S. has broad political support, there are also important and influential critics. Former prime minister Malcolm Fraser has denounced the U.S. approach to China as a rerun of Cold War–style "containment." He derides Washington for thinking of Australia as a "strategic colony, taken for granted, total support for whatever the United States may do." The most articulate criticism of U.S. policy in the region has come from Australia, by the former government adviser-turned-academic Hugh White. In a 2010 essay "Power Shift," he argues that if the U.S. does not find a way to accommodate China's interests in the region, it will slip into an open confrontation with Beijing. "As China grows, America faces a choice of Euclidian clarity," he writes. "If it will not withdraw from Asia and if it will not share power with China, America must contest China's challenge to its leadership." Canberra's role in all this, White says, is to help persuade Washington that it must accommodate China. Australia's debate on how to deal with China is not for the fainthearted. Greg Sheridan, the foreign editor of the newspaper *The Australian,* called White's essay "the single, stupidest strategic document ever prepared in Australian history" and an exercise in "appeasement." Discussions about the relationship with the U.S. will long reverberate, but that does not detract from the basic message behind the new deployment of marines. Australia has decided that, for the next generation at least, it will continue to bet on the U.S.

SWORD LAKE

The first time I visited Vietnam was as a tourist, and for a day or two my wife and I went to what seemed to us the obvious sites in Hanoi. We strolled along wide avenues still lined with trees the French had planted when they were the colonial power, and whiled away an afternoon in street-side cafés. Our hotel, the Metropole, was an imposing colonial building with a white façade, green shutters, and wood paneling that had been the focal point of French society in the city in the 1920s and 1930s. It was very proud of the fresh croissants it baked for breakfast. The next day, we went to the "Hanoi Hilton," the Hoa Loa Prison, where John McCain spent some of his five and a half years as a prisoner of war after his plane was shot down during the Vietnam War. It was built originally by the French, but the North Vietnamese used it as one of the main places for detaining captured American servicemen. Now it is a museum, its walls covered with photos of McCain, whose hair turned prematurely white in captivity.

It took a day or so for us to pick up on something that we would have known if we had been a bit more curious before arriving. However much the Vietnamese detested French colonialism, and however many millions had died in the war with the U.S., these had in many ways been but passing episodes in a much longer history of defending the country's sovereignty. In that longer story, the principal antagonist was China. Half a mile from our hotel was the Hoan Kiem Lake, a shimmering pond filled with water lilies that forms the focal point of the city center. It is also a somewhat mawkish memorial to the struggle against China. The name means "Lake of the Restored Sword," a reference to the legend that Emperor Le Loi was handed a magic sword which he used to fend off the Chinese invasion during the Ming dynasty in the early fifteenth century. Near the shore on the east side, there is a small island accessible by a red bridge. It houses the Ngoc Son Temple, built a couple of hundred years ago to honor a thirteenth-century general who helped defeat the Chinese Yuan dynasty. A couple of miles away, the Hai Ba Trung neighborhood in central Hanoi is named after two sisters who led a three-year-long rebellion against Chinese rule in the first century A.D. When we mentioned that we lived in China, several people immediately informed us how many times China had invaded Vietnam over the years, even if they sometimes offered different numbers.

In the annals of China's imperial history, Vietnam is the one that got away. The Han dynasty occupied a large part of what is today's Vietnam in the second century B.C., and China retained control of the country for most of the next thousand years. Vietnam eventually prized itself free from the Chinese embrace, but that long history has left traces of a sense of entitlement in China. A caption at the Shaanxi History Museum in Xian, one of China's premier collections of antiquity, reads: "Until 200 years ago, Vietnam was part of China, and even today in the homes of Vietnam people you can see Chinese characters." Like all such histories, Vietnam's links with China are full of complexities and discontinuities. Although it was Le Loi's victory in the fifteenth century over Ming invaders that cemented the independence of Vietnam, the decades that followed his triumph were the high point of Confucian cultural influence in Vietnam. But the Hanoi tourist sites underline the broader point; a significant slice of modern Vietnamese identity is rooted in the struggles to maintain autonomy from China. The anxieties stirred in Vietnam by the rise of China are in one sense the direct opposite of the response in Australia. Whereas Australia fears the end of a historical era it has been comfortable with, Vietnam fears a return to an older historical pattern it wants to avoid.

Vietnam is, therefore, one of the most interesting fault lines along the rise of China. More than any other country in the world, Vietnam has a political system that looks very similar to China's—an all-powerful party that is still run on Leninist principles but which has dumped Marx and embraced the market in a bid to modernize its economy and society. The Communist Party ties run deep. In his somewhat intimidating way, it was this spirit of fraternal political unity that Chinese Foreign Minister Yang Jiechi was trying to appeal to in his diatribe in Hanoi. Vietnam also knows that China's economy is one of the main potential growth engines that can drive its own prosperity. Huge public investments in the southwest of China are driving new road and rail links down into northern Vietnam, cementing the economic connections even further. A new high-speed train will soon link Hanoi to Nanning, the capital of the border province of Guangxi. Yet Vietnam is the country where China's great-power posturing is provoking deeper existential angst than almost anywhere else, as a new era of geopolitics collides with some very old Asian histories. Vietnam is thus an important barometer for both the mounting Asian backlash against China and the intricate balance of power that is taking shape in Asia. Hanoi believes it can both integrate its economy with China and seek new friends to help restrain China. Vietnam is working to have it both ways.

China looms large over every issue in Vietnam. Like China, Vietnam has a substantial claim over the South China Sea, including both the Paracel and Spratly Islands, and Hanoi has watched the expansion of China's navy with increasing unease. For Vietnam, the territorial disputes in the South China Sea are about much more than just control of some islands. With the exception of Chile, Vietnam is more dominated than any other country by its coastline, which stretches 3,260 kilometers— "a balcony looking onto the Pacific Ocean," as some Vietnamese describe its location. Vietnam's long-term economic plans talk about deriving 50 percent of its GDP from maritime activities, including fishing and exploiting natural resources in areas it claims as its own. The fate of the small group of rocks and islets in the South China Sea cuts to the core of Vietnam's vision of its own economic future.

Leaders in Vietnam run the constant risk of being accused of selling out to China. After Chinese ships cut the cables of the two Vietnamese oil-survey ships in mid-2011, large anti-Chinese demonstrations broke out in both Hanoi and Ho Chi Minh City. Afraid of being accused of appeasement, the Vietnamese authorities allowed the protests to continue every Sunday for twelve weeks—an eternity for protest movements in a one-party state. The protesters wore T-shirts and caps with the symbol for "No-U"—in reference to the Chinese map for the South China Sea. Others sported the slogan "Say No to the Ox-Tongue Line." Once the protests were eventually shut down by the authorities, some formed a "No-U" football club to play on Sundays.

The fissures of anti-China nationalism cut right across the Vietnamese establishment. In 2011, twenty prominent figures in Vietnamese society—terming themselves "patriotic personalities"—submitted a letter to the Vietnamese Politburo suggesting that Hanoi had been "too soft" on China. Their number included Major General Nguyen Trong Vinh, who had been the country's ambassador to China. Trong Vinh has also been a public critic of a controversial Chinese mining project in the Central Highlands region, which has proved to be a lightning rod for fears about Chinese economic domination. Trong Vinh was joined in that protest by an even more illustrious figure, General Vo Nguyen Giap, whose role as chief military planner in the victory over the French at Dien Bien Phu in 1954 and in the war against the U.S. makes him one of the nation's most celebrated military figures. Vietnam's leadership also has its pro-China faction, and some of the most senior leaders in the country are considered more sympathetic to Beijing. Yet, in both the Vietnamese Communist Party and in the military, analysts say that younger members tend to support closer ties with the U.S. Anti-Chinese sentiment is even stronger among Vietnam's large overseas diaspora, especially the population in the U.S. In some ways, one of the nightmare scenarios for the Vietnamese leaders would be for these different forces to be brought together by a dispute with China—popular nationalism, the anti-Chinese faction among the elite, and a significant section of the diaspora. A serious crisis with China could deal a potentially fatal challenge to the legitimacy of the Vietnamese Communist Party.

Vietnam's response to China's behavior should come as no surprise: it, too, is turning to the seas. Hanoi does not have the resources to mount a significant navy, even though the defense budget is rising sharply, but it can buy the sort of hardware that might allow it to conduct its own "asymmetric" challenge to China. In 2009, Vietnam placed an order for six Kilo-class submarines from Russia—a type dubbed a "black hole" by the U.S. Navy because special rubber tiles allow them to evade detection by sonar. The submarines will help Vietnam to monitor the movements of Chinese vessels in contested areas and to deter any Chinese attempt to grab islands currently occupied by Vietnam. To get a sense of just how seriously Vietnam takes the military challenge from China, it is worth considering that the order for the submarines was placed during the heart of the financial crisis, when the country's export industry was being decimated. And for a country of Vietnam's size, such a number of submarines does not come cheap—the $3.2-billion price tag is equivalent to a year of the entire defense budget.

In the summer of 2010, a U.S. Navy destroyer called the USS *John S. McCain* docked at the Vietnamese port of Danang. The vessel is named after both the father and grandfather of Senator McCain, both of whom were four-star admirals: the eldest McCain captained aircraft carriers in the Pacific War, and his son was commander of the U.S. Navy in the Pacific. Vietnam has not only been investing in its navy, it has also been assiduously making friends with other important naval powers, none more so than the U.S. The visit by the USS *McCain* capped one of the more remarkable turnarounds in Asian politics in recent years. Large tracts of land in Vietnam are still unusable because of unexploded bombs dropped by American planes. Yet, just over three decades after the Americans abandoned their embassy in Saigon, Vietnam has turned to the U.S. for support. The contacts began tentatively in the late 1990s but have gathered pace as concerns about China have risen. In 2009, Vietnam took one important step when several of its senior officers flew out to spend some time on the USS *John C. Stennis*, an aircraft carrier, to view its operations in the South China Sea. The appearance of the USS *McCain* marked the first time the two countries have conducted joint naval activities, in this case a training exercise and a search-and-rescue drill. (They also swapped tips about cooking on board a naval vessel.) If the substance seems a bit trivial, the message to China was not: it was a powerful statement that Vietnam sees the U.S. naval presence in the region as both legitimate and important. "China complains that the

U.S. is stirring up trouble," a senior Vietnamese diplomat told me, "but we think the increased U.S. presence in the region is important to help stabilize the situation."

China routinely denounces any exercise of U.S. military power in the region as evidence of a "Cold War mentality" and of a strategy to "contain" China, just as it once did with the Soviet Union. Washington's new friendship with Vietnam is further evidence to many Chinese that Washington is determined to maintain its hegemony. But China's anger misses the two most important points about Vietnam's rapprochement with the U.S.—both why it is taking place and the actual nature of their military cooperation. The uncomfortable truth for China is that collaboration with the U.S. is not being pushed on Vietnam; it is being solicited. Beijing also ignores the enormous subtlety with which Vietnam deals with China. Rather than shun its neighbor, Hanoi goes out of its way to try and engage Beijing, a delicate dance in which deterrence is mixed carefully with dialogue. Vietnam's suffocating history with China is, of course, an extreme example, but the pattern also fits many other countries in the region. Asia is now a continent of confident nation-states who cherish the autonomy they have won in the postcolonial era, and who want to make the most of the opportunities that globalization is bringing, including the rise of China. But they want to navigate this new era on their own terms, not as someone's "little brother." For Hanoi, setting aside wartime resentments of the U.S. is a price worth paying so it can establish its own path. This is not containment: Vietnam sees the U.S. presence as a way of getting its relationship with China on the right footing.

Hanoi takes elaborate care not to provoke China too far. Whenever Vietnam conducts some sort of exercise with the U.S. military, it usually does something similar with the Chinese shortly before or after. Vietnam and China have a defense hotline that they can use during periods of tension. The two Communist parties have also established a joint steering committee that allows officials from both countries to meet regularly and discuss ways to defuse problems. The party-to-party ties allow for a frankness of conversation that few other countries can achieve with China. Delegations of earnest experts in socialism and Marxism shuttle between the two capitals, glad for the rare chance to exchange ideas in another country. Even with the high level of anti-Chinese sentiment in the country, Vietnam exudes a certain confidence in its ability to cope with a rising China, the sort of self-assurance that comes from experience. In 2012, when China and the Philippines were locked in a tense standoff over the Scarborough Shoal, another disputed section of the South China Sea, a Vietnamese official commented to me, with a slightly world-weary air, "We have been coping with the Chinese for two thousand years. We know exactly how to deal with them." The comments were partly aimed at the Philippines, which was viewed in many quarters as having provoked a fight with Beijing it could not win, but it was also partly aimed at the U.S. This is the great paradox of modern Vietnam. Hanoi is the government that has the most sophisticated channels to talk with Beijing, but its combustible politics and deep-seated historical resentment make Vietnam the country one can most easily imagine fighting a war with China.

————

This complexity places considerable limits on the U.S. Into such waters, Washington should proceed carefully, fully aware of the way its rapprochement with Vietnam might be viewed in China. One of the surest ways for the U.S. to turn a budding rivalry with China into sullen hostility would be to make a big push to expand military ties rapidly with Vietnam. If the U.S. were to start stationing substantial military assets there, for instance, China would begin to think of this as a potential staging point for aggression against its territory. "Vietnam is to China what Cuba is to us," as one former senior U.S. official puts it. "When the Soviets flipped Cuba, we decided that it had profound national security implications. It almost caused the end of the world."

Pushing too hard would also alienate Hanoi. "We do not want to be owned by anyone," the Vietnamese diplomat told me. Closer ties with the U.S. give Vietnam a wedge to avoid being sucked further into a Chinese orbit, but Hanoi has no interest in becoming a new U.S. client state in the region. It wants enough, but not too much U.S. help. Hanoi is still hugely sensitive about allowing a U.S. military presence in the country: the American soldiers taking part in searches for missing personnel from the Vietnam War have to wear civilian clothes when they are outside of U.S. diplomatic compounds. Only once they are inside are they allowed to change back into uniform. Hanoi is also very particular about the use of the Cam Ranh naval base, a natural deep-water harbor near the strategic chokeholds of the South China Sea. Vietnam allows foreign logistics and survey ships to visit the port, but not battleships. Leon Panetta, the former U.S. defense secretary, went to Cam Ranh in 2012 in a high-profile visit that seemed like a major advance in military ties between the two countries. But the U.S. vessel he visited in the harbor was the USNS *Richard E. Byrd,* a cargo ship. For Vietnam, these little details matter a great deal.

Vietnam's relations with China may be unique in their historical complexity and intensity, but they set out the bigger patterns that are starting to shape Asian politics. Behind Vietnam's fervent diplomacy is a fierce desire to avoid being pulled into a Chinese sphere of influence. Yet the Vietnamese regard the U.S. purely as a balancing power, not as an ally, or as a nation they want to see dominate the region, or as a partner in containing China. For both Vietnam and Australia, the endgame is not to circumvent China and its booming economy, but to find ways to deal with China on their own terms. Military cooperation with the U.S. is not a new exercise in containment; it is a way of feeling comfortable about getting closer to China.

4

America's Choice

THERE ARE so many powerful nineteenth-century echoes in China's rise that it is easy to miss the most important exception. When the U.S. and Germany were establishing themselves as great powers, they had the luxury of a relatively benign regional environment. For the U.S. in the 1890s, the European empires which had once dominated its hemisphere, Spain and Portugal, were weak or crumbling, while its neighbors, Canada and Mexico, presented little security threat. "The Americans are a very lucky people," Bismarck liked to joke. "They are bordered to the north and south by weak neighbors and to the east and west by fish." Germany had to deal with a much more complicated set of neighbors, but it also enjoyed the good fortune that its rise was accompanied by decaying empires on its frontiers, from the Austro-Hungarians next door to the Ottomans to the southeast, or the Russian monarchy to the east. China faces a completely different backdrop, a region that is full of successful and ambitious states who also believe this is their time. From South Korea round to Indonesia and then to India, China is encircled, which places significant limits on its ability to get its own way. Japan, even after two decades of stagnation, is still the third-largest economy in the world, and has arguably the most capable navy after that of the U.S. China is not rising in isolation, but into a region of proud nation-states that want to stake their own claims in the modern world.

As a result, there is an iron rule to the new era of geopolitical competition in Asia, which Washington and Beijing ignore at their peril: do not ask the other Asians to choose sides. The government that pushes Asians to pick one power over the other will lose. Modern Asia has its own internal balance of power, which will make it hard for either the U.S. or China to dominate the region. Asians believe they can trade with China and at the same time encourage an active U.S. presence, and they will push back against anyone who tries to force their hands. Everything else follows from this simple understanding.

China's behavior over the last few years has been so counterproductive because it has run up against this iron rule. Beijing was in effect trying to suggest that America is the region's past and China the future, so Asian governments should fall in line with its wishes. Leaders in the Asia-Pacific responded by doubling up on their ties with Washington. The harder China pushes, the more the region's governments will band together into a loose coalition to deter a Chinese push for dominance.

Yet the new Asian reality also poses difficult questions for the U.S. American officials like to say that they have always been attentive to the regional balance of power, but the reality is that the U.S.'s unrivaled military superiority meant that it did not have to think too hard about diplomacy. The difficult process of coalition building seemed less pressing when most challenges could be addressed by sending in an aircraft-carrier group. All this is now changing. Even those who are skeptical about China's current capabilities do not doubt that, over the next two decades, American control of the western Pacific will be substantially loosened. That means the U.S. will have to develop different ways to maintain a favorable balance of power. The U.S. needs to rethink the way it exerts influence in Asia.

An Asia strategy first, not a China strategy. By focusing too closely on China, America tends to overreact to the country, a tunnel vision that leads to the assumption that the U.S. and China are the only central players. The result is a division into two different camps that favor either accommodating China or confronting it, neither of which is wholly realistic.

The hawkish response to China's military buildup is to call for a renewed effort to reassert American supremacy in the region. Pressure is building, especially on the right, for a decisive military response to push back against Chinese assertiveness. Yet down that path lies the potential for a permanent cycle of escalating tensions, of provocations and counter-moves and rising defense budgets. It is a recipe for a contest that would feel a lot like a new Cold War. It would also damage America's ties to the region. If the U.S. takes too confrontational an approach to China, it will lose support of some of its friends and allies, who will accuse Washington of pushing the region toward conflict. A strategy to contain China could not work. Asians want the support of the American military so they can feel comfortable engaging with China, not so they can isolate it.

At the same time, an excessive focus on China can lead America to lean too far in the opposite direction in an effort to accommodate Beijing, to search prematurely for a formula for sharing power between the two giants. The early years of the first Obama administration were full of talk of a G-2 between the U.S. and China to tackle global issues together. Such an effort would also fail the new Asian rule on several fronts. By transmitting a sense of weakness to China, it might actually embolden the more hawkish elements in Beijing, who would sense decline. And it would also terrify many Asian nations who dislike the idea of Asia's becoming a Chinese sphere of influence and who would feel abandoned by the U.S. If such fears took hold, Japan could seek its own nuclear weapons, maybe South Korea, too; Vietnam's existential crisis would deepen. Conflicts could become more likely, not less. Asians do not want the U.S. to confront China, but they also do not want the two governments to conspire to set the regional agenda. Even if Washington wanted to appoint China as a co-leader in Asia, that role is not America's to give.

Instead, it makes more sense to start not with China, but with Asia as a whole. If the U.S. is going with the grain of what most of a rising Asia wants, it will become much easier to fend off any Chinese efforts to alter the status quo. The good news for Washington is that ideas that it says it wants to promote in Asia—free trade, open navigation, legal protections for investment, economic integration across the Pacific, and an emphasis on human rights—are all things that most Asian governments also support. As its military dominance starts to wane, Washington's objective is to help build an Asian regional order based on these principles, which China could not overturn even if it wanted to. All this will require a delicate balancing act. As the iron rule dictates, the U.S. will need to avoid turning China into an implacable enemy. But it also needs to demonstrate to both China and its allies that it has staying power, and that, despite Chinese predictions, it is not about to retreat back across the Pacific for evening cocktails in Hawaii. China and the U.S. will eventually have to learn to live with each other, to find a way to respect each other's interests in the western Pacific, if they are to avoid a rivalry that feels like the Cold War. But that accommodation will be more favorable to the U.S. and more stable for the region if China believes any bid for regional dominance would come at enormous costs and regional isolation.

Elements of this approach are already being developed in what is now called the Obama administration's "pivot" to Asia. The president has left no doubt that he sees the Asia-Pacific as a central long-term priority for U.S. national security. But many of the details are not clear. As things stand, the U.S. economic agenda in the region is shaky, and the hints Washington has given of its new military strategy are downright alarming. This chapter will look at the four pillars of the U.S.'s approach to Asia—military, diplomatic, economic, and political.

HOW NOT TO FIGHT CHINA

In 1992, a young deputy air-force attaché at the U.S. Embassy in Beijing called Mark Stokes started to tour quietly around various parts of the country, looking for clues about what the Chinese military were up to. In those days, there were not nearly as many foreigners living in China as there are today, and in most cities a Western face soon attracted a lot of attention. But by hanging around cities with large military bases, such as Leping in the southern province of Jiangxi, and comparing impressions with what was being written in Chinese military literature, Stokes was able to gain some insights into what the PLA was actually planning. He started to accumulate evidence about what appeared to be the start of a major strategic bet by the Chinese military on medium-range and long-range missiles. It was the first sign that China was building a military that one day might seek to exert greater control over the western Pacific. "In many ways, we are still in the same position we were in then of underestimating China's ability for important breakthroughs in areas that directly challenge the U.S.," says Stokes, who now helps run a consultancy that monitors the Chinese military.

For much of the last two decades, the Pentagon has held an anguished internal debate about the nature of China's military modernization. Back in 1992, plenty of people in the Pentagon dismissed the analysis of people such as Stokes, rejecting the idea that a country as poor as China would have such clear-cut military ambitions. Others argued that China's ability to contest Asia's seas with the U.S. was heavily constrained by its dependency on the global economy. China could not afford to upset the apple cart, they said. In the 1990s, the debate was largely academic, because the U.S. still had a dramatic superiority, which it had coolly demonstrated in the 1995–96 standoff over Taiwan's election. After China launched several missiles into Taiwanese waters in order to intimidate voters, the U.S. sent two aircraft-carrier groups into the region as a demonstration of force. Beijing was furious, but it could not do anything, and Taiwan held its election without further threats. Yet, over the years, the Pentagon has consistently been surprised at the pace of China's military buildup, from its ability to take out satellites to the stealth fighter jet it tested while Bob Gates was in the country. Today, if you ask the question about how the U.S. would respond to a similar crisis, the answer from U.S. military officials often involves a lot of nervous fidgeting.

One of the jobs of a military is to plan for worst-case scenarios. The U.S. military conducts regular war games to test how conflicts with potential adversaries such as China might play out, and in recent years these have delivered some disturbing conclusions. In several of the simulations, the U.S. participants found that Chinese missiles quickly overwhelmed many American bases in the region, as well as sinking some of the aircraft carriers that the U.S. sent into the western Pacific. It is a measure of the rapid advance in China's air force and navy in the last two decades that, if a conflict did break out over Taiwan, it is now not at all clear that the U.S. would be able to intervene decisively in the Taiwan Strait.

The U.S. has not lost an aircraft carrier since the Japanese sank the *Hornet* in 1942. In both practical and symbolic ways, the aircraft carrier has been the symbol of American power projection over the six decades during which it has dominated the Pacific. The credibility of U.S. defense guarantees for the region has been carried on the backs of America's eleven carriers, with their decks each the size of three football fields filled with dozens of fighter aircraft. But it is those same vessels that are now potentially under threat by China's vast new array of missiles. The loss of a carrier would be a massive psychological blow to American prestige and credibility, a naval 9/11. The mere prospect that carriers might be vulnerable could be enough to restrict their use. Even if the U.S. Navy commanders thought their carriers would probably survive in a conflict, they might be reluctant to take the risk. As a result, the U.S. needs a Plan B.

Deep in the bowels of the Pentagon, that new plan is taking shape. It is not actually described as a plan—instead, Pentagon officials call it a new "concept" for fighting wars. But it does have a name, AirSea Battle, which echoes the war-fighting doctrine from the later stages of the Cold War called AirLand Battle, when the massive buildup in Soviet troops appeared to give the U.S.S.R. the capacity to overrun Western Europe. Many of the details about AirSea Battle remain vague. But the few indications that have been made public suggest an approach that, if pushed too far, could be a manifesto for a new Cold War.

———

In 2005, the American writer Robert Kaplan did a cover story for *The Atlantic* entitled "How We Would Fight China." I can remember receiving a copy in my office in Shanghai and tossing it angrily onto a pile of papers, the plastic wrapper still on the magazine. This was the high point of the debacle in Iraq, and the idea of talking up a war with China at that very moment seemed the height of neoconservative conceit. It made me uncomfortable for all sorts of other reasons. When you have recently moved to a country, are learning its language, making friends, and exploring its mysteries, it is unsettling to be asked to start thinking about how it might be defeated militarily. When I did eventually read Kaplan's article a few years later, it was not as hawkish as the title suggested and contained sensible recommendations about getting on better with the rest of Asia and dispersing U.S. military assets across the region. But I also began to realize that the question he raised was a crucial one. China does not have a grand imperial plan to invade its neighbors, in the way the Soviets did. But in any country with a rapidly growing military—one that is feeling its national oats and is involved in a score of unresolved territorial disputes—there is always the risk that its leaders might be tempted by some sort of military solution, the lure of a quick win that would reorder the regional balance. If China and its neighbors all believe that the U.S. has a credible plan for a conflict, this both acts as deterrence against any eventual Chinese adventurism and reduces the risk that anxious Asians will start their own arms races with Beijing. Or, as T. X. Hammes, the American military historian, puts it: "We need to make sure no one in the Chinese military is whispering in their leaders' ears: If you listen to me, we can be in Paris in just two weeks."

Alarming as it may sound, the question of how to fight China also forces Washington to reflect on its deeper objectives in Asia. Bob Gates, the former defense secretary, used to remark that the Pacific had "for all practical purposes been an American lake for our navy since the end of World War II." But relative decline means finding different ways to achieve U.S. goals. With its superiority now under challenge, Washington faces a choice: it can try to retain its primacy, or it can shift to a more defensive approach that is geared toward preventing another power from ever turning the region into a sphere of influence. Deterrence is not always the same as domination. Washington's answer to this question remains muddled. When asked to define their military objectives, American officials will say that deterrence is their principal goal, but they also give plenty of indications that they still aspire to a more maximalist role, to try and hang on to their unquestioned superiority. Shortly after he became head of the U.S. Navy in 2011, Admiral Jonathan Greenert issued a set of "Sailing Directions," which set out the navy's mission and made the claim that "we own the sea." When I asked another senior U.S. official about the objectives of AirSea Battle, he said, a little awkwardly, "It is part of a conversation we are having about the different forms we expect our pre-eminence to take."

AirSea Battle is a direct response to the war-game simulations that showed Chinese missiles taking out American carriers. Its target is the buildup by other nations of what in Pentagon-speak is known as "anti-access/area-denial," or A2AD for short, the weapons and ships that are designed to prevent an opponent from getting into the seas around its coasts in the event of a conflict. "We need to make sure that we can actually get to the fight," an air-force official explained. In public, Pentagon officials claim AirSea Battle is not aimed at China. One senior Pentagon official insisted to me, "This is not an anti-China battle plan." But when the Pentagon starts to describe the new threats it is facing—long-range, precision-strike missiles that can restrict the movements of its ships, advanced submarines, and skills in cyberwar—it becomes clear that AirSea Battle is primarily about China. The hypothetical threat that the Pentagon planners outline describes accurately the precise strategy that China has been developing to restrict U.S. access to the western Pacific. No wonder U.S. military officers sometimes refer to China as "Voldemort"—in the Pentagon's new battle plan, China is the enemy whose name they dare not speak.

Amid the military jargon there lies an idea that—if taken to its logical conclusion—is fraught with peril. The first time AirSea Battle was described in public was in a paper by an independent Washington think tank called the Center for Strategic and Budgetary Assessments. The paper said that if the U.S. and China ever came to blows, the U.S. should direct a "blinding campaign" at China's missiles and sophisticated radars. In early 2012, the Pentagon released a document called "Joint Operational Access Concept" (known in the building as JOAC), a 75-page paper which has a couple of recommendations that stand out. In the event of a conflict, the paper says, the U.S. should "attack the enemy's cyber and space" capabilities. At the same time, the U.S. should attack the enemy's anti-access forces "in depth."

The clear implication of this advice is that, if war ever were to break out, the U.S. should plan to launch extensive bombing raids across mainland China. To neutralize China's weapons that might prevent the U.S. from "getting to the fight," the U.S. would need to take out the missile bases and the surveillance equipment that they rely on, including land-based radar. These facilities are spread across the country, including many highly built-up areas. The basic idea behind AirSea Battle leads to a fairly uncompromising conclusion that, in the early stages of a conflict with Beijing, the U.S. should destroy dozens of military sites across mainland China.

There are several reasons why this would be a dangerous way to think about a conflict with China. For a start, it is a recipe for rapid escalation. Given that two nuclear powers are involved, there should be big incentives to leave room for diplomats to try and find a way to resolve the situation. Yet, in calling for U.S. forces to take out China's missile batteries as a first step, AirSea Battle is a formula to intensify any conflict quickly. It is not at all clear how China would interpret such a bombing attack. American commanders might rationalize their actions by saying that they were only going after the Chinese missiles that could hit their ships and satellites. But the Chinese might well conclude that the U.S. was also targeting its nuclear weapons. The fact that Washington knows so little about the Chinese decision-making process on nuclear war makes this even more risky.

Using AirSea Battle's ideas against China is an all-or-nothing battle plan. Military strategists talk about devising a "theory of victory," a war-fighting plan which will also create the sort of victory that can be translated into a realistic political settlement. But if AirSea Battle means swiftly ordering bombing raids across China, it does not provide any off-ramps that would create space for diplomacy. Short of complete Chinese capitulation, it is difficult to see how such a war would end.

As an approach to fighting, AirSea Battle would likely be very expensive, too. It would require the Pentagon to fast-track a lot of weapons projects, such as a new generation of stealth bomber, at a time when budgets are coming under pressure. It is not only the usual critics of the military-industrial complex who fear this is part of the hidden agenda of AirSea Battle. An analysis by the Marine Corps concluded that the plan would be "preposterously expensive." At the same time, Chinese hawks pushing for more aggressive defense spending would use the American investments as powerful evidence to push their own budget demands. The U.S. military objective should be to deter China, not provoke its hard-liners. Toward the end of the Cold War, the arms race ultimately bankrupted the Soviet Union before the pressures of high defense spending began to seriously undermine the U.S. But if a deeper arms race were to develop between China and the U.S., it is not at all clear that Washington would be starting from a stronger financial footing.

Then there are the allies. The iron rule of Asian geopolitics is to avoid forcing countries to choose, yet it is possible that AirSea Battle would oblige Washington to make some fairly hefty demands of its allies. Asian governments are keen on a U.S. military that can push back against Chinese aggression and are eager to enlist U.S. help in this regard. But some allies might balk at the prospect of a plan to attack deep into mainland China, especially if it involved launching bombing raids from their territory. Ben Schreer, an Australian military strategist, says AirSea Battle is suited to "a future Asian Cold War scenario." Winning the support of allies is even harder when the U.S. cannot tell them much about the plan. Given the high secrecy around AirSea Battle, I have met Japanese and South Korean officials who insist they have been forced to talk with the Center for Strategic and Budgetary Assessments—a think tank—in order to find out what it really means. Rather than providing assurance to its friends and allies, Washington's new battle plan could easily rattle some of them.

All these objections combine to create one final problem with AirSea Battle: Is such an approach politically viable? Whatever the level of international support the U.S. might enjoy at the beginning of a conflict would be sorely tested if the Pentagon were to escalate the dispute quickly into bombing runs on mainland China. Washington would likely face enormous international pressure to desist, putting it immediately on the back foot. Given all the risks, especially the chance of nuclear escalation, it is not at all clear that an American president would ever actually endorse a war plan that involves such a rolling bombing campaign. Successful deterrence relies on being able to demonstrate a military threat that is credible and realistic. Pentagon planners hope the Chinese military will be cowed by the mere thought of an American military strategy based on AirSea Battle. But, equally, the Chinese might come to see it as a one great big bluff.

———

At the very least, AirSea Battle concentrates the mind. It is prompting a much broader debate in the U.S. about how to construct credible deterrence. If the basic objective is to convince Chinese hard-liners that there is no path to a quick win in the western Pacific and to defend its allies, then U.S. strategy should be built around finding ways to raise the costs so that China's leaders would never be tempted even to consider such a proposal—and to do so in ways that are politically and economically realistic and which are not hugely provocative toward China. In its effort to force U.S. carrier groups into the seas around China's coasts, AirSea Battle fights the very war that Beijing has long been planning for. Instead, the U.S. and its allies will have to think about ways to invert that logic—to draw China's untested navy out of its comfort zone, using the region's geography against it and imposing high penalties that would give Chinese military commanders pause for thought.

The American naval historians Toshi Yoshihara and James Holmes suggest that the U.S. partly focus on what they call "war limited by contingent," smaller-scale operations which provide support to allies, preventing dramatic escalation but making life extremely difficult for the Chinese navy. They draw the analogy of the duke of Wellington's campaign in Spain and Portugal in 1807–14, which was in military terms a mere sideshow to the broader conflict with France, but which Napoleon complained gave him "an ulcer." The geography along different parts of the first island chain provides many strategic locations which can be used to construct a series of small-scale facilities with missile batteries, tunnels, and decoys that could create havoc for another navy in the vicinity. These facilities would be purely defensive and would present no direct threat to the Chinese mainland, but they could be used to make it extremely costly and difficult for China to exert control over the nearby seas. Under such an approach, the U.S. could also enhance the sense of deterrence by increasing the number of submarines it has operating in the region. "The ideas that China is pursuing about denying access can work both ways," Holmes told me. "There are many ways to give China an ulcer, which could be one of the best ways of deterring aggression before it ever happens."

In the event of a broader conflict, another option might be to reach back into the Pacific War playbook. During the Second World War, the United States imposed a blockade on Japan that cut it off from the rest of the world for four years, and the same approach could potentially be used again. Rather than seeking to smash China's mainland missile defenses quickly, the military objective would be to impose enough strain on the Chinese economy that China's leaders would be forced to the negotiating table. At first glance, such an approach might sound like an implausible suggestion, given the high degree of dependency between the two economies. But this would be a situation in which the two countries were already involved in a war that had devastated the global economy. The only question is how the U.S. would wish to conduct that war.

The region's maritime geography would help a blockade. Given that so much of China's energy comes from the Middle East, a blockade could be enforced by controlling only five strategic chokepoints—the Straits of Malacca, Sunda, and Lombok, which are the gateways from the Indian Ocean to the Pacific, and the routes to the north and south of Australia. A blockade forces the Chinese navy to come out: rather than operating from the protective confines of its coastal waters, the Chinese would have to launch operations far away from base. China's naval strategy is based on the "asymmetry" of not having to match the U.S. ship for ship, sub for sub. But the farther from China that its forces are required to operate, the greater demands are made on China's more inexperienced commanders.

There are plenty of strategic difficulties with a blockade. Without Russian support for the plan, China would have an overland route. Such a plan is also likely to enhance China's feeling of being under siege: this is, of course, the very "Malacca Dilemma" that China has long fretted about. However, a blockade would afford lots of ways that the leaders of both countries could bring the conflict to an end while saving some face. A slow process, it provides opportunities for both sides to back down while claiming some sort of victory. Such an outcome would be politically messy, with both nations claiming to have prevailed and nationalist tensions soaring. But the result could open the way to a return to the status quo of freedom of navigation in peacetime. In the disastrous scenario of a U.S.-China war, it is at least possible to imagine how such a conflict might end.

Even the proponents of these ideas acknowledge that they are at best half-answers, but they are kick-starting a broader discussion about strategies for deterrence. The debate is also raising difficult questions about how the navy should focus its investment in the coming years. Many of the possible options for a conflict in the western Pacific would require the U.S. to substantially rethink the sort of navy it needs. During one of their presidential debates, Barack Obama mocked Mitt Romney's defense-spending plans by telling him, "We have these things called aircraft carriers, where planes land on them." For almost a century, aircraft carriers have been essential platforms during conflict and powerful diplomatic statements during peacetime, as they roam the world from one harbor to another. But in areas like the western Pacific, their effectiveness could be coming to an end. As Henry Hendrix, a U.S. Navy captain and historian, puts it, aircraft carriers are "big, expensive, vulnerable—and surprisingly irrelevant to the conflicts of the time."

Some parts of the American navy believe that the U.S. should invest in a larger fleet of smaller and faster warships, which would increase the number of targets an opponent's missiles needed to take out but dramatically reduce the political and economic costs if one were hit. Other strategists propose much bigger investments in quiet, stealthy submarines, which would be harder for China's new surveillance technologies to pick up when they operate in the western Pacific. In a more defensive strategy that is designed to prevent another country from exerting sea control over the region, submarines are likely to be one of the main tools. And there are also strong proponents of weaponized drones—unmanned aircraft—which in the future might have the ability to operate at much greater distances from a base or a ship than fighter jets can. All three of these technologies could potentially give American commanders better options than sending in aircraft carriers. Yet downgrading the role of aircraft carriers is a decision fraught with difficulties. The fleet of carriers has become a symbol of American commitment to helping police the oceans. Any significant cut in their numbers would be viewed as a signal of retreat by some U.S. allies in Asia—precisely the people whom the new strategy is designed to reassure. Either way, there are no straightforward answers to the headaches China will cause the Pentagon in the coming years.

LEADING FROM BEHIND

The quest for a military Plan B dovetails with the second leg of American strategy, how to engage with the rest of Asia. As Chapter 3 indicated, the U.S. has the wind in its sails: China's behavior has provoked a powerful backlash in the region, mobilizing Asia's internal balance of power and pushing many of Asia's other rising powers much closer to the U.S. If constructed in the right way, Washington's web of friends and allies in the region could provide a parallel layer of deterrence against a Chinese push to dominate the region.

Yet, despite this fertile territory, the business of managing a coalition in Asia will be an extremely complex and delicate task. Even if it wanted to, the U.S. could not construct an Asian version of NATO. The potential partners are too diverse. They include a solid treaty ally, like Japan, but also a country like India, which would never sign up for anything that looked like a formal alliance, no matter how worried it became about Chinese naval power. Unlike Western Europe during the Cold War, these Asian powers have much less sense of a collective threat. Many countries have individual disputes with China, but they are less likely to intervene in one another's quarrels. Any effort to construct an Asian NATO against China would also break the iron rule: it would come across as the sort of confrontational step that could erode broader support for the U.S. in the region. A rigid alliance would feel a lot like an exercise in containment.

The U.S. also has to avoid being sucked into traps by its allies. Washington's objectives should be to maintain a favorable balance of power and to provide clear defensive arrangements against any potential aggressors. The big risk, however, is that allies will feel emboldened to pick fights with China because they think that the U.S. will bail them out if things get out of hand. Low-level standoffs such as the Scarborough Shoal incident in 2012 will provide dilemmas for Washington about whether or not to intervene. There will also be persistent pressure for the U.S. to pick up the bill for things that its allies are perfectly capable of paying for themselves.

One way to deal with these tensions is for the U.S. to take more of a backseat as new Asian political arrangements emerge. The default instinct in Washington is to try to organize everything, to put itself at the center of the conversation. However, it is also in America's interest to see the creation of robust regional organizations. Asia is a long way from replicating the sort of integration that Europe witnessed after the end of the Second World War, but there is a genuine move toward closer cooperation that, if successful, would help build a more predictable and stable environment. Stronger regional institutions can restrain bigger countries from throwing their weight around too much, and can act as shock absorbers during disputes.

In truth, both the U.S. and China have been lukewarm in the past about Asian regionalism. During the George W. Bush years, the U.S. was somewhat dismissive of the alphabet soup of different Asian organizations that have sprung up over the last three decades, many of which have thus far been ineffectual talking-shops. China, over the last few years, has openly played divide-and-rule at several summits of ASEAN, which brings together Southeast Asian countries, to prevent it from taking a common position over the territorial disputes in the South China Sea. At the July 2012 summit of ASEAN in Cambodia, China used its influence with the Cambodian government, which leans heavily on aid from Beijing, to block the joint statement that some of the members wanted ASEAN to issue. Chinese diplomats were sitting in a room next door to the main session, and the other delegations watched aghast as Cambodian officials shuttled between the official meeting and the Chinese to show them different drafts of the text. Yet, even as ASEAN has struggled to articulate strong positions, its more important members are quietly trying to create a more coherent organization. Indonesia, the potential anchor power in Southeast Asia, is starting to take a more active role in building a regional consensus, as is Singapore.

The same efforts at regionalism are beginning to take shape in the security field. One of the best ways to establish enduring deterrence is to encourage more security cooperation between Asia's other powers, independent of the U.S. China's hard-liners may always think that American presence in the region will be hostage to the next budget crisis in Washington, but its neighbors are not so easy to dismiss. There are already all sorts of signs that this kind of balancing behavior is starting to happen. In addition to its new efforts to collaborate with the U.S.

Navy, Vietnam has signed defense pacts with nine other countries in Asia. Hanoi is restoring its ties with Russia and increasing naval cooperation with India, which has started sending warships through the South China Sea. At the same time, South Korea is cooperating with Indonesia, the Philippines, and Australia. Perhaps the most important potential new axis is between Japan and India, where powerful voices in both countries are pushing the idea of a long-term strategic pact. India and Japan do not share the same disputes with China, but they do have one common interest: just as Japan does not want China to dominate the western Pacific, India does not want China to become a powerful force in the Indian Ocean. Both India and Japan also have burgeoning defense ties with Australia. It is early yet, but these initiatives have the potential to become an important means of balancing Chinese power in the region.

The difficulty for the U.S. will be to avoid getting in the way. Such agreements work in the same direction as American interests, but they run very much counter to the swashbuckling political style of the U.S. The Obama administration found itself on the sharp end of intense criticism when a White House official described the 2011 Libya operation as "leading from behind." Political opponents were quick to slam the idea as a failure of American leadership and of managing decline. Yet, in a future in which its military dominance is challenged and careful diplomacy becomes more important, leading from behind will sometimes be exactly what the U.S. needs to achieve. As Raja Mohan, the Indian analyst, puts it: "The U.S. needs to do less working 'on' Asia and more working with."

The eventual U.S. goal will be to help fashion a loose, informal web of collaboration across the region which is based on shared interests, and which makes it harder for any one country to try and overturn the status quo. Rather than an organized alliance structure, it will be more of a latent coalition, ready in the wings if needed. The central selling point is that it shifts the burden onto China. If Beijing behaves in ways that do not alarm its neighbors, the efforts to balance against it will be only modest. But if China continues to push hard and fans anxieties across the region, then a more robust coalition will take shape against it.

If Washington has the right military strategy and diplomatic arrangements in place, it will then be in a much stronger position to have a conversation with China about the long-term future of the region. The U.S. and China will eventually have to accommodate each other, but this will not be some diplomatic grand bargain, an Asian Treaty of Versailles for the twenty-first century. Instead, it will be a more mundane and long-term set of conversations about establishing rules of the road that allow both countries to live with each other. It will involve establishing limits on the sort of surveillance activities that navies can do, where China has some legitimate complaints. At the same time, the only way to find a way out of the myriad territorial disputes will be negotiations about joint development of energy resources, which the U.S. could conceivably help foster.

To help that process, the U.S. will need to try and establish as good a relationship as possible with the PLA, even while it is building its ties with other Asian countries. At present, the two biggest militaries in the world barely talk. "When we do meet, it hardly rises above the schoolyard," says one former senior officer in the U.S. Pacific Command. The U.S. is partly to blame. Particularly under Donald Rumsfeld, the Pentagon was deeply suspicious of having a closer relationship with China. More recently, it has been China that has put up the barriers, despite encouragement from the U.S. Some Chinese military officers worry about giving away secrets and suspect that U.S. insistence on closer ties is a sign that Washington sees the military balance moving against it. Yet the piracy operations off the coast of Somalia have shown that there is a potential opening for greater cooperation. Further efforts to build confidence should include inviting China to observe some of the naval exercises the U.S. Navy organizes in the region. If their navies work together more on issues such as humanitarian assistance, this could take some of the edge off the inevitable competition. Little will be lost and much potentially gained by being on better speaking terms with the PLA.

IT'S THE ECONOMY, STUPID

America's military presence alone is a thin reed on which to hang an entire Asian strategy. Trade is the lifeblood of the Asian economy, the source of its dynamism and decades of high growth. And it is through trade policy that many in Asia will ultimately judge American seriousness about the region.

During the last election, Asia was barely mentioned, and when it was, the tone of scorn was not hard to detect. China came in for particular criticism—Mitt Romney ran TV ads in Ohio on a constant loop about "Chinese cheaters"—but trading with Asia in general was often presented as a persistent threat to American jobs. As a senior politician in one Southeast Asian country puts it: "No one ever stood up and made the case in favor of globalization, saying that this is why Americans can buy so many cheap goods at Walmart." If Washington wants to remain central to the conversation about Asia's future, then it will need to tell a story about economic engagement with the region that is very different from election-time rhetoric. Asian politicians want to hear American leaders making the case for placing Asia at the center of the country's economic future. And they want to hear that case made in Ohio—and not just when American politicians are visiting the region. Nothing would demonstrate staying power more than long-term American commitments to reduce trade barriers with Asia.

Trade policy is another area in which the U.S. and China are quietly competing to construct the future path of Asia. Washington does actually have an ambitious trade strategy for Asia. The U.S. is now one of the leading proponents of the Trans-Pacific Partnership, a trade agreement that is being negotiated between a group of nations on both sides of the Pacific, including Singapore, South Korea, Australia, Chile, and Mexico. Japan is also hoping to join. The core idea is to establish rules on a series of issues that are not properly covered in existing trade agreements, and which will be at the center of economic governance in the twenty-first century—things like the protection of intellectual property, stronger protection for investment, and restrictions on the generous subsidies that some governments give to their industries. It aims to set high standards which would be binding on all its participants. Trade agreements are slow-burning exercises: TPP has been under negotiation since 2002. But American officials hope TPP can eventually become a template for broader trade integration for the Asia-Pacific Region.

China is pursuing a different path through an initiative called the

Regional Comprehensive Economic Partnership (RCEP). The goals are much less ambitious: a modest reduction in tariffs on some industries, leaving out more politically sensitive areas. It offers an easier but shallower form of trade integration. And from the U.S. point of view, it has the added disadvantage that it seeks to lower barriers only within Asia, not across the Pacific. The stakes are high. If the Chinese approach ends up prevailing, U.S. companies could find themselves at a big disadvantage in some of the world's fastest-growing markets.

America has some big advantages in this competition. Most Asian governments would prefer a model for trade integration that spans the Pacific rather than closing off the region. Yet there are two big sets of problems facing the U.S. trade agenda in Asia. The first is that it excludes so much of the region. Not only is China, the biggest Asian economy, absent from the negotiation, but so is India and nearly half of the members of ASEAN, the Southeast Asian group. It is hard to make the case that the U.S. is pushing regional trade integration when such a large part of the Asian economy is not at the table. Over the coming years, Washington will likely need to develop a second string to its trade agenda, one that complements TPP by finding ways to promote trade integration between the U.S. and other parts of the region. One idea would be a deeper trade partnership with ASEAN. Whatever the approach, however, the U.S. will need a trade strategy that does not give the impression that it is dividing up the region.

There are also lots of questions about TPP itself. Many in Asia question whether the U.S. really has the stomach to push through an important trade deal at a time when unemployment is so high and large sections of the electorate appear to be souring on the benefits to the U.S. of globalization. The success of TPP will also partly hinge on bringing Japan on board, the third-largest economy in the world, despite likely strong opposition from its agriculture lobby. That leaves the U.S. uncomfortably dependent on Japanese politics. If TPP does not progress, it would be an enormous setback to the U.S.'s efforts to demonstrate that it has more to offer Asia than just its navy. "If the U.S. rhetoric on trade is not matched by some action, it is hard to exaggerate the sense of disappointment this will cause," says another senior Asian politician.

BURMA AND HUMAN RIGHTS

On the day I arrived in Yangon, a large crowd was lining the streets of one of the main avenues near the center of town. They were there to greet the country's president, Thein Sein, who had just returned from an overseas trip. Only a couple of years beforehand, such a stage-managed stunt of support for the leader would have been evidence of the corrosive weakness of the Burmese military regime. But this was the autumn of 2012, and there actually was reason to celebrate. Thein Sein, the former general-turned-civilian-politician, had just become the first Burmese leader in four decades to visit the U.S., a political prize for the surprisingly brisk burst of political and economic reforms he had introduced since taking power in 2011. And while he was on American soil, he received an even bigger reward from his new American friends: the Obama administration announced that it would start lifting the sanctions which for most of the previous two decades had smothered its economy. Burma was being welcomed back into the modern world.

The trip was even more remarkable for the odd-couple act that Thein Sein put on with Burma's most famous resident. At the same time that the president visited the U.S., Aung San Suu Kyi was also making her first trip to the country since being released from house arrest in late 2010. For part of her fifteen years of isolation, Thein Sein had been the number-four leader in the Burmese regime that incarcerated her. Yet, as both of them toured the U.S.—he at polite diplomatic engagements at the United Nations, she at a series of rapturous rallies where she was greeted like a rock star—they went out of their way to say glowing things about each other. Whenever he was given the chance, Thein Sein praised her for the responsible role she was playing as the main opposition leader in Parliament. After she was presented with the Congressional Gold Medal, an honor which she had actually been awarded during her period of house arrest, Thein Sein said, "We are proud of her." For her part, Aung San Suu Kyi told audiences that Thein Sein was sincere in his efforts to promote reform, and that he needed all the help he could get from Burma's American friends. For several decades, he had been banned from visiting the U.S. and she had been prevented from trying, but here was the former dissident and her onetime jailer making the case for each other to American audiences. When they met at the Waldorf Astoria in New York, Thein Sein, wearing a V-neck sweater and comfortable shoes, came across as her kindly uncle.

Shortly before he left for the U.S., Thein Sein made another trip, this time to Beijing. In a meeting with Xi Jinping, he insisted that Burma's embrace of democracy would not affect its friendship with its "traditional neighbor" China. But the statement was not really true. The voyage that took Thein Sein to New York was also, in many ways, a journey away from Beijing. The powerful backstory to Burma's perestroika has been a desire to break free from overweening Chinese influence.

There are, of course, many reasons why the new civilian government in Burma has decided to change course after five decades of brutal military rule. There was the gnawing shame of isolation that kept its leaders from traveling to many parts of the world and left its economy hamstrung. In the 1960s, Yangon had been a thriving Asian hub, the sort of place where PanAm flights to the region stopped, but four decades later, the sense of stagnation was overwhelming. Zarganar, the country's best-known comedian, who was jailed four times by the military, described his disbelief when he was allowed to leave the country for the first time and visit Thailand in 2011. "When I saw the airport, I got a shock," he said. "When I saw a good road and big bridge, I got a shock. And seeing the big buildings, I got a shock." Yet, on top of the desire to modernize the country, the new government also wanted to escape from China's suffocating embrace. Burma's political revolution really began in earnest with an act of defiance toward Beijing, the decision to block a plan for a Chinese company to build a huge dam in the northeast of the country. At the time Aung San Suu Kyi was released from house arrest in late 2010, the political direction was still unclear: it could easily have been one more in the series of head feints the military had pulled in the past. The signal that this time things really were different came with the decision to stop the Myitsone Dam (pronounced *Mitso*), which had become the subject of an unprecedented political campaign within Burma. "It was a very significant step," U Han Thar Myint, one of the central committee members of Aung San Suu Kyi's National League for Democracy, told me. "It was the first time that the government had made a major decision based on the opinion of the people in fifty years."

Burma's tilt away from China is yet more evidence of the backlash against Beijing that has seeped across Asia in recent years. But it is significant in another important way. Burma has become a trial run for how much importance the U.S. will place on human rights and political reform in this new era of geopolitical competition in Asia. Burma's opening is raising some fairly fundamental questions about Washington's objectives in Asia. Thein Sein's visit to the U.S. has lent the impression that Burma is in the process of being "flipped," from a nation that sought patronage from China to one that takes direction from the U.S. As the U.S. seeks to shore up its diplomatic presence in the region in response to China, the temptation to try and draw Burma into the American camp is very strong. In a region where a new balance of power is taking shape, there is a certain cold, realistic logic to the idea of downplaying concerns about human rights in order to win new friends. That would be a big mistake. If Washington's objective were to contain China, then it would need the support of as many regimes in the region as it could muster. But if its goal is to foster an Asia of strong, independent states, then political reform and human rights will be a central objective. The endgame in Asia for Washington is not to have a bigger club of sometimes embarrassing friends than China; it is to forge a robust and stable set of rules and institutions laced with American values of openness and political pluralism which will be resistant to Chinese pressure. That is the real prize. And Burma is now the test case.

———

When Western governments imposed sanctions on Burma in the late 1980s, China was far from alone in filling Burma's gap. India has major interests in the country, and there has been a huge amount of Thai investment, including in controversial areas like teak and jewels. But, particularly during the late 2000s, the Chinese presence expanded rapidly. Some of those investments are quirky. Not far from the Shwedagon Pagoda, the gold-domed temple that rises from the center of Yangon, there is a Chinese-run entertainment center called Ice Wonderland, where you can pose beside ice statues of Mickey Mouse and descend slides made from ice. Residents of subtropical Yangon borrow long thermal coats to survive the minus five degrees Celsius. But there are also investments like the Myitsone Dam. The project is one of those jaw-dropping Chinese development schemes that speak to an almost mythical confidence in the power of engineering. The Myitsone Dam was planned to be one of seven in the mountains at the start of the Irrawaddy River that would in total have generated twenty gigawatts—more than the Three Gorges Dam itself. The Chinese group behind the project was CPI, part of one of China's most important energy groups, and run by the daughter of a former Chinese premier.

Right from the start, however, the project encountered resistance. Myitsone is in Kachin State, in one of the areas of the country that have been ravaged for decades by fighting between the government and the Kachin ethnic minority. As Ko Maw Tun Aung, an environmental activist originally from Kachin, told me, Myitsone is an almost sacred place in Kachin culture, considered to be a spiritual birthplace. "It is the sort of mystical place we hear about in bedtime stories," he said. The Chinese also found themselves in bed with some of the least savory elements of the former regime. Their partner was a Burmese company called Asia World, which is the subject of U.S. sanctions and has been accused of being involved in heroin smuggling. The U.S. Treasury Department describes the company's owners as "regime henchmen" and "junta cronies."

In a country where, until recently, politics had been tightly controlled, the dam quickly became a catalyst for an intense burst of campaigning. The well-known writer Ju began to hold events decrying the damage to the river valley. She was joined by cartoonists, artists, composers, and poets. "It is a different country now; it is not good enough for the Chinese just to do a deal with the regime," said the writer Ko Tar. The media also began to campaign aggressively against the dam—led by the Eleven Media Group, which started out publishing a sports weekly but now publishes the most dynamic newspaper in the country. The movement quickly took on a life of its own, largely bypassing the National League for Democracy, Aung San Suu Kyi's party, which was the nominal opposition. Sensing the shifting tide, "the Lady" lent her support. She released a public letter calling for an "amicable" resolution to the issue and made an appearance at a Yangon art gallery that was showing an exhibition about the dam.

Not only did the campaign against the dam open unprecedented space for political activism, it was also notable for the stridently anti-Chinese sentiments that it exposed. The project struck a chord across many sections of society that felt that China had become far too influential during the years of isolation and that it was time to take a stand. U Tin Oo, one of the leading figures in the NLD, described the broader issue as being whether Burma becomes "not just China's satellite state, but China's vassal state." The media coverage of the campaign played up the anti-China angle. Than Htut Aung, chairman and CEO of the Eleven Media Group, said in one interview: "I informed the government and the opposition of the real situation in our country. In the 19th century, the superpowers were the British and the French. They colonised India and us. In the 20th century, the superpower was the US and they took Vietnam, Korea and Germany. In the 21st century, it's China and we cannot sacrifice our country to China. I told the generals and Aung San and she knows." Even among the military, some of whose members have become very rich doing business with China, there was resentment about the regime's closeness to Beijing, which in the 1960s had backed a Communist insurgency and had denounced the Burmese military as "fascist." Thein Sein had himself commanded a unit of the army which fought against the China-backed Burmese Communist Party.

Yangon has some of the buzz of the cool, new thing these days, the best hotels packed with Westerners who have decided to take the chance of looking around. When I met one of the anti-dam activists in a café called Coffee Circles, we were surrounded by hip, young Americans and Europeans, typing on their MacBooks and talking enthusiastically into headphone sets, the sort of frontier atmosphere that you could see in Shanghai a decade ago. Burma is also the exciting new topic in American foreign policy. The dramatic political opening has presented a big strategic opportunity for the U.S., which it has grabbed with both hands. The then secretary of state Hillary Clinton visited the country in late 2011, and Barack Obama followed suit in 2012. But just how the U.S. chooses to engage with Burma's government—and how quickly it withdraws remaining sanctions—will have a big influence on the sort of society that emerges. Plenty of pitfalls lie ahead. The reforms that have been introduced so far to open the economy are only partial, and their success is not assured. Cronyism is easy to catch, but difficult to get rid of. Lots of members of the old regime and the business interests connected to them would be happy to see the government give the impression of reform, allowing sanctions to disappear, while changing little in the way the country is really run. Momentum could easily be lost. The U.S., therefore, faces a lot of difficult decisions. If Washington lets its companies rush in quickly to Burma with few questions asked, it could retard the pace of reform. But if it puts a lot of pressure on the government, some leading figures might seek to tilt back toward China.

In his latest book, *On China*, Henry Kissinger warns that "an explicit American project to . . . create a bloc of democratic states for an ideological crusade is unlikely to succeed." Kissinger has long criticized the Wilsonian tradition in American foreign policy for its missionary, evangelical quality, which he argues alienates potential partners and allies and frustrates national interests. In Asia, he believes that the American promotion of human rights as a central goal is bound to complicate the cool-headed negotiations that Washington will need to have with China in the coming years. The Chinese, he argues, will view this as a threat to their own legitimacy, creating even more competition between the two great powers. Kissinger believes there is too much at stake for the U.S. to indulge in an emotionally satisfying but counterproductive campaign for democracy.

This brand of realism holds strong appeal for many in Washington who are less optimistic than Kissinger about the prospects of doing diplomatic business with China. If the goal is to push back against Chinese adventurism, some argue, that exercise will be made much harder if human rights are treated as a central issue. It will be more difficult, for instance, to improve relations with Vietnam or Cambodia if Washington is constantly harping on their political failings. If the U.S. pushes too hard on human-rights issues, so the argument goes, it could help carve the region into rigid camps, authoritarian and democratic. No one in Asia likes the U.S. when it is delivering shrill lectures about political values that it has been happy to ignore in many other parts of the world. The Obama administration has at times appeared to support parts of this view, especially when dealing directly with China. "Successive administrations and Chinese governments have been poised back and forth on these issues, and we have to continue to press them," Hillary Clinton said before her first visit to Beijing as secretary of state in 2009. "But our pressing on those issues can't interfere with the global economic crisis, the global climate change crisis, and the security crisis."

Yet, in the long run, it would be a mistake to downplay human rights. It is obviously important to get the tone right and to avoid hectoring, but political reform should still be a central plank of U.S. strategy. In some cases, close attention to human-rights issues could aggravate rivalry with China, but the bigger risk for the region is that Washington and Beijing get drawn into a contest for influence in which they are constantly lowering the common denominator in order to avoid "losing" a country to the other side, the cynical logic attributed to Franklin Roosevelt of "he may be a son of a bitch, but he is *our* son of a bitch." In the end, promoting good governance is a way of keeping U.S. policy makers honest. If Washington starts backpedaling on the need for reform in places like Burma, those countries could find themselves pawns in a great-power confrontation between China and the U.S. Elements of the old regime in Burma would be delighted to play Beijing and Washington against each other, allowing them to fend off the pressure for further reforms while maintaining a hold on power. Indeed, some of the activists who helped stop the Myitsone Dam worry that this is already happening. "We are already being used," says Ko Maw Tun Aung. "It feels that we are being played with, that we are slowly being dragged into these regional games."

This debate is already being played out in Washington as the Pentagon tries to revive contacts with a host of militaries around Southeast Asia as part of the Obama administration's "pivot." The U.S. military has reopened links with Indonesia's armed forces, which had been put on hold because of human-rights abuses in East Timor, and it has paid for the sons of Hun Sen, the authoritarian leader of Cambodia, to attend the West Point military academy. Washington is also reviving military-to-military ties with its Burmese counterpart, which over the last two decades has been responsible for a host of crimes against humanity. The Pentagon is confident that, through these sorts of relationships, it can help mold the culture of the military in Burma and boost the careers of younger officers who want to make a break from the past. But it is treacherous terrain, where it is easy to fall back onto the habit of turning a blind eye on abuses in return for political support.

Washington has played this game with Burma before. In the Cold War 1960s, when the U.S. was worried about both Soviet and Chinese influence in Southeast Asia, the U.S. saw the Burmese military as an important counterweight against the spread of communism. The last Burmese president to visit the White House was Ne Win, the very man who ushered in the country's five decades of military rule with the coup he launched in 1962. In 1966, he visited Washington at the invitation of the Johnson administration, which had arranged for him to play golf in Maui for four days on the way. Ne Win was given the keys to the city of Washington, and he and his wife had a private dinner with the Johnsons at the White House. Over the years, Ne Win proved adept at navigating between the U.S. and China as he cemented his hold on power; the Burmese military eventually secured weapons purchases and training from both countries.

———

Burma is an important test in another way. The sort of politics that emerges in countries like Burma will influence the kind of Asian regionalism that develops. Asia will be much more immune to the machinations of great powers if the region is dominated by well-run, independent, and stable states that are free from the sort of crony-vested interests that outsiders can manipulate. States with strong institutions are better able to stand up for themselves. A strong consensus behind transparency and good governance can place limits on the worst elements of the Chinese system—the more ruthless, cash-rich state-owned companies, which support extravagant projects that appeal to some elite interests but have little popular support. Through the remaining sanctions, the U.S. still has the leverage to nudge Burma toward introducing stronger rules for monitoring huge investment projects, such as large dams. In the process, Washington might lose some of its new friends in the Burmese elite, but in the long run it will help Burmese society. If the U.S. appeared to be trying to impose democratic reforms on a reluctant region, it would be breaking the Asian iron rule and creating problems for itself. But the reality is that, across the region, there is strong popular pressure for more transparent and less abusive government. Indeed, if China tries to push back against this trend, it will only intensify the backlash against its influence. Even from a realist's point of view, promoting good governance is also good politics for the U.S. It plays to American strengths and Chinese weaknesses.

If Washington really wanted to "flip" Burma to its side against China, it would fail, if for no other reason than geography. The U.S. is thousands of miles away, but China is right next door—a consumer market of 1.3 billion that is still growing fast. Burma's leaders do not want the Chinese breathing down their necks, but they also realize that China's economy is one of the main keys to Burma's own future prosperity. The controversial Myitsone Dam is only one of a string of major investments that China is conducting in the north of the country, including the twenty-eight-hundred-kilometer rail-and-pipeline project to Burma's Bay of Bengal coast. The government has been eager to gain the good graces of Washington to help dismantle the sanctions that have strangled parts of its economy, but Burma cannot and will not close the door on China. As Aung San Suu Kyi put it: "You must not forget that China is next door and the U.S. is some way away."

The real irony is that the foreign government with the biggest stake in seeing improved human rights in Burma is China. Even though the political opening in Burma has allowed an outburst of anti-Chinese sentiment, there are actually good reasons why China would want a more representative and liberal government in Burma. China's investments in the country have given it a direct stake in several of the uprisings and conflicts between the government and ethnic minorities that have scarred Burma for decades, including the pipeline that runs right across several areas of unrest. Geography also makes China a party to some of these disputes, given both its long, loosely policed border with Burma and the fact that some of its own ethnic minorities in southwestern China are related to groups within Burma. In early 2012, tens of thousands of refugees from Burma fled across the border into China after fighting escalated between the military and the Kachin Independence Army. If a civilian and more representative government can bring some stability to these regions and begin to draw the poison out of long-standing ethnic conflicts, China would stand to gain enormously.

More than any other issue, the promotion of human rights and democracy has to be done with a light touch. Preachy rhetoric does little to change minds, in China or anywhere else. But in the long run, the promotion of more transparent and open government is a central U.S. interest. The more well-governed states there are in Asia, the more resilient and stable the region will be.

Section II

POLITICS AND NATIONALISM

5

China's Brittle Nationalism

A S MIDNIGHT STRUCK to usher in the Chinese New Year, the firecrackers were almost deafening, but Li Yang continued to teach his English class as if nothing were going on. Outside the school gymnasium, the local residents were celebrating the most important holiday of the year, the one day when Chinese families make a special effort to be together. As many as 150 million people return to their hometowns, making the Chinese New Year the biggest annual human migration on the planet. It is also the largest spontaneous fireworks display; the next morning's streets are lined with ash and debris. The roar did not prevent Li Yang from holding his three hundred students in thrall. Standing below a basketball net on an impromptu stage, he shouted out English words in his raspy voice, which they then repeated. "Success!" he called. *"Success!"* they called back. "Sux—sess," he boomed, pausing between the two syllables. *"Sux-sess,"* the enthusiastic audience replied. Li uses a method of language teaching that involves shouting the words—"exercising the tongue muscle," as he calls it—which he believes is essential to overcoming the awkwardness of learning a foreign language.

"Opportunity!" Li shouted. *"OPPORTUNITY!"*

"All right, *bu cuo da jia*. Well done, everybody." He joined them in a loud round of group applause.

Li is at the forefront of the "English fever" that has been sweeping China for the last decade. Learning English has become one of the main paths to social mobility—the key to getting a good job, getting married, and getting on. Researchers estimate that there are between two and three hundred million people studying English throughout China, not far short of the population of the entire U.S. The British Council has calculated that there may be more English speakers in China than there are in India, even though English is the secondary official language of India. English has become the touchstone for the ambitions of China's aspiring middle class. Li Yang, who speaks with an almost pitch-perfect American accent, is the best-known popular English teacher in the country, a cult figure who is treated like a film star, stopping to give autographs to young fans in airport lounges.

The class was taking place in a suburb of Guangzhou, the main city in the south of the country, where the students were attending a week-long "boot camp" that Li runs over the Chinese New Year. Some had traveled from as far away as Xinjiang in the west and Inner Mongolia in the north, a four- or five-hour flight. Throughout the year, Li tours schools across the country to give seminars, visiting as many as two hundred cities each year. His blog was the most popular education-related Web site in the country before he lost interest in daily postings. In the past he has filled entire sports stadiums with his classes, an improvised performance of jokes, advice, and interactive shouting—part teasing and part scolding his students. Beside the stage, one of the teachers wrote a series of inspirational slogans that were projected onto a screen, and Li then used these as the basis for his classes. "Education is the secret to success!" the teacher wrote.

Li has won a broader fame in China for two reasons. His unorthodox teaching methods have attracted a good deal of attention, especially during China's pre-Olympics burst of learning English. More recently, he gained a different kind of notoriety when his estranged American wife won damages in a Chinese court for assault, a 2012 case that broke new ground in the prosecution and discussion of domestic violence in China. Kim Lee, originally from Florida, had helped Li build up his teaching business. She posted pictures on the Internet of her damaged face and ear and described in detail how he "beat me" and then "slammed my head into the floor ten more times." But when I met Li, he had yet to be accused of wife beating, and I was curious about a different aspect of his teaching style. Along the wall in the main classroom were a series of large photographs of soldiers in uniform with slogans such as "Integrity!" and "Duty—It is our Duty to give something back to our great country." The schools are called "boot camps" for a reason. The group of three hundred students is divided into classes of around twenty, each of which is assigned a monitor dressed in army fatigues. The monitor wakes the kids at 6:30 a.m. and brings them downstairs for their first, pre-breakfast shouting exercise. For the large sessions in the main hall with Li Yang, the monitors march the different classes of students in at precise times, with a military anthem blaring, and each monitor carrying a red flag. The cosmopolitanism of "Crazy English" is laced with a harder-edged nationalism.

Li peppers his talks with casual put-downs of America and the English-speaking world. "We Chinese are victims of English—so difficult, but we have to learn it," he tells the audience. He is obsessed with what he sees as the growing softness of young Chinese. Over the New Year holiday his company ran two boot camps—a cheaper version in downtown Guangzhou, and a more expensive, "platinum" camp at a private school in a distant suburb. While driving between the two campuses, he told me that he much prefers the students at the cheaper program, because they work harder. "Chinese kids are becoming spoiled," he says. "We cannot become like the West." Li exhorts his classes to improve their English not just as a means to self-improvement but as a form of patriotic duty. He wants to use language training to stiffen the national backbone. Every one of the students in his courses wears a red windbreaker with Li Yang's signature motto on the back: "Conquer English to Make China Stronger!"

The literary quote most often repeated to me by Chinese friends and acquaintances is not from Mao or Confucius, but from the novelist Lu Xun. "Throughout the ages Chinese have had only one way of looking at foreigners," Lu wrote in the 1930s. "We either look up to them as gods or down on them as wild animals." One of the most interesting, perplexing, and important aspects of the rivalry between Washington and Beijing is modern China's simultaneous admiration for and resentment of America. The three decades of economic reforms have created a tidal wave of Western influences in Chinese cities, from the cars that people drive, to the supermarkets they shop in and the suburbs they now flock to, with their wide roads and neatly spaced uniform houses. The "English fervor" is one part of that mindset. There is no prouder parent in China today than one whose child is studying at a brand-name American university. But there is a parallel instinct that is equally powerful, a desire to stand up to the West, to make up for past injustices, and to restore China to its natural position of superiority.

Every nation's nationalism has a blind spot, a raw nerve that is all too easily tweaked, which reveals a deeper angst. Post-colonial societies have an obvious and natural sense of injustice that colors their view of the West. And rising powers are often particularly touchy, hypersensitive about condescension from the established players. But none of this really captures the potentially toxic quality of modern Chinese nationalism, the nervous energy that is constantly just beneath the surface. China's worldview is being nurtured by an often abrasive brand of nationalism that is informed by deep historical wounds, and which is infused with a desire for payback. "A weak country will be bullied and humiliated," warns one popular Chinese history textbook. China's sense of itself as a great power is closely wound up in this parallel feeling of victimhood. This brittle nationalism provides the emotional underpinning for the emerging contest with the U.S., a constant psychological tension which is shaping many of China's interactions with the world. As Peter Hays Gries, author of a book on modern Chinese nationalism, puts it: "The West is central to the construction of China's identity today: it has become China's alter ego."

Li Yang has positioned himself exactly at the sweet point of this identity crisis, the on-off romance with American-style modernity. The first day I visited the school, Li was wearing a brown suede jacket over a mauve turtleneck sweater, smart jeans, and brown lace-up boots. Along with the designer glasses he was sporting, it was the sort of moneyed, smart casual you see more often in Santa Monica than in mainland China. His classes can sometimes feel like an American civics lesson. Before one of Li's teaching sessions, the screen on the stage was filled by a large video of Barack Obama giving his first election victory speech at Grant Park in Chicago. "If there is anyone out there who still doubts that America is a place where all things are possible . . ." Obama pronounced. Li provided the simultaneous translation when Tony Robbins, the American "life coach," came to China, and there is a strong element of self-help philosophy in his teaching. The students carry around marker pens and ask teachers to write a comment on their "Crazy English" windbreakers. On the shoulder of one of the students, a teacher had written: "Don't forget me when you become President!"

Yet Li delights his students by taking potshots at the foreign teachers in his school, who sat in a circle behind him onstage when he was giving his lectures. He called on one of the teachers to stand up, an American named Shawn who was considerably overweight. "America is a ridiculous country," he boomed. "Why do you people get so fat? Why do you eat so much?" The audience roared with laughter. "Are you offended, Shawn?" he asked. Shawn smiled gamely—a slice of humiliation is clearly part of the contract for teaching at Li's schools. "I hate going to America," Li later told me in his car, a black Buick sedan. "I mostly stay at home and watch TV. What is there to do apart from going to Sam's Club? I find America boring." As the car pulled up to the second school, the driver nearly knocked over one of the teachers by accident. "These foreign teachers, they are so lazy," Li muttered. "They become language teachers because they are too lazy to do anything else. I always tell them this."

NEVER FORGET OUR NATIONAL HUMILIATION

Blame it all, if you like, on Lord Elgin.

China and Greece have one powerful thing in common—a deeply held grievance over the cultural vandalism of the British Empire. In both cases, their resentment is focused on the Bruce family from Fife in Scotland, inheritors of the earldoms of Elgin and Kincardine, and colonial adventurers of the most notorious brand. For Greece, it is the seventh earl, Thomas Bruce, who dominates the family's share of historical infamy. It was he who in 1801 removed the marble sculptures from the Parthenon that are still housed in the British Museum. For the last few decades, Greece has viewed Britain's refusal to return the marbles as an acute form of post-colonial condescension. For modern China, it is his son, the eighth earl, James Bruce, who has a central place in the gallery of foreign villains. It was this Lord Elgin who gave the order in 1860 to set fire to the Yuanming Yuan, the Garden of Perfect Brightness, a vast complex of Qing dynasty gardens and buildings to the northwest of Beijing which were known in English as the Summer Palace.

James Bruce has received much less attention than his father in the U.K. over the years. When Britons reflect on the history of empire, we focus heavily on India and to a lesser extent on East Africa, but we rarely discuss the episodes in China. At my school, we only learned about the Second Opium War, 1856–60, in which Elgin was a central figure, because of the way Lord Palmerston used it for domestic political gain in a general election. When Elgin sailed in 1856 on board the *Furious,* he almost did not make it to China: when they stopped on the way in India, the Sepoy Mutiny, one of the biggest uprisings against colonial rule, broke out, and the governor of Calcutta pleaded with him to use his seventeen hundred troops to help put down the uprising. They were delayed for several months. But their voyage to China culminated in an incident of imperial arrogance that still reverberates a century and a half later, even if it is largely forgotten at home.

Uncomfortable in the claustrophobic confines of the Forbidden City, which had been the focus of power under the Ming dynasty, the Qing dynasty rulers constructed a new compound to the northwest of Beijing on an area of eight hundred acres. Amid the palaces and pavilions, there were opera houses, fountains, waterways, and intricate gardens. The complex also boasted extensive hunting grounds and riding trails, which were among the favorite haunts of Xianfeng, who became the seventh Qing emperor in 1850. He was born at the Summer Palace, by which time it had already become the main seat of power.

Elgin had been dispatched to China after a dispute over a ship called the *Arrow,* which had been impounded by the Chinese authorities. The British used the incident as a pretext to push for greater opening of China to European trade. By September 1860, a British and French force was on the outskirts of Beijing and threatening to invade if Xianfeng did not grant their demands. Elgin sent a small team to conclude an agreement with Xianfeng's envoys, which included a senior British official, Harry

Parkes; Elgin's secretary, Henry Loch; a group of Sikh cavalry; and a journalist from *The Times* called Thomas Bowlby. Instead of reaching a deal, they were imprisoned and tortured. Parkes and Loch were later released, but fifteen of the twenty-six taken prisoner were killed, including Bowlby. According to one of the Sikh soldiers imprisoned with him, Bowlby's dead body was eventually fed to dogs and pigs.

The British and French armies decided they needed to extract symbolic revenge. Elgin later said that he wanted to find a way to punish Xianfeng personally without hurting the residents of Beijing. His solution was to burn the Summer Palace. Xianfeng had already fled, and the compound was unguarded when the French and British troops arrived. At first, the soldiers went on a spree of frenzied looting and plundering, smashing porcelain vases and jade ornaments. After a day, the officers reasserted control over the troops and organized them to complete the main mission: to methodically destroy the elaborate Summer Palace complex.

Outraged at the death of its correspondent, *The Times* supported Elgin's actions, but even at the time, at the height of empire, the Anglo-French force was denounced at home. Victor Hugo said that Elgin was worse than his father and famously warned that the incident would come back to haunt the British and French. The marquess of Bath described it as an act of "vandalism" that was comparable to the sacking of Rome or the burning of the Alexandria Library. On his way to China three years earlier, Elgin had written, "We have often acted towards the Chinese in a manner which is very difficult to justify." But although he later regretted burning the Summer Palace, he defended the decision on the grounds that it was necessary to set an example, so that other Europeans in China would remain safe. It had been a "painful duty," said Elgin, who went on to become viceroy of India. Some of the soldiers he commanded realized the consequences. "The people are very civil, but I think the grandees hate us, as they must after what we did to the palace," Charles George Gordon, who was then a young army captain, later wrote. "You can scarcely imagine the beauty and magnificence of the places we burnt. It made one's heart sore to burn them. . . . It was wretchedly demoralising work for an army."

China's rulers tried to restore many of the buildings that had been destroyed, even if a shortage of funds meant they had not quite completed the job by the time the Boxer Rebellion broke out in 1898. Called I Ho Ch'uan in Chinese or Righteous Harmonious Fists, the Boxers— as they were known in English—were a secret society that called for the expulsion of "foreign devils." The initial target was Chinese Christians, but some British missionaries were also killed. By 1900, the violence against foreigners was so intense that hundreds took refuge in the Legation Quarter in Beijing, where foreign diplomats resided. To relieve the siege, a twenty-thousand-strong army from eight countries made its way to Beijing—six European countries, Japan, and this time the U.S., which had troops in the region following the conquest of the Philippines. After they relieved the Legation Quarter, the foreign armies embarked on what one American marine called an "orgy" of looting, so extensive that the troops later held open-air markets to trade the gold, silver, and silks they had stolen. (Again, the actions of the foreign armies were denounced in their home countries, this time with Mark Twain to the fore.) Before they left Beijing, the armies decided they needed to perform one last act to rub in their victory. They looted, ransacked, and burned down the Summer Palace again.

In some ways, it is surprising that the Summer Palace has been turned into a symbol of the wonders of Han Chinese civilization. The Qing rulers were Manchus, who were considered by many of their Chinese subjects to be foreign barbarians, and the ravishing complex they built was full of overseas influences. A series of marble pavilions in the northeast of the complex, including one known as View of Distant Seas, were actually designed by Jesuit missionaries. The destruction continued for many decades after the foreign armies had left, this time at the hands of ordinary Chinese people, who quietly took away many of the remaining treasures. During the Cultural Revolution, the Summer Palace continued to be thoroughly ransacked. The Zhengjue Temple, one of the few buildings that remained intact, became a boiler factory. But in the late 1970s, as China started to breathe again after the nightmare of the Cultural Revolution, historical interest in the Yuanming Yuan site picked up.

A petition was circulated in 1980 to get funds for its protection—120 years after the duke of Elgin's fateful order. The Chinese historian Wu

Hung described the pavilions of the View of Distant Seas, by then crumbling and smashed columns, as China's "national ruin." A picture of the destroyed pavilions became a regular fixture in popular culture, reproduced on playing cards and cake tins. As interest in the stories of Elgin and the anti-Boxer armies spiked, the Summer Palace site gradually evolved into an emotional symbol of both cultural unity and patriotic outrage. So it was not a complete surprise that, when the G-7 imposed sanctions on China after the 1989 Tiananmen Square Massacre, Deng Xiaoping reached into this collective memory of anti-imperial anger to frame his response. "I am familiar with the history of foreign aggression against China. When I heard the seven Western countries had at their summit decided to impose sanctions on China, my immediate association was to 1900, when the allied forces of the eight powers invaded China," he said.

———

The stories that a country tells about itself say a lot about how it views the rest of the world. Tiananmen was a fundamental break in the way Communist China has decided to describe its own history. During the Mao years, China was the proud winner in a revolutionary struggle against imperialism and its internal class enemies. The Chinese people had stood up, as Mao declared in 1949. There was plenty of anti-foreigner sentiment—during the Cultural Revolution, Red Guards burned down the British embassy—but China presented itself as victor, not one of history's injured parties. After Tiananmen, however, Chinese history-writing started to reflect a very different self-image, a form of anti-Western nationalism that adopted the tone of an aggrieved victim. Jiang Zemin, who took over from the ousted Zhao Ziyang as party secretary-general after the massacre, announced that the education system "must prevent the rise of the worship of the West." In a speech entitled "Patriotism and the Mission of the Chinese Intellectual," he thundered that the U.S. and its allies were "trying to turn China into a vassal state dependent on the Western superpowers." Deng, who continued to pull the strings behind the scenes, gave a speech to the PLA in which he blamed the protests on the way history had been taught to young people. "During the last ten years, our biggest mistake was made in the field of education, primarily ideological and political education," he said. The students had occupied Tiananmen Square and had called into question the very legitimacy of the Communist Party for one simple reason: they had not been taught how to be sufficiently patriotic.

The new patriotic education had a name: National Humiliation History. *Wuwang guochi*—or "Never forget our national humiliation"—had been a popular phrase in the 1920s, after Germany's colonial possessions in China had been handed to Japan at the 1919 Versailles Conference. With their backs to the wall after 1989, the Communist authorities started to lean on the same emotional memory of national humiliation. The school curriculum began to emphasize the "Century of National Humiliation," which started in 1840 with the First Opium War and ended with the Communist takeover in 1949. This time frame knits together the different invasions, unfair treaties, economic exploitation, and other indignities that a weakened China suffered at the hands of the Western powers. The destruction of the Summer Palace, first by Elgin, then by the anti-Boxer armies, became a central episode in the narrative.

The bullying, war crimes, and injustice were real, of course, the genuine story of a proud civilization humbled by foreigners who had become more powerful without anyone in China realizing it. Yet it is also a version of history that leaves out as much as it includes. Qing China (1644–1912) ruled a country twice the size of the one controlled by the Ming dynasty that preceded it (1368–1644). Long before British warships ever sailed up the Yangtze, China's frontiers had been a constantly shifting map that contained their own stories of expansion and aggression. One of the foundational myths of modern Chinese identity is the benevolence of imperial rule, the belief that China expanded as a result of the superiority of its culture rather than the strength of its armed forces. Today's official histories also have little to say about the Taiping Rebellion, a civil war in the 1850s which Elgin stumbled into, and which took as many as twenty million Chinese lives, making it one of the most brutal episodes in China's or any country's history. In the "national humiliation" canon, Qing China was neither an expansionary empire nor a dynasty whose writ was crumbling, but a victim of history—a defenseless and naïve innocent plundered by a warmongering West.

To mark the 150th anniversary of the First Opium War, a book entitled *The Indignation of National Humiliation* was published in 1990, the first in a series of new textbooks that aimed to provide the patriotic lessons Deng thought China's youth needed. The 1998 text *Never Forget National Humiliation* set as its goal the rejuvenation of a Chinese nation that would "rise again to be an awesome and gracious great power like in the past that will stand lofty and firm in the Eastern part of the World." Another school textbook implored its student readers: "In modern Chinese history since the Opium War, foreign powers have launched invasion after invasion, act after bloody act of coercive pillage, occupying Chinese sovereign territory, slaughtering the Chinese masses, looting China's wealth, and stealing China's cultural artefacts. All this stained China with blood and tears." Jiang Zemin ordered that the curriculum start in kindergarten.

The new emphasis on National Humiliation History proved hugely popular; its themes were used to frame major political events. During the 1997 handover of Hong Kong from British rule, Jiang Zemin described the occupation of Hong Kong as "the epitome of the humiliation that China suffered." Speaking to a huge crowd in Beijing two days after the handover, he announced: "The return of Hong Kong marks an end to the 100-year national humiliation." When a NATO bomb hit the Chinese Embassy in Belgrade, a *People's Daily* article thundered: "It is 1999, not 1899. . . . This is not the age when Western powers plundered the imperial palace at will. . . . The Chinese people are not to be bullied. . . . In the veins of the Chinese people circulate the blood of the anti-imperialist patriots over a period of 150-plus years." The slogan "Never Forget National Humiliation, Rejuvenate China" started to appear on signs in parks. An aerial photo shows a group of Chinese police forming the phrase with their bodies as part of a parade-ground drill. In the aftermath of a 2001 diplomatic standoff between China and the U.S. after China shot down a U.S. spy plane, the government declared a National Humiliation Day in mid-September. Thousands of students turned out to celebrate the occasion at the Summer Palace. "This is the national phrase of China," says the historian Zheng Wang. "It is the key to [the] cultural and historic formation of Chinese nationalism."

———

At first sight, it seems an odd sort of political project, to encourage national regeneration by constantly harping on past suffering. Not only is history written by the victors, but it usually dwells on the victories. Instead, China has developed a form of hair-shirt nationalism, the manipulation of the authority that comes from past suffering to forge a permanent sense of victimhood. The Communist Party has faced a slow-burning threat to its legitimacy ever since it dumped Marx for the market and dropped the Mao cult of personality, a threat that was only exacerbated after it turned the army on its own people in Tiananmen. Chinese sometimes talk about their *xinyang weiji*, a crisis of faith which has eaten away at society as the old Confucian or socialist sense of order has eroded. The emphasis on humiliation has helped the Communist Party create a sense of unity that had been fracturing, and to define a Chinese identity fundamentally at odds with American modernity. This strand of nationalism has become an important part of its claim to maintaining a monopoly of political power, a deliberate project to mold the historical instincts of young Chinese.

The crude version of history that is portrayed in Chinese textbooks is scorned in private by Chinese academics, but it is a dangerous orthodoxy to oppose. One of the most dramatic acts of censorship in recent times involved the writing of history—and not just any history, but the story behind the burning of the Summer Palace. In 2006, the authorities closed a magazine called *Freezing Point* after it published an article by Zhongshan University historian Yuan Weishi which took issue with what he saw as the blind nationalism and anti-foreigner sentiment of school textbooks. The official Chinese histories, he said, completely glossed over the mistakes made in the later years of the Qing dynasty. Professor Yuan did not doubt the official version of how the palaces and gardens at the Summer Palace had been destroyed. But he suggested that China broke its word by arresting the diplomats and killing the soldiers. The Qing rulers, he said, had been asking for trouble. He also objected to the way the Boxer Rebellion was constantly praised as "a magnificent feat of patriotism," while the violence against foreigners was ignored. "Our youth are still drinking wolf's milk," Yuan wrote, a reference to the excuse people gave during the Cultural Revolution for violent excesses. The new generation of textbooks "suggest that the current Chinese culture is superior and unmatched and that outside culture is evil and corrodes the purity of existing culture. . . . To use this kind of logic to quietly exert a subtle influence on our children is an unforgivable harm."

For daring to criticize the official verdict, Yuan Weishi was vilified. He had "attempted to vindicate the criminal acts of the invading powers," as the propaganda authorities put it. Li Datong, managing editor of the magazine, was fired. *Freezing Point* was later re-opened under new editors, but only on condition that its first issue carry an article entitled "The Main Theme of Modern Chinese History Is Anti-Imperialism and Anti-Feudalism." Sipping Coca-Cola in a café next to his apartment a couple of years later, Li Datong described to me how control of history had been so central to the party's hold on power and its legitimacy. He went through a long list of historical subjects, from the decline of science in the Qing and Ming dynasties to the Korean War, about which it was impossible to have an honest debate. "The legacy of a ruling party is the right to define history—they use history to brainwash people," he said. "The textbooks say that history proved that such-and-such happened, that history chose the CCP to be the ruling party. They think this can convince people how great the CCP is."

———

Totalitarian regimes are able to completely invent their own histories. North Korea can get away with claiming that Kim Jong-il wrote fifteen hundred books and composed six operas because no one can say otherwise. But China is no longer that sort of regime. Though dictatorships censor their histories, they cannot create them in a vacuum. The CCP may have manipulated the idea of "national humiliation" after Tiananmen for its own ends, but it did not make it up. To understand the force of modern Chinese nationalism, it is important to recognize that the CCP has helped revive an older intellectual tradition that had its roots in the early years of the Chinese republic and the attempt to forge a modern nation-state after the collapse of the Qing dynasty in 1912. The patriotic-education campaign has been so influential in part because it taps into a long-standing emotional reflex about what it means to be Chinese. As the historian William Callahan puts it: "It would not be an exaggeration to say that when the idea of 'modern history' took shape in China in the 1920s, it was guided by the history of national humiliation."

The seminal event in the early years of the republic was the May Fourth Movement, a youthful protest which encapsulated the new country's search for a place in the modern world. The ideas behind May Fourth came to be characterized by the slogan "Mr. Science and Mr. Democracy," but it was also steeped in the nationalism of bruised pride. At the end of the 1919 Versailles Conference, which awarded Germany's possessions in China to Japan, Chinese students who were living in Paris surrounded the hotel of the Chinese delegation to prevent them from leaving to sign such a humiliating treaty. On hearing the news from France, a group of around three thousand students in Beijing met at Tiananmen Gate on May 4 and decided to march on the house of Communications Minister Cao Rulin. According to one of the demonstrators, a student named Luo Jialun, the crowd started cursing Cao as a "traitor to the country" when they arrived at his door. They then proceeded to storm into his house. Cao changed into a policeman's outfit and escaped over the back wall, injuring his leg along the way. Zhang Zongxiang, a former minister to Japan who had been visiting that day, was not so lucky: he was beaten with iron rods torn from an old bed and left nearly dead. Cao's house was then burned to the ground. The historian Rana Mitter summed up the launch of the May Fourth Movement this way: "The combination of these factors—youth, internationalism, and violence—would shape not just the day of the demonstrations, but much of the path taken by twentieth-century China."

As republican China struggled to find its way in the 1920s and 1930s, the feeling of injured national honor was a powerful political reflex among the new urban middle classes being established in cities like Beijing and Shanghai. Political leaders used this aggrieved nationalism as a way to appeal to the new constituencies and social organizations that were developing. When Chiang Kai-shek's Nationalists asserted control over the country in 1927, they decreed a National Humiliation Commemoration Day. It is worth noting that the controversial "nine-dash line" map of the South China Sea was drawn up during this period, one example of the way China's current territorial claims are wrapped up in this mentality of restoring injured pride.

Chiang Kai-shek kept a daily diary for two decades, and at the top right corner of each page he wrote the same words—*xue chi,* "wipe out humiliation." The weaker he got politically, the harder he pushed the humiliation narrative. Shortly before he lost the Civil War to the Communists, he published a book called *China's Destiny,* which blamed much of the country's ills on foreigners. The text was scorned even by the Chinese intellectuals who still supported his regime, but it was priced cheaply and proved a huge hit. "During the past hundred years, the citizens of the entire country, suffering under the yoke of the unequal treaties which gave foreigners special 'concessions' and extra-territorial status in China, were unanimous in their demand that the national humiliation be avenged, and the state be made strong," he wrote. When this nationalist potboiler was released, his wife, Meiling, happened to be in the U.S., trying to raise money for the anti-Communist cause, and Chiang himself was about to be awarded the Legion of Merit. An English-language version of the book was first shelved and then heavily edited to take out the fire-breathing passages. Lest Chiang's views about the West gain too wide a circulation, the State Department classified its copy of the Chinese original as "top secret."

The emphasis on humiliation and suffering in these histories actually has even deeper roots. China celebrates many of the usual sorts of historical heroes—brave generals and great thinkers. But it also reserves a special place for Goujian, the king of the state of Yue in the Warring States period (around the fifth century B.C.), whose story strikes a very different emotional chord. Having been captured by the rival king of Wu, Goujian set about trying to be as submissive as it was possible to be. He slept amid the horse manure of the rival king and even tasted the king's excrement. When he was eventually freed and allowed to return home, he spent the next two decades submitting himself to one humiliation after another in order to keep his desire for revenge intense. The Chinese phrase *woxin changdan* ("sleeping on brushwood and tasting gall") stems from Goujian's nightly exercise in self-flagellation, when he would sleep on a bed of brushwood and lick a gallbladder full of bile. It was this regimen of suffering and self-victimization that gave him the strength finally to defeat the king of Wu. The story of Goujian is "as familiar to Chinese schoolchildren as the biblical stories of Adam and Eve or David and Goliath are to American youngsters," wrote Paul Cohen, the American historian who has brought the mythical story to the attention of a wider Western audience. Perhaps it is no coincidence that the Goujian story was particularly popular in the 1920s and 1930s, when National Humiliation History began to take off. It also gained another lease on life in the 1990s and 2000s.

———

Though it is always tempting to think that everything in China is mapped out by an all-powerful Communist Party, the reality is that modern nationalism is very much a two-way process. The Communist Party has been happy to fan the sense of victimhood to buttress its own legitimacy. Yet the foundational myths that are at the heart of today's nationalism have their origin well before the Communists took power, and will not disappear if they should ever fall. At the same time that the party has been pushing its own "patriotic education," the themes of victimhood and resentment at the U.S. have flourished in their own right among young educated Chinese. The publishing industry has had a series of huge successes with potboiler polemics, in the Ann Coulter style, raging against the West. They started with the 1996 hit *China Can Say No*, written by a group of young intellectuals, which warned that China risked being "culturally strangled" and turned into a "slave" if it did not resist its infatuation with America. Two of the authors had taken part in the 1989 Tiananmen Square protests, but in the book they turned their ire on activists such as Fang Lizhi, the astrophysicist who inspired some of the 1989 protesters and ended up an exile in the U.S. after spending a year in the U.S. Embassy in Beijing.

Chinese intellectual life in the 1980s had been dominated by a fascination with the West and a thirst for political experimentation, but in the years after Tiananmen there has also been a strong counter-reaction, a popular clarion call that China needs to stand up for itself and to find its own path, resisting the temptations of the West. A string of popular anti-American titles have been released in recent years, with titles like *The Plot to Demonize China*. In 2009, the authors of *China Can Say No* published a follow-up, this time called *Unhappy China*, which was just as big a hit. Detailing a long list of tales about continued Western condescension toward the Chinese, the book urges China's leaders to turn the nation into a hegemon, or be cast aside. The writers and audience for these books, mostly young, are not party apparatchiks. They see themselves as loyal to a China that is a great and respected nation, not to the Communist Party.

The most famous megaphone of modern Chinese nationalism is the *Global Times*, the third-most-popular newspaper in the country. With a mix of conspiracy and indignation that has echoes of Fox News, *Global Times* has built a huge successful franchise by fanning the flames of any perceived slight to China and by criticizing the weaknesses of the U.S. and Japan. It has come to dominate the market for full-throated populism. Hu Xijin, the paper's dynamic editor, once described Chinese liberals as "the cancer cells that will lead to the demise of China" and "a key tool in the hands of the Americans who want to topple China." However, it can also be quite critical of the government, especially concerning Beijing's dogged support of North Korea. In a way, *Global Times* is the perfect example of the two-way nature of Chinese nationalism. It is published by the same group that produces the *People's Daily*, the party's mouthpiece and distiller of official truths, which gives it an official stamp of approval. But it is also far more interesting and controversial than the dreary *People's Daily*, projecting its own abrasive worldview and building its own constituency among the public. *Global Times* does not provide the official China line, but it is the Communist Party's nationalist alter ego. That alone makes it essential reading.

MEMORIES OF A HOLOCAUST

When we moved to Shanghai in early 2005, my wife and I rented a flat on Huai Hai Road, one of the main streets running through what in colonial days was known as the French Concession. In a city that has become overrun by skyscrapers, the area is a museum of prewar Western architecture. One block away from our flat was the Normandie Apartments, a wedge-shaped building reminiscent of the Flatiron Building in New York; three blocks in the other direction was a Russian basilica. Its avenues lined with plane trees planted by the French, the area has an unhurried feel that is a welcome break from Shanghai's frenetic pace. It has become a popular neighborhood for foreigners, including the tens of thousands of Japanese who now call Shanghai home. Many of the shops along Huai Hai Road had Japanese writing in the windows to attract customers, including the tailor on our block and the tobacco store run by a couple from Anhui Province.

At about the same time that we arrived in Shanghai, a group of right-wing historians in Japan published a new textbook which downplayed important aspects of the war crimes committed by Japanese soldiers in China. One of the books described the evidence behind the massacre in Nanjing in 1937 as "inconclusive." It was not the first revisionist text-book in Japan to minimize war crimes, and it was only taken up by a small number of schools. But it caused a furor in China. Meetings with Japanese politicians were canceled, official protests lodged. After a few weeks, messages started to circulate on the Internet about a demonstration in Shanghai on the following Saturday. "A lot of people are talking," one of our new Chinese acquaintances told us a couple of days before the demonstration.

At around 10 a.m. that Saturday, we headed out to try and find the protest, only to discover that our section of Huai Hai Road had already been totally closed off to traffic. After walking up the street, we could eventually see the beachhead of a demonstration that looked to be much bigger than the modest protest we had been expecting. The group had started near the Bund and had already halted the traffic in some of the city's busiest shopping and business areas. The demonstrators were all young, mostly university or high-school students. Older residents watched from the sidewalk, a little bemused, not quite knowing what to think. The protest gathered numbers along the way until it had at least ten thousand people by some counts—making it one of the biggest public demonstrations since the 1989 protests in Tiananmen Square. The students carried banners and shouted slogans such as "Down with Little Japan," "Japan Out of Asia," and "We Love Our China, We Hate Your Japan." By the time they reached our stretch of town, they had developed a distinct sense of impunity. When they passed a little sushi restaurant a block away from our flat, they threw eggs and plastic bot-tles at the windows, as well as red paint. At the cigarette shop with the Japanese script, they smashed the window. There were plenty of police keeping an eye on the protest, and occasionally they would move people along. But mostly they stood back and laughed.

The demonstration carried on three miles farther, through another of the city's busiest areas, before it reached the Japanese consulate in Hongqiao, in a modern office building. By then a couple of Japanese cars had been overturned, and there was a report that a few demonstrators attacked a police car which they believed was protecting a Japanese citizen. Some local shop owners had put up Chinese flags, not as a patriotic act but to try and convince the protesters that their businesses had no Japanese connection. At the consulate, a large contingent of police was waiting, including some from an anti-riot squad in special protective equipment. But although they made sure no one entered the consulate, they, too, stood aside as the demonstrators threw rocks and bottles at the premises.

For a while, I walked alongside a young woman called Wang Hongli, who said she was sixteen and in high school. Her dark hair was cut in a bob, she was carrying a knapsack on her shoulders that was covered in "Hello Kitty" stickers, and she wore round John Lennon–style glasses. "You must think this is all very strange," she said at one stage. She told me how word of the protest had spread rapidly by text message over the previous two days. At first she had not thought about attending, but she kept getting more and more messages. A friend of a friend, who was a student at Fudan University, had said he was going. Eventually, she and a couple of schoolmates had decided to come along, although the friends had given up after a while. When I asked her why she was so keen to stay with the march, her mood darkened and she fixed me with a severe look. "We hate the Japanese, just hate them," she said. Most of the students thought the whole thing was quite fun, and there was a day-out-of-school feel about the event. This was probably the first chance they had ever had in their lives to walk through the streets chanting political slogans, and many reveled in the experience. The good humor could not disguise, however, that this was an exercise in political mob violence.

———

One of the more peculiar aspects of the "national humiliation" mindset is that it allows Chinese officials to decide when the country has been offended. Officials at the Foreign Ministry will announce with a straight face that a particular government has "hurt the feelings of the Chinese people." The phrase often prompts a bemused sneer from foreigners, but makes some sort of sense within the emotional framework of victim nationalism. In 2008, Danwei, a Beijing-based Web site, reported on a fascinating piece of research conducted by a Chinese blogger. He had gone through the archives of the *People's Daily* since 1946 and collected all the instances in which the Chinese government had accused someone else of "hurting the feelings of the Chinese people." In total, nineteen countries and organizations had committed the sin—representing around two-fifths of the world's population. The United States had done so twenty-three times, with another ten from NATO (mostly to do with the 1999 Belgrade bombing), which were really the U.S. as well. Only one country had managed to offend China more—in fact, on a total of forty-seven occasions. That nation was Japan.

Japan is the epicenter of China's victim complex. It is Japan that is most likely to turn young, cosmopolitan, Internet-savvy Chinese into fire-breathing protesters, Japan that is most likely to elicit reactions that mix inferiority and superiority. Japan is also the area of foreign policy where nationalism has its greatest potential impact, a populist anger that is at times encouraged by the government but which is also increasingly tying its hands. Nationalism is becoming a major force in the relationship between the two richest countries in Asia. After the 2005 protests and another round of demonstrations in 2010, the protests reached a new intensity in late 2012, as the dispute over the Senkaku/Diaoyu Islands flared up again. In one incident, a Chinese man was paralyzed after a mob of anti-Japanese protesters in the city of Xian attacked his car. His crime was to drive a Japanese vehicle.

The immediate source of such anger is the catalogue of grotesque war crimes committed by Japanese soldiers during the occupations and wars of the 1930s and 1940s in China. Japan operated labor camps and conducted medical experiments on Chinese prisoners. At one stage, Japanese planes dropped fleas infected with the plague onto a Chinese city. In Nanjing in 1937, the invading Japanese army slaughtered a significant part of the local population. The estimates of casualties range from fifty thousand to three hundred thousand, the latter figure being widely accepted in China. In an era of jaw-dropping, shocking crimes, Nanjing was one of the great crimes. When the Japanese were finally defeated, however, hostility toward Japan remained surprisingly restrained. Mao's China was the victor, not a victim that wanted to linger on war crimes. When Japanese Prime Minister Tanaka Kakuei visited in 1972 to reopen relations with China following the Nixon trip, Mao is reported to have observed that, without the war with Japan, his Communist revolution would not have succeeded. In keeping with that mood, the massacre at Nanjing was deliberately downplayed. In some ways, it is a natural human reaction to avoid thinking about such events when they are still raw. Sometimes, survivors of an atrocity just want to carry on with their own lives: it is often the next generation who feels the urge to guard memories. But by the 1980s, the official tide had started to shift. With economic reformers under pressure by leftists for their diversion from Marxist truths, a spot of Japan-bashing nationalism was a useful crutch. After the 1989 massacre, official attention to Japanese war crimes snowballed as the National Humiliation History canon was launched.

The war crimes from the 1930s would be reason enough for modern China's antagonism toward Japan, but the roots are much deeper, stretching back into the emotionally strained history of the nineteenth century. The Opium Wars with Britain may have been a huge jolt to Chinese self-esteem, but in a sense they were a warm-up act for the real psychic shock that imperial China suffered: the rise of Japan in the second half of the nineteenth century. China had always looked upon Japan as a "little brother" nation, one of the countries which had been brought under the civilizing realm of Confucian culture and Chinese script. Chinese emperors thought of themselves as the center of a world where nations like Japan offered them deferential respect. Defeat in the 1894–95 Sino-Japanese War was a double blow: not only did China lose to one of these junior nations, but Japan had fortified itself precisely by choosing Western over Chinese culture. (It was after this war that Japan took control of the Senkaku Islands.) The Meiji Restoration in Japan, from the 1860s, was a modernization project that deliberately turned its back on Asia and sought to learn from the West, importing everything from military organization and engineering colleges to fashions. The protests after the Versailles Treaty in 1919 were not just about continued imperial interference in China: they were in a pique of rage that Japan was now a member of the club of imperial bullies. Sun Yat-sen and several other senior figures from the early years of the Chinese republic actually spent time in exile in Japan and were inspired by its zeal for modernization, but they also felt the loss of the Sino-Japanese War deeply. One of them, Kang Youwei, described it as "the greatest humiliation in two hundred years." Modern Chinese nationalism began with defeat by Japan in 1895.

China's anti-Japanese tilt has not taken place in a vacuum, of course, but has had its own mirror in Japanese society. For the last couple of decades, Chinese nationalists and right-wing Japanese revisionists have fed off one another. In the decades immediately after the Second World War, Japanese textbooks included an open discussion of events such as the Nanjing Massacre, as Japanese society and its American occupiers sought to erase the vestiges of imperialism. But from the 1970s, with the Cold War in full flight, revisionist versions of Japan's role in the war started to gain some ground both in the academy and in popular culture, including *manga* comics. Japanese efforts to fudge history produced a resentment in China that reached a peak during the prime minister-ship of Junichiro Koizumi—the idiosyncratic Elvis Presley fan—who led Japan from 2001 to 2006. Unlike his predecessors, Koizumi made a habit of visiting Yasukuni, a Shinto shrine not far from the presidential palace in Tokyo, which honors the war dead. Koizumi described his visits as "a matter of the heart," but the Yasukuni Shrine also honors many of the military leaders from the Second World War who were later branded as "war criminals." Among the portraits of kamikaze pilots at the shrine's war museum there is also a portrait of General Tojo Hideki, head of the Imperial Japanese Army. In late 2012, Japan returned to power Shinzo Abe, another leader with strongly nationalist tendencies, whose grand-father was arrested as a war criminal after the Second World War but never charged. Members of his cabinet have resumed visits to Yasukuni.

China saw these visits as a crude insult, and it was not alone in thinking this way. Distaste for revisionism in Japan has also been strong in South Korea, which has its own painful memories of Japanese occu-pation, and which threatened at one stage to break off diplomatic relations with Tokyo because of what it saw as Koizumi's provocations. The deep sense of hurt in South Korea about continued Japanese efforts to massage its wartime past show that these emotions are not merely the product of China's propaganda authorities. Japan's attitude to the war remains a deep sore across Northeast Asia.

China's response has been to gradually turn up the emotional temperature. It was Iris Chang's 1997 book, *The Rape of Nanking,* that first really brought the events of 1937 to the attention of many Americans. As well as documenting the atrocities, the book made a central intellectual claim that was clear from its subtitle: *The Forgotten Holocaust of World War II.* Over the last couple of decades, China has gradually begun to use the idea of a holocaust to frame the memory of the Japanese invasion and the retelling of the Nanjing Massacre. In 1985, the local authorities in Nanjing built a museum to commemorate the massacre, which includes a large display of bones from bodies found at a nearby location which was dubbed "the pit of ten thousand corpses." In the mid-1990s, the museum was expanded, and it now includes a series of powerful sculptures. Qi Kang, who helped design parts of the reformed memorial, says that he was influenced by the Holocaust museums that started to appear in the U.S. in the 1990s, and the Nanjing memorial has a similar bleak and desolate aesthetic. Near the entrance, the figure three hundred thousand—the official estimate of the number of deaths—is carved into a wall. Ian Buruma, who has written extensively on both Japan and the Holocaust, argues that the only real parallel with the way the Chinese Communist Party has started to use this history is in Israel's Likud Party. "The humiliations of the past must act as a spur to national strength and unity," he wrote. "The more people are told about the terrible things inflicted on their people by foreign enemies, the more they will follow their 'patriotic' leaders." There is no higher form of victimhood than a holocaust.

The emotionally charged atmosphere of the Nanjing memorial is even more intense at the September 18 History Museum in Shenyang, established to celebrate the 1931 Mukden incident that was used as a pretext for Japan's invasion of northeastern China. The museum's catalogue calls on visitors "not to forget national humiliation and to invigorate China." The main gate is a huge stone carved with the date September 18 and riddled with bullet holes. There is a picture of a blood-red tear-drop, and beside it an inscription which blames the "criminal Japanese militarists" who invaded "Great China with its five thousand years of history." At the end of the museum, the text reads: "As we are about to leave the exhibition room, everyone's heart is dripping blood, and every drop of blood seems to congeal into a question mark: How could Japanese imperialism dare to lift a butcher's knife against our great and vast China?"

A WOLF IN MONK'S CLOTHING

When we arrived in the center of Lhasa, the air still held the scent of burnt timber. The old Tibetan quarter of the city is little more than a handful of narrow streets lined with two-story stone buildings. On every block there were several black, singed frames where once had been small storefronts. It was ten days since the Tibetan capital city had been shaken by the worst outburst of racial violence since the 1960s, but the old section of the city remained in near lockdown. On every street corner, armed guards looked on, demanding to see the credentials of the few passersby.

Four days before the riot, around three hundred monks from the Drepung Monastery, just outside Lhasa, had staged a march toward the city—the first open political protest in the streets of the city in more than a decade. Fifteen monks were arrested. On March 14, 2008, a Friday, monks from the Ramoche Monastery also started a small protest. Ramoche is located near the center of the city, and this time the protest attracted many followers. With rumors spreading that the monks arrested earlier in the week had been beaten, some members of the crowd started to attack the police. The police initially held back, perhaps because there was no one to give them orders—most senior officials from the province were in Beijing at the time, for the National People's Congress. At some stage, the ethnic Tibetans who were protesting turned their attention from the police to the large population of migrants who have moved to the city in recent years—mostly Han Chinese, but also some Hui Muslims. They used gasoline to burn the shops and businesses of the migrants. By chance, the Beijing correspondent of *The Economist*, James Miles, was in the city at the time. He watched dozens of different businesses being burned, looted, or destroyed. "It was an extraordinary outpouring of ethnic violence," he wrote.

Foreign journalists are only allowed into Tibet on tightly controlled visits, an indication of just how sensitive the political situation is. Miles happened to be on one of those visits—his first reporting trip to Tibet in fifteen years of covering China. Ten days after the riot, I was lucky enough to get one of the four places for Western reporters on another government-organized trip. The Foreign Ministry hoped the visit would help explain to the world its version of events in Tibet. Things did not quite work out that way. Instead, we found ourselves at the center of a firestorm that cast a long shadow over that year's Beijing Olympics and brought out the very worst aspects of China's brittle, anti-Western nationalism. The Beijing Olympics were supposed to be the occasion when China cast off much of the emotional baggage that feeds its nationalism. China had spent the best part of a century trying to secure the chance to host the Olympics. As far back as 1908, Chinese writers saw the Olympics as a perfect vehicle to erase the country's image as the "Sick Man of Asia." By 2008, that moment had come. The Games were the perfect opportunity to showcase the country's many achievements and to cast off any lingering sense of inferiority. But five months before the opening ceremony, in the streets of the Tibetan capital of Lhasa, that dream started to go sour.

In the days after the Lhasa riot, Chinese TV was broadcasting an almost constant loop of images of the "3/14 incident," as it was known, showing how Han Chinese had been victims of the violence. We were taken to one clothes shop that had been set on fire, where five young women—four of them Han and the other Tibetan, according to reports—had been burned alive. The only things left were the charcoal frame of a storefront and bouquets of flowers lined up against what remained of the outside wall. A shopkeeper, who was a Hui Muslim, told me about the horror he had experienced on seeing a mob start to set his business alight, before they decided to go elsewhere. All the shops on his street were still shuttered, but most of the ones that were untouched had white silk scarves tied around the padlocks, a signal to the protesters that they were owned by Tibetans. The narrative that the Chinese authorities wanted us to believe was indeed true: there had been an ugly race riot in Lhasa, and Han Chinese had been the principal victims.

Except that the official story stopped there. For all the gory details about what had happened, no convincing explanation was put forward as to why the protest took place. Government officials simply told us that the rioters were all common criminals and that they would be dealt with according to the law—"*kuai zhua, kuai shen, kuai sha,*" as Tibet Party Secretary Zhang Qingli later put it—"quick arrest, quick trial, quick execution." There was no discussion about why such an ugly episode in racial violence had actually taken place, no reflection on why ethnic Tibetans had turned on the other residents of Lhasa in such a brutal manner. With the rioters dismissed as common criminals, there was no need to ask probing questions about how Tibet was governed. Moreover, the obsessive attention given to the "3/14 incident" obscured the reality that the Lhasa riot was not an isolated event. Instead, there had been a wildfire of protests across the Tibetan plateau. According to Robert Barnett at Columbia University, there were at least ninety-six different protests during that month, in which thirty thousand Tibetans took part. "The question that now faces China's leaders, if not the world, is 'Who lost Tibet?'" Barnett wrote shortly afterward.

The official story started to unravel when we were taken to the Jokhang Temple, in the center of the city, one of the centers of Tibetan Buddhism. A senior abbot, portly in his purple robes, met us in an entrance hall and launched into a long explanation about how calm had been restored. "Everything is back to normal," he insisted. As he was speaking, a group of maybe twenty young monks began to swarm around us. It was unclear at first what was happening, but we soon realized that it was an impromptu protest. The monks seemed in a state of extreme distress, some shouting while others cried. The state media at the time had been going out of their way to demonize the Dalai Lama ("a wolf in monk's clothes," Zhang Qingli called him), but the monks wanted to convince us of their undimmed affection for him. They told us that they had been under effective house arrest since the protests began and that the temple was still in lockdown. And then they dropped the real bombshell. The monks told us that everything going on in the temple that day had been arranged for our benefit. At the time, we were standing in a large hall outside the main temple. Through the door, we could see a throng of people who seemed to be going through their daily prayers, many with prayer beads in their hands. It was all a lie, the monks said. The people inside the temple were all Communist Party officials who had been brought in for the day and told to pretend to be regular worshippers.

Our government minders were apoplectic, but with TV cameras running, they could not afford to break up the protest. So they tried to chip away at the edges. On a couple of occasions, I had to fend off attempts to pull me out of the tumult. After the monks had been talking for about fifteen minutes, two large security officials came up behind me, placed their hands on my shoulders, and lifted me away. The image from the temple proved explosive. The official Chinese narrative about Han Chinese being the victims of the Lhasa riot was true as far as it went. But the elaborate deceit at Jokhang exposed just how much effort the government was exerting to prevent any discussion of the simmering political problems that lay behind the rioting across the Tibetan plateau.

The Chinese government's response was effectively to go to war against the foreign press. In the days after the Lhasa riot, most foreign journalists reported as best they could on the event, even though they were not allowed to visit the site. But there were also plenty of mistakes. One German newspaper used a picture of a violent clash between protesters and police which had actually taken place in Nepal. CNN was accused of having cut out part of a photo of Chinese armed police that showed rioting Tibetans. The government jumped on the errors as decisive proof that the foreign media were irredeemably biased against China, and most Chinese of my acquaintance believed the authorities. Before long, witch hunts were being conducted against any foreign journalist who had been deemed to offend the honor of the nation. For a few days, the target of the campaign was Jane Macartney, the correspondent of *The Times* of London. (This was particularly unfair as she had not written the article that appeared to cause offense, but it at least had a certain historical irony—she is a direct descendant of Lord Macartney, the British envoy in the late eighteenth century who refused to bow to the Qianlong emperor, a standoff that proved to be a precursor to the Opium Wars.) Geremie Barmé, the Australian academic, correctly described the exercise as "a radical demonisation of the western international press." The four Western reporters who had been on the trip in Tibet also started to come under attack. When I arrived at the office in the morning, I would find abusive messages and a few death threats waiting on the answering machine. My colleague who runs the *Financial Times'* Chinese-language Web site called one day, after reading the volume of hate mail that was coming into the site. He suggested that I maybe start to change the route I took to and from the office, just in case. At the time, I shrugged off the threats, assuming them to be from young men in Internet cafés who were letting off a little steam. But one of the other reporters who had gone to Lhasa received a rather more intimidating threat. Someone got hold of a photo of him, cut off the head, and then posted the two images on a Web site.

Before long, the furor spilled over into the preparations for the Olympics. A few weeks after the Tibet riot, the Olympic torch was due to travel through several European capitals, part of an elaborate global tour. In London, a few pro-Tibetan protesters tried to disrupt the torch relay and were pushed away by Chinese police in track suits who were running alongside. In Paris, the protesters were more aggressive and tried to grab the torch from a young Chinese woman in a wheelchair. Jin Jing, a twenty-seven-year-old from Shanghai who was due to compete in Paralympic fencing, became a national hero after fending off the attack, "an angel in a wheelchair" as the Chinese media dubbed her. "I still feel very angry now, and I think the man was very irrational," she said the next day. "Hosting the Olympics is such a good thing for our country, so why do they want to ruin it?"

Back in China, a new wave of angry popular protests broke out, once again with the urban, educated youth at the forefront. Some of these young Chinese had an idealized view of the foreign media and were deeply upset at what they believed to be the obvious bias of the coverage of the Tibet riots. ("Don't be so CNN" became a popular retort.) The disruption to the torch relay just added to their ire. After a rumor circulated that a Carrefour executive had made a large donation to a radical Tibetan group, a boycott campaign was organized online. Huge demonstrations of young people erupted at some of the chain's Chinese stores. In Hefei, a provincial city three hundred miles inland from Shanghai, ten thousand people congregated one Saturday afternoon in the car park of a Carrefour to demonstrate their displeasure. An Internet video about the history of Tibet which went viral among young Chinese was entitled "Tibet WAS, IS, and ALWAYS WILL BE a part of China."

In some ways, tempers were even more frayed among young Chinese studying at overseas universities—precisely the constituency that some in the West hope will be an eventual bulwark for liberal reform in China. At Duke University in North Carolina, a young Chinese student named Grace Wang attempted to intervene in a fierce debate that had broken out between Han Chinese students at the university and ethnic Tibetans. Her intervention went viral on the Internet, and she was subjected to a vicious hate campaign, in which she was labeled by other Chinese students a "race traitor." After her parents' home address in Qingdao was circulated on the Internet, a photo appeared online which purported to show feces smeared all over the door. They had to go into hiding.

It is hard to understand the intensity of the 2008 events without seeing how deeply rooted Tibet is in the framework of national humiliation. One of the flip sides of modern China's victim mentality is a ferocious defense of its sovereignty, which was impugned by foreign powers in the nineteenth century, the invaders who "carved up China like a melon." In the periods when China has been weak, its ambiguous influence over Tibet has loosened further, including when the British invaded in 1903. Control over Tibet is tightly linked to the urge to restore national pride. It is that mindset that can turn a dispute between Han Chinese and one of the country's ethnic minorities into a struggle against imperialism. Since the early years of the republic, China's leaders have been faced with the dilemma of trying to forge a modern, unified nation-state from the loose, saggy terrain of a multinational empire. The new national identity has leaned heavily on a strong sense of shared suffering, which Beijing has then imposed on all the country's ethnic groups, even those whose historical connections to the Chinese state are full of nuance, complexity, and in some cases conflict. For Beijing to recognize deep political problems in Tibet or among other ethnic groups would be to undermine the narrative of China as a victim of outside interference. When Tibet explodes, the West sees a Beijing government floundering in a very different political culture; official China sees such complaints as a challenge to its core identity.

The Olympics were supposed to provide the catharsis from this psychological burden, to show that China could move from victim to victor. Instead, the buildup to the Games made many Chinese feel that the country was being subject to a series of damning judgments, as if the West did not yet believe China was good enough. After all the changes and successes of the last three decades, many Chinese felt that the country was still not considered truly respectable. This was another reason to be furious at the Tibetans: they had tried to spoil the party. Beneath their bureaucratic exterior, the Tibetan riots exposed a kind of emotional rage among Chinese leaders, who experience such setbacks as a form of personal humiliation. At the same time, the contortions to avoid an open discussion about Tibet led even the more sensible members of the Chinese bureaucracy to take the most addled, paranoid positions. On one occasion, a very senior Chinese official was asked to explain why foreign journalists were banned from visiting Tibet except on carefully organized tours. Journalists could not be trusted, she said, because all the photos of the Dalai Lama hanging on the walls of homes and offices in Tibet had been brought in by foreign reporters. Tapping her finger on the table for emphasis, she repeated: "Every single photo."

SHALLOW AND INTENSE

Li Yang was about halfway through a three-hour teaching session at the English-language boot camp when he started calling attention to me. "We have an important guest, Jiefu, from a British newspaper," he announced, using a Chinese transliteration of my name. I was sitting at the back, and all the students turned round to look at me. They laughed when Li told them, "He has come down here to taste our *jiaozi* [dumplings]." Gradually, more and more of his comments seemed to be aimed in my direction. "The best place to teach English would be in church, but I do not think that Comrade Hu would allow this—don't you think, Jiefu?" he said, smiling.

Li insists that his entire routine is improvised, even when some of the sessions last for hours. To prove it, after a while he decided to summon me to the stage. Several hundred young Chinese students looked around at me with an expectant gaze, perhaps suspecting some sport might be in the offing. It would have been extremely rude to refuse, so, somewhat embarrassed, I wandered onstage. Li started questioning me about my life in China. Then he asked me what I thought to be the most impressive thing about China. I mumbled something, I believe, about the striking ambition and energy of ordinary Chinese people to improve their lives. *"Wow!"* thundered Li. "Listen to this. Jiefu, say that again. Repeat that, please, Jiefu. Everyone, listen closely." My onstage ordeal continued for another ten minutes, during which Li anticipated one of my strongest reactions—and something that has also been a persistent criticism of his school. Looking out at the rapt audience hanging on his every word, with red flags lined up all across the auditorium, and monitors in army fatigues standing in the aisles to watch over the students, Li turned to me and said, "Jiefu, you must think this is a lot like the Cultural Revolution."

Class eventually broke for dinner, a school meal served on metal trays with four different compartments, one each for the meat dish, vegetable, rice, and fruit. The Chinese New Year was only a few hours away, which the students would spend in a class, but there was time for one more entertainment: a torch rally. The students assembled in drill formation on an adjacent sports field to watch some fireworks and to listen to a short speech by Li. Then, with their monitors each carrying a torch, they marched in formation around the campus, chanting slogans in English about "Success" and "Achievement." I watched, unsure what to think. If there had not been so much laughter in the air, if the students had not been so charming and curious, and if these kids had not been sacrificing the most important holiday of the year to learn a foreign language, then there might have been something just a little fascist about the spectacle.

After two days in his company, I still could not decide whether Li Yang was really tapping a deep vein of nationalism, or whether his anti-American shtick was just performance art, a ritual about humiliation and sacrifice that his students understand and laugh at but which they do not really believe. That is the broader challenge in trying to understand Chinese nationalism. The last decade has seen a series of angry fits at the rest of the world, full of bitterness and bile, but these have quickly subsided. Is there a volcano of resentment waiting to explode, or are these just tantrums that will ease, the growing pains of a new great power adjusting to its place in the world? One of the most important questions about modern China is whether the nationalist chorus is relatively small, a rump of 10 percent of the population, who get more attention than they deserve, or whether it is the reflection of a set of attitudes that are ingrained into the national DNA.

Prasenjit Duara, an Indian scholar of China now based in Singapore, described the mood of some of the young Chinese nationalists this way: "Day 1: Eat at McDonald's; Day 2: Throw rocks at McDonald's; Day 3: Eat at McDonald's." There is, he says, "a simultaneous superficiality and depth of nationalist feelings" in modern China. In each of the big nationalist outbursts, the Communist Party has for a moment looked vulnerable, as if the events might spin out of control, but it has then managed quickly to turn off the tap. After a NATO bomb hit the Chinese Embassy in Belgrade in 1999, hundreds of Chinese students spent the next few days protesting outside and vandalizing the U.S. Embassy in Beijing. The atmosphere was feverish. Western residents of the city at the time said that for a couple of days they felt under threat if they stepped outside. And then the protests stopped. A Chinese friend of mine who was at university in Beijing at the time recalls turning up for class one morning to be told by a teacher to get on a bus, which dropped all the students off outside the U.S. Embassy. The next day, the bus was there again to take them to the embassy. On the third day, lectures went on as normal.

The anti-Japan protests in 2005 followed the same path. The week before the big Shanghai demonstration, there was a large protest in Beijing, and the week after, Guangzhou and Shenzhen held demonstrations. Then the movement fizzled, and the students returned to their classes. When we left Shanghai three years later, the cigarette shop on our block still had Japanese characters in the window. Duara's observation also captures the central ambiguity at the heart of the Li Yang phenomenon, the simultaneous fascination with and distaste for the West. The generation of Chinese who have been through "patriotic education" is the same generation that is exposed to the world through the Internet in ways that their parents could never have dreamed of and is attracted to all the same symbols of American consumerism. A year or so before I left Beijing, a new Apple Store opened, which I must have walked past fifty times. But I never once entered, for the simple reason that there was always a queue outside to get in.

Yet, at the same time, each cycle of nationalist spasms seems to get a bit bigger and a little more autonomous, further outside the control mechanisms of the state. Nationalist pressure has been an important factor in some of the disputes in the South China Sea, and has become increasingly influential in the argument with Japan over the Senkaku/ Diaoyu Islands. In both cases, the populist online pressure found common cause with the sections of the military that want to take a more confrontational approach. As the protest waves become more intense, the leadership finds its room to maneuver more limited. The events that have produced demonstrations in recent years have been relatively minor—a stray bomb, a handful of textbooks, some unruly protests during an Olympics torch relay—yet each managed to create a paroxysm of angst that left the country temporarily off-balance. It begs the question of what might happen in the event of a major international incident—a 9/11-style terror attack, or a genuine confrontation with the Japanese navy in the East China Sea. The raw, popular nationalism does not dictate Chinese foreign policy, but at the very least it makes it hard for the government to back down or make concessions.

For the U.S. and other Western countries, the broader lesson is that they have to be aware that there will always be this emotional tension in the background of their relations with Beijing, a trauma which has yet to be fully resolved, and which makes its leaders at times hair-trigger sensitive to perceived slights. One of the most difficult tasks for American politicians will be to find a way to engage with the Chinese people over sensitive issues, from political reform to territorial disputes, in a way that does not step on any of these trip wires. At the same time, the U.S. has a responsibility to pressure its ally Japan to, at the very least, refrain from provocative gestures that revive historical tensions. By inflaming South Korea as well as China, such stunts harm not only Japan's influence in the region, but also that of Washington.

Chinese liberals argue that it is the political system that nurtures the particular virulence of today's nationalism. Hard-line views are very much a minority, they suggest, but, because political and historical debate is so curtailed, there is no room for nuance or context, and emotions are easily manipulated. Japan has a nationalist right wing whose views are often toxic, but their impact is diluted and absorbed by a more open political debate. If that liberal view is correct, then it is possible to imagine that, in the long run, political reform might draw some of the poison from Chinese nationalism. The anger of a small minority can multiply in strength under an authoritarian government that does not want to appear weak; but in a more open system, shrill voices find it harder to dominate the debate.

That is the theory, at least. Maybe a democratic China would have a more comfortable sense of its own identity and place in the world, as liberals and many in America hope. But it is equally possible to imagine a very different scenario, in which a loss of control by the Communist Party leads to even stronger nationalist pressures. The students who have taken part in anti-U.S. or anti-Japanese protests know one basic truth, that this is almost the only way they can safely take part in popular demonstrations. The Communist Party's most vulnerable flank is at the nationalist, populist right. A party that loudly claims the mantle of national salvation cannot afford to look weak in the face of perceived slights. If the Communist Party's grip on power ever did start to loosen seriously, it is not too hard to imagine an embattled Chinese leader searching for an anti-America or anti-Japan cause and placing it at the center of his agenda.

6

Soft Power

HARMONIZING THE WORLD

THE LARGE NEON SCREENS on the corner of New York's Broadway and Seventh Avenue are among the most visible and prestigious advertising sites in America. The signs are sixty feet high by forty feet wide and are seen by many of the half-million people who daily pass through Times Square. The spaces have been rented by Coca-Cola and by the Prudential insurance company; HSBC had its name in lights for a decade. The new name on the signs is not quite so familiar to most New York tourists: Xinhua, China's state-run news agency, the propaganda arm of the Chinese Communist Party. As well as renting the neon advertising screen, Xinhua has also taken the top floor of the forty-four-story skyscraper at 1540 Broadway—only a block away from the sumptuous new *New York Times* building designed by Renzo Piano with silver birch trees in the atrium.

The financial pressures that are slowly strangling many of the world's media groups do not appear to be hampering Xinhua. In 2010, the agency opened a new twenty-four-hour English-language news channel called CNC World, which the group's president, Li Congjun, described as an attempt to "present an international vision with a Chinese perspective." Beijing has long complained of unfair treatment from what it calls "the Western media." Officials believe that if the world could just find out more about the reality of China, about its history and progress, then people would think very differently about the country. They want more good news, and if the BBC and CNN will not provide that service for the world, then Xinhua and the other arms of the official Chinese media will.

A decade ago, China was thought of as an inward-looking, developing country with modest international ambitions, whose leaders cared about little other than the next month's GDP figures. But it is hard to think in quite the same way about a country that has such grand global ambitions for its media groups. China wants to crack the Western monopoly on news. According to several informed reports, China spent around $8.7 billion in 2011–12 on the overseas operations of just four news organizations—Xinhua, Chinese Central Television (CCTV), the English-language *China Daily*, and China Radio International. The entire budget for the BBC World Service is around $400 million a year. With big budgets come big goals. Beijing mainly wants to improve China's image in the world, but it also hopes that Chinese news organizations can loosen the grip that American values of democracy, individualism, and human rights have on the international media business. "While our media empires are melting away like the Himalayan glaciers, China's are expanding," Orville Schell, the director of the Asia Society's Center on U.S.-China Relations, was quoted as saying—in the *New York Times.*

Like many of the trappings of modernity, from Maglev trains to the Nobu restaurant chain, soft power has become an obsession in contemporary China. Originally coined by the American academic Joseph Nye, soft power is the idea that the more attractive a country's culture and society, the more influential it will be. America's international dominance, so the theory goes, rests not just on its military power or its economic weight but also on the fact that so many other countries around the world have sought to copy its rules, institutions, and way of life. Nye defined soft power as "the ability to get what you want through attraction rather than coercion or payment." In some ways, China takes the basic idea of soft power more seriously than the U.S. The first academic in China to take up the theme was Wang Huning, a scholar at Fudan

University in Shanghai, who has since become one of China's most senior foreign-policy officials and a member of the party's Politburo. His ideas have been adopted at the top levels of the Chinese leadership. In his keynote speech to the important Communist Party Congress in 2007, Hu Jintao gave the concept his official stamp of approval, telling the audience: "We must enhance culture as part of the soft power of the country." Whole university departments in China are now devoted to soft power, and the Foreign Ministry has opened a special department to improve the country's image. There is even a new museum in Beijing celebrating public diplomacy, the art of national image boosting.

For Beijing, soft power is a tool to present a less threatening image to the world, to massage anxieties caused by the country's rise. But there is also a hard edge to the soft-power fascination. Some Chinese scholars argue that it is also an essential part of a project for challenging America. Shen Jiru, an academic at the Chinese Academy of Social Sciences, argues that soft power was central to the U.S.'s winning the Cold War, the mass appeal of its popular culture helping to curtail international support for the Soviets. The Soviet Union had been equal to the U.S. for a time, he says, but "lost the whole game due to a flaw in its soft power." China, he urges, should not make the same mistake. For many of the officials and academics pushing the promotion of Chinese soft power, this is much more than just a PR campaign, but part of a broader struggle for influence and respect. China is taking on the U.S. at its own game in a global cultural contest.

China's soft-power push is both a window onto its expanding ambitions and an important emotional crux in the emerging rivalry with the U.S. If the feeling takes root in the U.S. that China is presenting a worldview that will be attractive to large parts of the world, this will add real political edge to the competition. The temptation will grow in the U.S. to elevate the rivalry to a form of ideological contest, with echoes of the Cold War. There are already a few hints of this in official American reactions to the investments China is making in its media sector. "During the Cold War we did a great job in getting America's message out. After the Berlin Wall fell we said, 'Okay, fine, enough of that, we are done,' and unfortunately we are paying a big price for it," Hillary Clinton told Congress in 2011. "We are in an information war and we are losing that war. Al Jazeera is winning, the Chinese have opened a global multi-language television network, the Russians have opened up an English-language network. I've seen it in a few countries, and it is quite instructive."

Soft power can come in lots of shapes and sizes. Some academics in China believe that the country should be promoting its model of economic management, particularly to other parts of the developing world, as a way of making the country more influential. A few even suggest that China's political system could be exported. But most of the discussion about soft power in China has focused on culture and the idea that the best way to make the country seem more attractive to the outside world is through the potential magnetism of Chinese civilization. The big media investments are the most visible element of China's soft-power project, but beneath the surface there are, in effect, two central ideas about the attractiveness of Chinese culture: an attempt to establish a sort of modern Chinese aesthetic that the rest of the world might find enticing, and an effort to tap into the wisdom of ancient thinkers to flesh out a non-Western worldview. China wants to present itself to the world as a culture that is both new and old.

———

When he was sixteen, Yan Xuetong was sent to work on a farm in the northeastern province of Heilongjiang, right near the border with Siberia. It was the height of the Cultural Revolution, and, like many members of his generation of urban youth, he was taken from his home and school and instructed to learn the greater wisdom of a peasant life. It was an unimaginably harsh existence. During the winters, they sometimes had to haul around large sacks through the snow, barefoot. For months, they would go without vegetables. The brutalities of the Cultural Revolution changed young Chinese in different ways. Some never overcame the emotional scars from that time, and suffered an adult life of depression or even suicide. Others developed a toughness and resilience that, in a perverse way, have served them well as society and the economy opened up. For Yan, who was from a family of scholars, the conclusions he drew were more philosophical. Mao Zedong's mad experiment with enforced anarchy, he decided, had destroyed the country's ancient ethical tradition of sincerity and replaced it with lying and hypocrisy.

Nearly four decades later, Yan is one of the most prominent public intellectuals in China and a professor of international relations at Tsinghua University in Beijing. He has written extensively about American foreign policy and Chinese military strategy. In recent years, however, he has turned to a project that has its roots in his disillusionment during the Cultural Revolution. He is trying to find ways to reconnect with what he sees as China's ancient ethical traditions, in particular the idea that China and the world should be governed by what he calls "humane authority." China, he believes, needs to re-establish the sense of morality that used to guide its behavior, both at home and abroad.

If that sounds a little esoteric, Yan has some fairly robust ideas about why it is a subject worth paying attention to. The quest to recover a Chinese ethical tradition, he believes, is a central part of the soft-power contest that a rising China faces with the U.S. The U.S. and China are in, he says, a "race for global supremacy," and an integral part of that competition will be a "battle for the hearts and minds" of people around the world, which will "determine who eventually prevails." The search back into China's philosophical traditions is not just an academic exercise, but part of a broader effort to present a vision of China and Chinese-inspired ideas that can challenge American modernity. "America's ideology is still much more influential around the world than China's," he told me. And he wants that to change.

These are interesting times in China's universities. After three decades during which Chinese society kept its head down and concentrated on getting ahead, it is starting to come up for air. Among some Chinese intellectuals, there is a hankering to generate new ideas about how global society is organized, to provide Chinese solutions to the world's problems. In a similar vein to Yan Xuetong, Zhao Tingyang at the Chinese Academy of Social Sciences has become a star of the Beijing intellectual scene with a series of works about the concept of *tianxia*—literally, "all under heaven"—another idea from the classical philosophy that attempts to define a vision of international harmony. Just as the Chinese authorities have embraced soft power to present a more positive image to the world, some Chinese intellectuals are brimming with optimism about the lessons that Chinese ideas can present to the world.

One of the striking features of the way China has embraced soft power is the suggestion that China now sees its values and culture as exportable. China and the U.S. have one very powerful thing in common, a sense of exceptionalism, the deeply felt belief in the superiority of their cultures and societies. American exceptionalism has an evangelical quality, the idea that its institutions and values are by their nature universal and should be copied by others; in recent times however, Chinese culture has been presented as being more exclusive. Chinese have tended to believe that their strengths were tied up in a history and set of values that are unique to China and which cannot be easily adopted by outsiders—at least by those countries outside the traditional Sino-centric world of East Asia. But the soft-power push indicates the beginning of a very different sort of attitude to Chineseness, a confidence that China now represents something that can be introduced in other countries, that it has things to teach the rest of the world. Amid official rhetoric about the "revival" or the "rejuvenation" of China, which has been given new impetus under Xi Jinping, China is reconnecting with an older tradition when it considered itself a natural cultural magnet for the world that surrounded it. "The Chinese have always prided themselves on being civilized as bearers of universal ideals," Wang Gungwu, the doyen of overseas Chinese historians, has written. China is dabbling with its own ideas of universal values.

"Five years ago, no one talked about this. People said it was crazy to talk about these sorts of things, that only our grandchildren might have to address these sorts of issues," Yan told me. "But when you are the biggest power in the world, you have to provide leadership. The new leaders that are taking over in China now, they will face a debate about future strategy and how we use power that the leaders of the past two decades did not."

During the Cultural Revolution, Red Guards destroyed the temple dedicated to Confucius, whom Mao scorned for his "feudal mentality," but over the last decade the ancient sage has witnessed a remarkable revival. The academic Yu Dan's book *Confucius from the Heart* sold ten million copies. Among party elders, there is still some token resistance to the veneration of Confucius: a statue was unveiled in Tiananmen Square in 2011, outside the reopened National Museum, only to be taken away a few weeks later. But it is another example of the extreme intellectual dexterity of the Chinese Communist Party that, having spent three decades denouncing everything Confucius stood for, it now presents itself as the legitimate inheritor of the millennial cultural tradition he represents. Yan Xuetong is one of the many intellectuals who have tried to tap into this surge in popular enthusiasm for ancient wisdom. He has mined Confucius and Mencius, as well as the less well-known writers from a similar era, such as Xunzi, Laozi, and Hanfeizi, to look for lessons about how a powerful China should behave. The most influential states, he concluded, were not necessarily the ones with the most powerful military, but the ones who won over the most hearts and minds of people at home and abroad. And this ability rested on the "humane authority . . . the superior moral power of the ruler."

The conclusions he draws for China are blunt. "An increase in wealth can raise China's power status but it does not necessarily enable China to become a country respected by others," he writes. "For China to become a superpower modeled on humane authority, it must first become a model from which other states are willing to learn." Some political reforms will be required, he believes, but that does not mean China should copy the U.S. "If China wants to become a state of humane authority, this would be different from the contemporary United States," he writes. "The goal of our strategy must be not only to reduce the power gap with the United States but also to provide a better model for society than that given by the United States."

If Yan is often blunt about his objectives, Zhao Tingyang is more oblique. The title of Zhao's best-known work is *The Tianxia System: A Philosophy for the World Institution*. In his elliptical style, Zhao describes the current international order as one which contains not just the odd "failed state," but a "failed world" that is rendered unworkable by excessive competition between nations and endless wars. Like Yan, he thinks the solution is for one country to provide an impeccable moral and political example. The world institution he envisages would be a voluntary order, based on the attractiveness of that country's "magnanimous" thought and behavior. International harmony would be established not by violence or power, but by the demonstration of virtue and good governance. "Tianxia theory," he writes, "is a theory for transforming enemies into friends where transformation seeks to attract people rather than conquer them."

The sorts of ideas that people like Yan and Zhao have started to discuss come with some very dangerous trip wires. *Tianxia* is an idea with deep roots in two thousand years of Chinese empire that was based on hierarchical relations between China and the other nations and peoples in the region. It reeks of a certain kind of cultural superiority and of a return to hierarchy. Most of the writers now championing ancient thinkers also leave open big questions about how China would be governed. Does "humane authority" require the sort of accountability that only democracies have been able to offer? As a result of these obvious problems, there has been a tendency among China-watchers to dismiss much of the work of the neo-Confucian writers, to see them as willing supporters of government propaganda. But these discussions are important for two reasons. They demonstrate a growing appetite among public intellectuals in China for devising ways of interpreting the world around Chinese precepts and history and forging a Chinese worldview. They are also a serious attempt to mold a language for China to explain its ambitions to influence the world and the role it wants to play. "Ancient Chinese policy will become the basis for much Chinese foreign policy, rather than Western liberalism or Communist ideology, both to justify and to be understood by Chinese people," Yan says. "It is easier to teach common people why they are doing certain things if it is explained in these terms. It makes it different from the U.S."

———

Before the opening ceremony for the 2008 Beijing Olympics, Zhang Jigang, the event's deputy director, made the following prediction: "I really hope that the people of the world can . . . get to know China, to understand China, to love China, to long for China." If trying to revive a Chinese intellectual tradition is one part of the underlying project, the other is an effort to present it as modern and hip, to define China Cool. The emotional high point of China's soft-power push was the ravishing Olympics opening ceremony—another beneficiary of a budget stretching into the hundreds of millions of dollars. Zhang Yimou, the country's most famous film director, was instructed to demonstrate the richness of traditional Chinese culture, the sort of brief that has produced many a tired, bureaucratic show for foreigners. Yet, with the help of fifteen thousand immaculately drilled performers and luminous lighting to tell the story of paper, printing, and the compass, he provided a vision of modernity China-style, with a powerful state rooted in Confucian wisdom yet also married to modern technology. After the ceremony, Zhang admitted that the only other country that could have put on a performance of such scale and discipline was North Korea, and they could not have mastered all the high-tech visual trickery that went along with it. Steven Spielberg, who had withdrawn as an adviser to the ceremony in protest against Chinese policies in Sudan, called it "arguably the grandest spectacle of the new millennium."

When visitors to the Olympics got tired of the sport, they were able to do a side trip to see some of the newest wonders of modern architecture. They would probably have seen the recently opened Norman Foster airport terminal, whose roof is shaped like a dragon. Beside the Great Hall of the People in central Beijing, they could visit the new titanium-domed concert hall, which goes by the name "the Giant Egg." And of course, there was the "Bird's Nest" stadium at the Olympic site, by Swiss architects Herzog and de Meuron, which is encased in twenty-eight thousand strips of structured steel, like a woven basket. But the biggest architectural draw was not even finished: the new China Central Television headquarters in the city's main business district. CCTV is the principal state-run broadcaster in China and, in the eyes of many Chinese, a reliable mouthpiece of stale government propaganda. It has spared neither money nor effort in its quest for a prestige building with the sheen of brand-name modernity. The $800-million project, on which work started in 2004, is the brainchild of the Rotterdam-based Office for Metropolitan Architecture and its principal architect, Rem Koolhaas. It is as much an exercise in engineering as in architecture and might only have been possible in China.

The building is made up of two L-shaped towers made of glass and metal, pieced together to create a cantilevered corridor that seems to hang in the air. Beijingers have bestowed many nicknames on the project, the most popular of which, *da kucha*, means "big shorts." Other, less flattering names include a play on the words for hemorrhoids. The design would have violated the building codes of most developing countries, but the architects managed to convene a meeting of the different

Beijing agencies to talk them through the idea. One of the quirks of modern China is that so many senior officials are qualified engineers, and that allowed them to follow all the technical details as Koolhaas and his thirty-something protégé, Ole Scheeren, walked them through the computer models. The building was approved. Even then, there was still huge anxiety about joining the two towers together, which was done before dawn in case the daytime heat caused the steel to expand slightly. It was a moment of "early-morning intimacy," as Scheeren told me.

A week before the Beijing Olympics, the *New York Times* architecture critic Nicolai Ouroussoff had this to say about the host city: "If Westerners feel dazed and confused upon exiting the plane at the new international airport terminal here, it's understandable. It's not just the grandeur of the space. It's the inescapable feeling that you're passing through a portal to another world, one whose fierce embrace of change has left Western nations in the dust. The sensation is comparable to the epiphany that Adolf Loos, the Viennese architect, experienced when he stepped off a steamship in New York Harbor more than a century ago. He had crossed a threshold into the future; Europe, he realized, was now culturally obsolete." The gushing about Beijing's new architectural triumphs (each one, as it happens, built by a European architect) might be an extreme example, but the article underlined the trepidation and awe that some in the West feel about China's rising cultural attraction. China is now beginning to promote its values and culture abroad just at the time when the West is undergoing a profound crisis of confidence. The financial crisis has not only inflicted huge damage on the economies of the Western world, it has also sapped confidence in the ability of democracies to solve their deepest problems. While China appears to be steaming ahead with its modernization plans, barely missing a beat during the crisis, the U.S. and other democracies are beset with doubts about corrosive political partisanship, about the power of vested interests, and about the inability of politicians to see beyond the latest headline. According to Ian Buruma, one of the most perceptive writers on modern Asia, "China's success story is the most serious challenge that liberal democracy has faced since fascism in the 1930s."

Amid such disillusionment, China's campaign to sell its cultural vitality around the world could not be better timed. Yet it will fall short. China's efforts to mobilize soft power misunderstand the forces that actually make societies attractive. The flaw is nowhere more evident than in the huge amount of money China is spending on taking its media groups overseas.

FOXIFICATION

In forty years in the television news business, Jim Laurie has done just about everything there is to be done. He spent two decades touring the world as a foreign correspondent for NBC and ABC. He was the only American network journalist in Saigon when the Vietnamese Communists took the city in 1975. Laurie has done breaking news and long-form documentaries, taught journalism, and helped set up News Corporation's news channels in India. In his locker, there are two Emmys and a George Peabody Award. It is a CV that any aspiring journalist would die for. And now he has a new challenge. He is one of the senior executives for CCTV America, the recently established U.S. operation of the Chinese state broadcaster.

In China, CCTV's showcase program is the main 7 p.m. news broadcast, which is a template for political power in the country. The broadcast begins with a rundown of the activities that day of the secretary general of the Communist Party, describing his meetings with foreign leaders and regional bosses and noting any comments he might have made. Then it moves to the number-two leader in the Communist Party Standing Committee, before describing the day of the number three in the list. The set is gray; the newscasters are unsmiling and stolid. A Chinese friend likes to joke that the broadcast is designed to persuade older Communist officials that nothing has actually changed in the country over the last three decades. CCTV runs a dozen or so channels, and some of its programming has tried to push boundaries. A few of the scandals about shoddy consumer products in China in recent years have actually been first aired on CCTV shows. But it can never escape its principal purpose, as the state's main tool for dictating the national news agenda.

Laurie was teaching journalism to students in Hong Kong when he got the offer to help start CCTV America. "The Chinese want to play catch-up," he says. They saw the global impact of Al Jazeera, the Qatar-based channel that broadcasts in both Arabic and English and which has won any number of accolades in recent years. Russia and Japan also have English-language channels vying for foreign audiences. Al Jazeera's success persuaded Chinese executives that there was a huge potential demand for "non-Western" news. The Chinese took the view that U.S. networks seemed to be shunning more conventional news in favor of Hollywood gossip and stories about celebrity addiction. They also observed what Laurie calls the "Foxification" of news in much of the West, where the once straitlaced presentation of facts has given way to different points of view and much more attitude. "The Chinese want to have their own perspective represented," Laurie says.

When Chinese Communist Party leaders met in October 2011 for their annual plenum, they issued a document with the following title: "Central Committee Decision Concerning the Major Issue of Deepening Cultural System Reforms, Promoting the Great Development and Prosperity of Socialist Culture." It was the most definitive in a series of policy statements over the last few years which have endorsed the promotion of cultural soft power. The document concluded: "Whoever owns the commanding heights of cultural development and soft power will enjoy a competitive edge internationally." Such high-level endorsement helps loosen budget strings. Over the last few years, Beijing has thrown a huge amount of resources at projects aimed at reaching the "commanding heights" of global soft power. There are more than four hundred government-sponsored Confucius Institutes around the world, promoting the Chinese language. When Hu Jintao visited the U.S. in 2011, the government rented another of the huge screens in Times Square to run a series of expensively produced promotional videos to show a more appealing side of China. There were images of "award-winning Chinese talent" such as pianist Lang Lang and "thrilling Chinese athletics," including Yao Ming. Another section of images of successful entrepreneurs was entitled "Chinese wealth," which, in retrospect, was probably not the best message to win over skeptical New Yorkers.

Of all the initiatives that have been launched to support the government's soft-power campaign, the overseas expansion of Chinese media is the biggest and most ambitious. The injection of resources into the international divisions of Chinese media has been striking. *China Daily*, the party's English-language daily, is now sold widely across the U.S. and Europe. Friends have reported that at times it is the only English-language paper available free in certain European hotels. It partners with a host of other papers that allow *China Daily* sections to appear across Asia. Readers of the *Washington Post* also receive a weekly "paid supplement" inside their paper which is written by *China Daily* staff. At the same time, China Radio International provides programming for a number of radio stations in the U.S., having started out with a station in Galveston, Texas. The Xinhua News Agency moved its journalists from a Queens suburb to Times Square. As well as its more traditional print and news-wire services, it is developing a Web-based TV service in foreign languages for a hundred countries. In a number of African countries, for instance, newspapers which in the past used Reuters or Associated Press articles for many of their news pages now lean heavily on Xinhua. CCTV is just as ambitious. It has recently opened a broadcast center in Nairobi, and since early 2012, it has been employing around a hundred people in Washington to put together programming for the U.S. market from a new studio just a few blocks from the White House.

Laurie says that CCTV spent a huge amount of time studying the BBC and CNN, looking at how they present news and trying to establish a "professional look." It also went about hiring journalists with internationally respected credentials. Cutbacks in the West have helped. In Latin America, CCTV picked up the former BBC Brazil and Cuba correspondent Mike Voss, who was laid off in one of the organization's cost-cutting rounds. While in China, I saw Voss giving an interview to the main CCTV channel, explaining his decision to join them. "I have already done more live takes in two months with CCTV than I did in the last year with the BBC," he said. "This shows they are really committed to the news." When Tom Brokaw was booked to appear on one of CCTV America's shows, the conservative *Weekly Standard* made a gibe about how China was "trying to buy good coverage for its Communist regime." Laurie is well aware of the baggage that his new network carries. "We are CCTV—and all that comes with it," he says. But he insists that the new channel is pushing back barriers on what a Chinese network can cover. During the week of their first broadcasts, the Pope happened to be visiting Havana, and Voss pitched a story on the trip.

China's relations with the Vatican are a politically treacherous subject in Beijing, and so a visit by the Pope to another Communist country is delicate territory. But CCTV America broadcast the item.

As well as the look, CCTV America has paid close attention to tone. Russia Today, Moscow's alternative to CNN, takes an aggressively anti-Western point of view and takes pleasure in its potshots at the American networks. One regular feature is about a piece of news that U.S. news channels have chosen not to cover, which usually includes a dig at America's presumed moral authority. In 2012, WikiLeaks founder Julian Assange was given a show on the channel. The Russia Today Web site is even more dismissive. One column about the U.S., by a writer called Robert Bridge, concludes: "What we are left with is an obese, drug-addled Burlesque Empire, bursting at the seams with electronic circuses, cocaine and corn puffs, physically and mentally incapable of finding the remote control when the scenes of war become too unappetizing." Alongside such competition, CCTV America is altogether more straitlaced. On a typical night, the news is heavy on economic themes and avoids sensationalism or gossip. It is straight, professional, maybe a little dull, but not without authority. If there is an implicit criticism of the U.S. and the West, it is not a full-throated one. Instead, the underlying politics are more subtle, an exercise in the sort of relativism that Chinese officials often adopt—an argument along the lines of "Your society has problems, our society has problems, so let's not be too judgmental about each other's political systems."

No one has a monopoly on providing the news, of course, but the identity of the leading broadcasters is still a matter of some importance. Imagine, for a second, if such important international stories as the protests in Cairo's Tahrir Square or the war in Bosnia had been beamed to the world not by the cameras of the BBC and CNN, but by the producers and correspondents of CCTV. Would the events have played out in the same way? Would the pressure on the Egyptian government not to use violence against the protesters have been the same? Would Washington have felt obliged to get involved in Bosnia had the dominant broadcaster in Sarajevo been Chinese? The high-minded goal behind China's overseas media splash is to try and frame the global conversation, to push a news agenda that is not so laced with Western values. Beijing does not want to evangelize the world against democracy, but it does want to shift some of the terms of the global debate. At the same time, lurking behind the project there is a certain animus for what Chinese officials routinely denounce as the "Western media," a term of abuse that lumps together journalists from any democracy, be they American, German, or Japanese. Beijing is trying to counter what it sees as the systematic bias in how foreign reporters portray China and the Communist Party to the rest of the world. The heads of foreign media bureaus in Beijing are summoned to the Foreign Ministry for periodic dressings-down by a senior official, and during one meeting I took notes. "Lots of good things happen in China but they do not interest you," the official complained. "You pick on anyone or anything that seems to support your views, which makes people think you have an agenda. You only seem to see the problems, so that makes people nervous." The lecture went on: "The Chinese people are getting more and more bored with this arrogance. They think it is unfair."

———

CCTV America's first show aired on February 6, 2012. Two days later, a man named Wang Lijun walked into the U.S. consulate in the Chinese city of Chengdu and set off the biggest political scandal in China since the 1989 Tiananmen Square Massacre. In the process, he also exposed why CCTV America and China's overseas media push will likely fail.

Wang was the police chief in Chongqing, a large city in the center-west of China, a few hundred kilometers from Chengdu. He sought refuge in the U.S. consulate after falling out with Bo Xilai, the local party boss. And he started talking. Wang brought a series of stories about corruption, legal abuses, and power grabs in Chongqing. The most explosive tale involved Bo's wife, Gu Kailai, who he claimed was responsible for the death a few months earlier in a Chongqing hotel room of Neil Heywood, a British businessman. The son of a famous Communist revolutionary, Bo had been considered a shoo-in to be promoted that autumn to the Politburo Standing Committee, the Communist Party body that really runs the country. Instead, Bo was relieved of his duties and expelled from the Communist Party, and his wife was charged with the murder of Heywood. It was the most damaging and open split in the top levels of the party in two decades.

Before long, the revelations were falling thick and fast. Elite-level politics in China is still something of a black box, but for once foreign journalists working in China had a glimpse inside. Within weeks, Bloomberg had revealed the $240-million family fortune that the Bo clan had managed to build up, my colleagues at the *Financial Times* had talked to a Chongqing billionaire who had been tortured and squeezed out of his fortune by rivals friendly with Bo, and the *Wall Street Journal* had detailed the complex relations between Heywood and the Bo clan. It was a tour de force of foreign correspondence. It was also the biggest political story in China in two decades. And yet almost none of it appeared on CCTV America. "There are certain issues that will not be covered by state TV in China," Laurie admits.

A couple of weeks after CCTV America started broadcasting from its new Washington studio, I got to meet Wadah Khanfar, the former director general of Al Jazeera and the man who helped turn it into an internationally recognized network. Al Jazeera demonstrated that there really is a market for non-Western news. Yet, in describing the network's early brushes with the U.S. authorities and its empathy for the stories of ordinary people, Khanfar talked about Al Jazeera in a way that could not have been more different from CCTV. The network first came to prominence during the Iraq War for broadcasting stories that the Western press were unable to. As security deteriorated across Iraq after the invasion, Western reporters found that important parts of the country were simply too dangerous to spend much time in. Al Jazeera filled this gap. While the Bush administration was still insisting that ordinary Iraqis had been liberated, Al Jazeera articulated the mounting rage against the occupation. Its message was implicitly anti-Western, which infuriated the Pentagon. But it was also largely correct.

A decade later, now with its own English-language channel, Al Jazeera hit another journalistic gold mine when the Arab Spring started. The self-immolation of a disgruntled trader in rural Tunisia became the unlikely spark for an astonishing wave of political change from Cairo to Benghazi, fueled by ordinary people standing up to despotic leaders. Al Jazeera was there once again to record their frustrations. Khanfar talked passionately about how grassroots political movements were finally changing a region whose politics had been ossified for so long. And he made no attempt to hide the network's role in pushing their agenda. "We were the voice of the Arab Spring," he proudly declared. Some of that spirit has spilled over into its coverage of China. Over the last decade and a half, the Chinese authorities have expelled only one foreign correspondent working in the country. Hassling and lectures are common, and some journalists have been beaten by local thugs. But only one reporter has actually had a visa rescinded because of official displeasure at the reporting. Her name was Melissa Chan, and she worked for Al Jazeera.

To be sure, the Western media do a partial job in China. Sometimes that is down to our prejudices, which can push some reporters to only see events through a narrow human-rights prism. Sometimes it is down to our personal limitations, in language or education. But mostly it is down to the nature of the political system, which still remains largely impenetrable. There is a global audience that would love to have more information about what is really happening in China—not out of hostility toward the Communist Party, as Beijing officials imagine, but out of genuine curiosity. That means there is endless demand to know more about the thoughts and personalities of the people who lead the second-most-important country in the world. But there is little appetite for insipid propaganda. The best way for a new network or paper to establish itself is to identify a huge story where it has some advantage and to plunge wholeheartedly into that story. Al Jazeera won itself an audience by broadcasting important tales that the Western media could not match. The gap in the international market where CCTV America could really make its name is the real story about China. But that is a story CCTV cannot tell.

VELVET PRISON

On the December day when his close friend Liu Xiaobo was awarded the 2010 Nobel Peace Prize, the Chinese human-rights lawyer Teng Biao found himself staying at the upmarket Shengping Yuan Hotel, just over an hour's drive north of Beijing. At that time, Liu was one year into an eleven-year sentence for "subverting state power," which he was serving at a prison in the bitterly cold northeast. Back in Beijing, the authorities operated on the principle of guilt by association. Liu Xiaobo's wife, Liu

Xia, had prepared a list of 143 friends and family members whom he would like to represent him. Everyone on the list who was still in China was barred from leaving the country. The crackdown on Liu's supposed sympathizers sometimes verged on the surreal. A few days before the ceremony, Mao Yushi, an eighty-one-year-old economist and occasional government critic, was supposed to travel to Singapore to give a speech on the development of rivers in the Himalayan region. He was stopped at Beijing airport and told that his planned trip was a "threat to national security." The climate of intimidation, he said, "reminds me of the Cultural Revolution," when his wife's hair was shaved by Red Guards and he was tortured and imprisoned.

Teng Biao's prison was of the velvet kind. A lecturer at Beijing's University of Politics and Law, Teng had also worked part-time for the previous decade as a lawyer, taking on cases about forced abortions and illegal land seizures. He was also one of the original signatories of Charter 08, the pro-democracy petition that Liu Xiaobo helped write, which was based on Czechoslovakia's Charter 77 and was the real reason for his long prison sentence. The Beijing authorities wanted to prevent Teng, who keeps copies of the political writings of Václav Havel on his bookshelf, from holding any public celebration of the Nobel. They also wanted to stop him from talking with the foreign journalists in Beijing, whose daily dispatches on the prize were a constant embarrassment for the government. So, along with a large number of activists, he was taken on an enforced trip out of Beijing, at the taxpayers' expense. The hotel where he was staying is just north of Badaling Station, on the Great Wall, one of Beijing's most visited places, and right next door is the Longqing Gorge, a beautiful limestone canyon with a fifty-meter-high waterfall.

One of the least understood powers of authoritarian regimes, but one which Havel knew well, is arbitrariness. In their bid to intimidate and punish Liu Xiaobo's friends, the Chinese authorities mixed subtlety with crude thuggery. Hua Ze, an independent journalist who used to make documentaries for state TV, had a black hood thrust over her head by the police, who took her into detention for nearly two months, during which she was also beaten. Yu Jie, another close friend of Liu's who was writing his biography, suffered a similar fate. The day before the prize ceremony, he was taken in a hood by state security agents to a prison, where he was burned with cigarette butts. "Right now, foreigners are awarding Liu Xiaobo the Nobel Peace Prize, humiliating our party and government. We'll pound you to death to avenge this," the leading security official told him. "If the order comes from above, we can dig a pit to bury you alive in half an hour, and no one on earth would know." Yu now lives in exile in Washington.

Yet, like Teng Biao, the poet A'Er had a more luxurious brush with the law. He was kept for several days at a holiday villa to the west of Beijing in Pinggu and wrote a poem about a tree trapped in rock that he could see from his window. When he was released, A'Er fled to Lijiang, his hometown, a popular tourist spot in the southwest much prized for its moderate climate and mountain walks. Eight plainclothes policemen followed him and stayed to keep an eye on him during his three-week stay. Teng Biao was held at his Beijing resort for three days. At first he was allowed to make phone calls, though not to receive them. From his bathroom, he called a friend, gave him the sign-on to his Twitter account, and asked him to write some messages commemorating Liu Xiaobo's award. He got four tweets published before the police discovered the ruse and took away his mobile. "They were incredibly angry," he later told me. "But I was very pleased with myself."

At the heart of Beijing's soft-power drive is the notion that if China somehow had better PR its image would change. If Chinese media only had a higher profile overseas, or if China had an appealing set of values to sell to the world, or if the leaders had a snappier phrase with which to frame China's ambitions, then people would start to think differently about the country. They might start to "love China, to long for China," as the Olympics deputy director had hoped. But the harsh truth is that China's ability to project soft power is hampered by the reality of life in China. The effort to project some form of "humane authority" is constantly undermined by the real-life capriciousness of China's leaders. It is hard to make a society seem attractive when those who disagree with the carefully policed mainstream are persecuted in such a way, when dissent is criminalized, and when those who seek to criticize are brushed aside so ruthlessly. The problem is the messenger, not the message. One of the strategic goals of the soft-power push is to present an unthreatening vision to the world of what a powerful China might portend, but it is persistently undercut by the reality of what a powerful China means for the more awkward members of Chinese society.

Liu Xiaobo and his friends missed a somewhat melancholic ceremony in Oslo. Thorbjorn Jagland, the head of the Nobel Committee, brought in the red binder with gold trim that holds the Nobel citation. He then placed it on an empty chair. What they witnessed at home was an outbreak of paranoia. On the day of the ceremony, the prize was described as a "political farce" by Foreign Ministry spokeswoman Jiang Yu. "Prejudice and lies are untenable and the Cold War mentality has no popular support," she said. Chinese officials warned Norway that business deals were now under threat. Ambassadors in China were called in by the Foreign Ministry and told that their governments should not have anyone present at the ceremony in Oslo. In the end, nineteen of the countries said that their ambassadors would not attend the prize ceremony. Most were obvious bedfellows of an irate Beijing—for instance, Cuba, Russia, and Sudan. But there were a few surprises as well, such as Colombia, the Philippines, and Sri Lanka. Chinese officials claimed that 101 countries in total had expressed opposition toward having the prize awarded to Liu Xiaobo. The *Global Times*, a nationalist tabloid and sister publication of party mouthpiece the *People's Daily*, wrote: "All the applause has come from the West and the citizens of the third-world countries are all now China's allies." Dai Bingguo, China's senior foreign-policy official, told Hillary Clinton that the prize was part of an American conspiracy to weaken China. Speaking a few months later, a senior Chinese official captured the tone of self-pitying victimization that underpinned Beijing's aggressive reaction. "The Nobel Prize was a wake-up call about the existence of a difference over ideology that many here thought had fallen away as a result of the growth of the Chinese economy," the official said. "This prize makes us think that maybe the Cold War is not entirely over. The cloud is still there."

China treats soft power as a problem that can be solved by bureaucrats. Beijing throws money at it, just as it has with high-speed rail or wind power, attracting brand-name international architects with big-ticket commissions. But modernity is not something that can be bought off-the-shelf. Soft power is generated by society from the creativity of its citizens, not created by culture ministries. China hopes its soft-power investments will blunt criticism of its political system, but it is the political system that is holding back its soft power. The cast of people who were harassed during the Nobel ceremony underlines the central dilemma. Among the political activists, there were also poets, writers, journalists, lawyers, and other members of the intellectual elite. (Before he became more involved in politics, Liu Xiaobo was the *enfant terrible* of Chinese literary criticism.) China is fighting a soft-power battle with one hand tied behind its back. It wants to channel the energies of the country's leading thinkers into helping define a vision of a modern China that will appeal to the rest of the world. But it also punishes those who step too far out of line from the official script.

Take the two artists most closely associated with the Beijing Olympics, the film director Zhang Yimou and Ai Weiwei, the sculptor who helped two Swiss architects with the design of the stunning Bird's Nest stadium. These are the sorts of figures with the talent to shape a distinctive and attractive Chinese modernity, to persuade the rest of the world that the future will be shaped by Chinese and not American imaginations. Yet Ai Weiwei spent two months in jail in 2011 because of his criticisms of the government and is now banned from talking to the media. (He was "harmonized," as ironical young Chinese activists say whenever one of their number is harassed by the born-again Confucian authorities.) A few weeks before his arrest, he told me: "Mao used to say that the Communists came to power on the back of the gun and the pen. But the pen is not working anymore." If Ai revels in the status he has now as a leading dissident, Zhang Yimou is still very much in favor with the establishment. He has become the Communist Party's in-house creative director. After his Olympics success, he was asked to put on a grand pageant in Tiananmen Square on the evening of the 2009 military parade. But even this status does not afford him any more real creative space. I once asked Zhang why his recent films had all been period pieces that shunned the fascinating complexities of contemporary China. If he made a film about today's China, he said, he would have so many problems with the censors that it would not be worth his trouble.

Winning a Nobel Prize had long been a Chinese obsession. Delegations were sent to Sweden to investigate what the judges were looking for. Conferences were held and a national literature prize established to seed local talent. The push to win a Nobel Prize "had become a cause of a psychological disorder, a token whose value and authority as imagined in China was inflated out of all proportions to its real importance," the China scholar Julia Lovell wrote in a 2006 essay. In a way, the Nobel obsession demonstrated the way China has got things the wrong way round, a bureaucratic-led push for recognition taking the place of actual creativity. As they did most years, in 2010 the main Chinese news Web sites ran special pages for the Nobel awards, including long profiles of the winners for medicine, chemistry, and economics, as their names were announced. When the award of the peace prize to Liu Xiaobo was unveiled, however, the special Web pages quickly disappeared. Official China craved a Nobel Prize: just not *that* prize. Some disgruntled Chinese took matters into their own hands. A group of academics founded the inaugural Confucius Peace Prize, which was awarded the day before the Nobel ceremony in Oslo and was designed to demonstrate displeasure with the Norwegian committee's decision to honor Liu. According to Qiao Damo, a poet who was one of the prize organizers: "We thought it better to have a prize that suits Eastern values of peace, which are different from Norway and the West"—a sentiment somewhat undermined by the fact that Qiao was also on the short list of winners. The prize brochure put it slightly differently: "Norway is only a small country. With over one billion people, [China] should have a great voice on the issue of world peace." In the end, the event had a farcical air. The aging Taiwanese politician who was given the award, Lien Chan, declined to attend because he did not take it seriously. His place was taken by a surprised-looking six-year-old girl who stepped up to collect the cash award.

Validation of a sort eventually came when the 2012 Nobel Prize for Literature went to the Chinese author Mo Yan. Television programs were interrupted to announce the news, and the *People's Daily* gushed the next day that the prize was "a comfort, a certification and also an affirmation—but even more so, it is a new starting point." Mo is a particularly unusual talent, an internationally respected writer whose work is full of social criticism but who is also a vice chairman of the state-run Chinese Writers Association. It is a testament to his skills, both literary and political, that he has managed to walk this tightrope. But it has not always been easy. His reputation at home was damaged when he took part in the 2009 Frankfurt Book Fair, another one of those events which exposed the limitations of China's soft-power push. As the guest of honor that year, Beijing saw the festival as an opportunity to promote Chinese literature and spent $7.5 million on the event, sending two thousand publishers to Frankfurt to promote the country's authors. Mo gave a speech to the opening session, which was attended by then vice president Xi Jinping. Yet, from the start, the festival was marred by behind-the-scenes fighting between Chinese officials and the organizers over what would be discussed at the events. At a symposium before the festival, the German hosts asked dissident writers Dai Qing and Bei Ling to speak, but then withdrew the invitations after Beijing objected, only to reinstate them following a protest by German journalists. In the end, when the two writers stood to speak, the official Chinese delegation walked out. Mo was among that group.

A similar furor erupted at the closing ceremony, when Dai and Bei said they had initially been invited to speak, only to be barred again after another protest from Beijing. The result was a huge own-goal, with much more attention paid to Chinese political interference than to any of the writers actually present. As long as Beijing tries to control the definition of Chinese culture and to decide who will speak on its behalf, China will continue to punch well below its weight. "I had no choice," Mo said in an interview a year later with a Chinese magazine, when asked to explain why he had walked out on other writers. "A lot of people are now saying about me, 'Mo Yan is a state writer.' It's true, insofar as . . . I get a salary from the Ministry of Culture, and get my social and health insurance from them too." He added: "That's the reality in China. Overseas, people all have their own insurance, but without a position, I can't afford to get sick in China."

It was a Chinese liberal intellectual and diplomat, Hu Shi, who in the 1930s provided the best answer to those afraid of Chinese soft power. He was writing in another era of intense debates in China about how to modernize its society and whether it should follow a Western path. If there was anything really valuable in traditional Chinese culture, Hu Shi told his compatriots, then it would easily survive the entry of

Western ideas into the country. "If our culture really contains priceless treasures that are able to withstand the power of the cleansing foreign attack, this indestructible part of our culture will naturally emerge even more fully after scientific culture washes over it," Hu wrote. The threat to America's soft power does not come from China, but from its own seeming inability to solve basic issues of governance. The U.S. should worry less about the attractiveness of China and more about getting its own house in order.

A few months before he left office in 2012, Hu Jintao gave another speech about soft power, this time with much harder edges. "We must clearly see that international hostile forces are intensifying the strategic plot of Westernizing and dividing China, and ideological and cultural fields are the focal areas of their long-term infiltration," Hu warned. Gone was the confident vision of a proud culture winning its due in the world, replaced instead by an insecure, enemies-under-the-bed nervousness. Hu added: "We should deeply understand the seriousness and complexity of the ideological struggle, always sound the alarms and remain vigilant, and take forceful measures to be on guard and respond." The speech was an appropriate bookend for the hidden agenda behind the soft-power push. As a result of its slow-burning legitimacy crisis, the Communist Party has reached for any number of new props to replace its socialist ideals, from economic managerialism to nationalism. Confucius, the Olympics, and Nobel Prizes are all part of the same search for legitimacy. China is not really selling itself to the world: the party is trying to justify itself to the Chinese people.

7

"We Are Not the World's Savior"

Humanitarian Intervention and the UN

WHEN BARACK OBAMA MADE his first-ever trip to China in November 2009, he got to meet most of the country's top leaders, with one very notable exception. That same week, Zhou Yongkang decided it was the right moment to take a large Chinese delegation to Sudan. A member of the all-powerful nine-man Communist Party Standing Committee, Zhou had the day job of running China's vast security apparatus. It was he who orchestrated the arrest of Liu Xiaobo. But Zhou [pronounced *Jo*] also occasionally dabbled in foreign policy. When the ailing Kim Jong-il unveiled his twenty-something son Kim Jong-un as his successor during a mass rally in Pyongyang in 2010, Zhou was standing right next to him on the platform. Zhou has also been one of the linchpins of China's close ties with Sudan. During his trip to Khartoum, Zhou met with Omar al-Bashir, the Sudanese president, who, partly as a result of U.S. pressure, had been charged four months earlier by the International Criminal Court in the Hague with genocide and crimes against humanity.

Back in Beijing, Obama was enduring a frustrating visit, every stage of which was carefully stage-managed by the government to limit open contact with ordinary Chinese people. At a joint "press conference" in the Great Hall of the People, there were no actual questions allowed from either the American or the Chinese media. Instead, the two presidents read out short statements and walked away in silence, looking as if they had just been to couples counseling. On the same evening, Bashir, who now faces an international arrest warrant, held a banquet for Zhou and the Chinese delegation in Khartoum. "As an old friend of the Sudanese president," Zhou said in an after-dinner speech, "I got a full sense of the profound changes that have taken place in Sudan under your leadership as soon as I stepped on Sudanese soil."

It is not hard to see why some in Washington might feel China is becoming the cheerleader for the world's more authoritarian and anti-Western regimes. In the last few years, Beijing has gone out of its way to protect the Kim regime in North Korea, despite its increasingly dangerous behavior. China provided a financial lifeline to Hugo Chávez in Venezuela, and helped reduce international pressure on the Syrian regime as the country's civil war escalated. China has even become an important backer of Robert Mugabe in Zimbabwe, helping protect him from censure in the United Nations and elsewhere. When Mugabe celebrated his eighty-sixth birthday in February 2010, the Chinese Embassy in Harare put on a party for the president to mark the occasion, with more than a hundred guests invited. Mugabe was presented with a large cake, made from eight different layers. A group of Chinese diplomats sang the Zimbabwean national anthem for him in the Shona language. It was the first time Mugabe had visited an embassy in the capital in the three decades he has been in power.

Among all these relationships, however, the Sudanese connection has been the most controversial. Over the last two decades, China has invested $7 billion in the oil industry in Sudan, making it both the main customer and the biggest investor in Africa's largest nation. With the possible exception of North Korea, Sudan is the nearest thing China has to a client state. Shortly after Omar al-Bashir took power in a coup in 1989, he found himself the subject of international sanctions as a result of his links to terrorism. (During the 1990s, Sudan provided a home for Osama bin Laden for several years.) As Western oil companies pulled out of the country, China stepped into the vacuum. China's oil companies were in the first throes of their "go out" strategy, where Beijing encouraged selected companies to operate overseas, and Sudan provided the perfect opportunity, a country with ample reserves not already tied up by China's Western rivals. Within a few years, the Chinese companies accounted for more than 70 percent of Sudan's entire exports. As it happens, one of the executives at the helm of the oil industry who helped set up the Sudan investments was Zhou Yongkang, the security boss who in the 1990s ran China National Petroleum Corporation, the largest oil group. Relations between the two countries started to go well beyond oil. In its bid to curry favor with Khartoum, China trained Sudanese helicopter pilots and became one of the government's main suppliers of arms. Twice during the Darfur conflict, a UN panel of experts noted that Chinese weapons were being transferred to Darfur by the Khartoum government. When Hu Jintao visited Sudan in 2007, at the height of the international furor over Darfur, he offered an interest-free loan to build a new presidential palace.

At the same time, China has also become the political protector of the Sudanese regime. During the very worst years of the slaughter in Darfur, in 2003 and 2004, China provided crucial political support using its position on the United Nations Security Council to block or water down measures aimed at the regime in Khartoum. At the UN, Darfur was a hugely divisive issue. The conflict exposed the stark difference between the way the U.S. and European nations now understand the world, and the way China does. For many in Washington, the events in Darfur were "genocide," a grotesque series of crimes by the government against its own citizens, which made some sort of outside intervention a moral imperative. Beijing argued that the violence was an internal affair of Sudan and that heavy outside intervention in the country would only destabilize it even further. The rest of the world had no right to override Sudan's sovereignty. China effectively put up a large sign saying: "Keep out."

If the twentieth century saw fierce ideological battles between fascism and liberal democracy and between capitalism and communism, then one of the central dividing lines in this century will be the issue of state sovereignty. As China has become more powerful over the last decade,

Washington and Beijing have started to compete over the basic rules at the heart of the international system, about the duties and responsibilities of what is sometimes called "the international community." In part, it is a battle for the soul of the United Nations, where many of these disputes are played out, but it is also a bigger discussion about the role of human rights in international affairs. In one corner, the U.S. and Europe urge greater outside intervention in states that are conducting massive abuses against their citizens; in the other corner, China and Russia defend a belief that absolute sovereign rights are the bedrock for a stable international system. Sudan was a warm-up act for this clash between two very different philosophical views about the way the world should work. Beijing would like to use its new influence to set the tone for how international politics will be organized and to check what it sees as Western moralizing and meddling.

This tension has been at the heart of the UN ever since it was founded in 1945, created out of the ashes of the Second World War by men scarred by the experience of Nazism. The UN's architects aimed to establish a world free from foreign invasions by territory-hungry great powers. The defense of sovereignty was proclaimed as a core value. Article II, Part 7, of the UN Charter reads: "Nothing contained in the present Charter shall authorize the United Nations to intervene in matters which are essentially within the domestic jurisdiction of any state." Over the next decade, the UN was closely involved in the process of decolonization, which added to its doubts about outside interference in the internal affairs of sovereign nations. The number of member countries has risen from fifty at the start to 194, and the leaders of these new nations had little intention of letting the UN become a rubber stamp for meddling in their politics by former colonial masters. Decolonization, as the Indian writer Pankaj Mishra puts it, was "fueled by an intense desire among humiliated peoples for equality and dignity in a world controlled by a small minority of white men."

Yet, right from the start, the UN was also squarely focused on human rights and the protection of minorities. The same shattering war experiences encouraged world leaders to sign in 1948 the Universal Declaration of Human Rights at a conference in Paris. Having seen the paralysis of the League of Nations, the UN's founders did not intend to create an organization that would be impotent in the face of wide-scale abuses. This debate about sovereignty lay dormant during the Cold War, when the U.S.-Soviet rivalry neutered the effectiveness of the UN. But by the time the Berlin Wall fell, it was clear that many of the greatest humanitarian problems in the world were caused no longer by wars between nations, which had declined, but by abuses taking place within nations—from Uganda to Cambodia. The growing awareness of environmental degradation has only added to the perception that sovereignty has its limits.

The end of the Cold War prompted a wave of optimism about the creation of a new, coherent international community which could put the stale arguments of the previous decades aside, and which would never again be too late to the scene. Yet this confidence was short-lived. The recurring crises in Bosnia, Kosovo, and especially Rwanda, where eight hundred thousand people were massacred, reinforced the uncomfortable reality that the UN lacked the tools to deal with the worst humanitarian crises. Stung by its failure to do anything to stop the bloodshed, then UN secretary general Kofi Annan launched a discussion about when it was right for the international community to intervene to protect vulnerable populations. The negotiations were tortuous, in part because of the objections of those developing countries which did not want to provide an excuse for the U.S. and other Western powers to send in the marines every time there was a crisis. But in the end, a committee led by Gareth Evans, a former Australian foreign minister, and the Algerian diplomat Mohamed Sahnoun, came up with a formula which was approved unanimously at a UN summit in 2005 and which became known as the "Responsibility to Protect."

The end result was a carefully crafted compromise. Military action was held out only as a very last resort; instead, there would first be a whole spectrum of policy options for the UN to take, from pressure and diplomacy to sanctions and referring leaders to the International Criminal Court. But, for all the caveats, the governments of the world committed themselves to take action in cases of genocide or grave crimes against humanity. The combination of the Rwanda disaster and the disappearance of Cold War ideological divisions gave the UN an opening to promote a new international philosophy about the defense of innocent civilians from rapacious governments. Robert Mugabe may have denounced it as a "phony principle," but for its supporters, "Responsibility to Protect" was an attempt to enshrine a series of basic guidelines that would underpin the international community in a new century. Martin Gilbert, the British historian of Winston Churchill and the Holocaust, called it "the most significant adjustment to national sovereignty in 360 years."

China voted in favor of "Responsibility to Protect," but right from the start Beijing was deeply anxious about the whole project. Under Mao, China had been a revolutionary power that occasionally looked to export its model around the world and saw international forums as a stage for occasional tantrums. But since the late 1970s, it has put its firm support behind the old Westphalian notions that sovereign nations should keep out of one another's affairs. The survival instincts of the party demanded as much. During an era when democracy has spread rapidly, this aggressive defense of sovereignty is a way to deflect attention from China's own affairs and to help make the world safe for the Chinese Communist Party. After all, how can Communist China shield itself from overseas criticisms of its own political arrangements if it routinely sticks its nose into the affairs of others? China has worked assiduously to make sure that the UN Human Rights Council, which is supposed to report on abuses around the world, has remained a toothless talking-shop.

Yet there is more to China's position than just opportunism. China has its own arguments for why a policy of strict nonintervention is a strong foundation for the international system. Rather than weakening the international community, China believes it is creating a more equitable world, a "democracy between nations" in which each state is treated equally by the rest of the international community. Beijing sees its friendship with dictatorial regimes as part of an approach that is better for the developing world than the bullying interventionism of the West. Whereas the West values human rights and transparent governance, China places emphasis on stability. Beijing argues that only when a poor country has a solid government, whose sovereignty is respected by other nations, can it then introduce the sorts of coherent, long-term policies needed to promote growth and reduce poverty. Even when the

Western powers have a good point about abuses, Beijing claims, the initial intervention on humanitarian grounds often becomes an excuse for prolonged colonial interference that makes the situation worse. For Beijing, nonintervention is a firewall against destabilizing meddling.

The irony is that, from Beijing's point of view, the U.S. is the radical, revolutionary power trying to change the rules of the game. While the West has become more animated about tackling humanitarian catastrophes since the end of the Cold War, China believes it is defending tried and tested ideas about how states should behave, which took root in Europe four centuries ago and are a better guide for international stability. From Sudan to Zimbabwe, China believes it is defending a status quo the West once established but now wants to tear up.

In conversations and interviews about this subject, Chinese officials would occasionally try to play Europe off against the U.S. "We want the same multipolar world that Europe wants," a senior diplomat once told me. "Europe's view of the world emphasizes system building, rules, dialogue, and discussion, as opposed to a view of the world that stresses confrontation." But mostly I would be on the receiving end of a finely honed series of talking points about how Western or American interference was a big part of the problem in the developing world. "Look at Liberia," a lunch companion from the Foreign Ministry told me. "It has had lots of U.S. help and influence and money, but it is not a mini-America. You cannot govern another country from the outside."

China also has its own list of grievances about American obstruction at the UN, starting with the large number of vetoes that Washington has exercised to protect Israel from criticism about human-rights abuses. And, like many other developing countries' governments, China is quick to point out the double standards in American moral leadership. Washington does not like our support of Mugabe, Chinese officials would say, but it backed Mubarak for so many decades. The U.S. complains when we buy oil from Iran, they ask, but is the situation in that country really much different from Saudi Arabia? Or Equatorial Guinea? Chinese diplomats can play these games all night. Beijing is also not shy about using the anti-colonial card, suggesting that noninterference is a bulwark against the sort of exploitation China itself suffered at the hands of the imperial powers in the nineteenth century. At the United

Nations, China often listens closely to what other developing countries are saying and then, if it does not have big issues of its own at stake, will follow their views. It has become very skilled at channeling anti-colonial resentment in the developing world against America's messianic tendencies. "We are very different from you," a senior official at the Foreign Ministry once told me. "We do not think that we are the world's savior."

China's defense of sovereignty has a lot of support at the UN from developing countries with colonial pasts. There is even sympathy among such big democracies as Brazil and India, on whom the humanitarian evangelism of the West often grates, and who were appalled by the aggressive unilateralism of the Iraq War. Plenty of developing countries, democratic and authoritarian, would like to see limits placed on the moralizing interference of the U.S. in the affairs of others. All of this makes nonintervention an extremely important policy for China. It provides international protection for the Chinese Communist Party. At the same time, it gives the government a powerful anti-colonialist calling card as it seeks to expand its international influence. We will do business with you and not ask any questions about how you run your country, China tells other developing nations. It is not just autocrats who find this extremely appealing.

But then there was Darfur. The fierce debates about Sudan in the early years of the 2000s put China at the center of UN politics in a way it had never been before. China came under intense political pressure because its support of Sudan appeared to be making a mockery of the post-Rwanda "never again" rhetoric at the UN, even as diplomats were drafting the "Responsibility to Protect" doctrine. For all the attractions that China's opposition to outside interference holds for many governments, there is also a powerful downside—in the hands of a veto-holding, permanent member of the Security Council, it can render the UN mute at the very moment when it should be at its most active.

The burden of proof for genocide is a very high one, and for some of the most informed observers of the events in Darfur, that bar was not reached by the Sudanese government. Human Rights Watch, for instance, declined to define what happened as genocide. It is also true that the complex events in Darfur were not a one-sided affair—the government in Khartoum was responding to a rebellion in the province. At the same time, there exists ample documented evidence to show that, between 2003 and 2010, widespread and grotesque human-rights abuses were committed by the Sudanese government or by the local proxy it used, a militia group called the Janjaweed. There is extensive testimony of villages burned to the ground, the men then killed and the women raped. In a country that had seen constant outbreaks of civil unrest since its independence, this was more than the usual burst of violence. A decade after Rwanda, Africa was witnessing again an organized campaign of ethnic cleansing.

Yet the early years of the conflict were also the time when China's oil investments started to bear real fruit, and Beijing did everything it could to shelter its Khartoum ally from international pressure, often with the support of Russia. In 2003 and 2004, when Kofi Annan was trying to draw the world's attention to the emerging catastrophe, China tried to keep the Darfur situation off the agenda at the UN. In 2004, it threatened to veto a resolution which merely raised the prospect of sanctions. A year later, with African Union peacekeepers struggling to control the situation, it blocked the idea of a UN peacekeeping operation. Chinese officials argued that, however bad things were in Sudan, they would become much worse if heavy-handed intervention by outside powers led to the downfall of the Khartoum regime. "The country would have become another Somalia," a Foreign Ministry official told me a few years later, still with a tone of indignation that China had come in for such intense criticism.

In the near-decade since the Darfur crisis, the same debates about outside intervention have continued to rage. The fiercest dispute has been over the civil war in Syria that started in 2011. In this case, Russia took the lead in blocking sanctions on the Assad regime as it waged war on its people, but China moved in lockstep at each stage in the process—both countries vetoing three separate UN Security Council resolutions. The international community remains deadlocked. Almost a decade after the "Responsibility to Protect" was negotiated, the leading powers at the UN are no closer to agreeing on how to respond to these types of crises.

The bruising arguments over Sudan and Syria have prompted anguished discussion in the West about a new "axis of authoritarians," with China and Russia using their vetoes at the UN to protect dictators around the world from outside pressure. There is widespread criticism in the West about the deadening impact that China's noninterference principle is likely to have on international politics. As François Godement of the European Council on Foreign Relations puts it, the effect of China's growing influence is a "hollowing out of the international system." Michael Ignatieff, the Canadian intellectual-turned-politician who was one of the leading voices in the interventionist debates of the 1990s, has also become one of the fiercest critics of the new axis between China and Russia. "Syria tells us that the era of humanitarian intervention, 'responsibility to protect,' is over, because it assumed a historical progression that has turned out to be false," he wrote. "When they look at the world this way, the Russian and Chinese regimes mock our view of history."

This is a powerful view, and one that is deeply pessimistic about the ability of the West to continue to shape the values at the heart of the international community. It fits into the narrative of decline, of a West that is now powerless to turn its ideas and instincts into coherent action in the face of the influence of rising powers. Yet it is also a mistaken view, because it misses two essential features about the emerging international environment, both of which are potential game-changers. It ignores the way in which China's rapidly expanding interests around the world are undermining its reluctance to get involved in crises. And it also downplays the potential for the U.S. to find common ground with some of the other new rising powers, who are likely to have considerable influence in the coming years over the shape of the new global order.

ENTER THE SWING STATES

To the other members of the guerrilla group, she was known as Estela. When the Brazilian military arrested her in 1970, one of the worst years for violence during the two-decade-long dictatorship, she was subjected to a ferocious array of torture techniques. Her head, thighs, and breasts were given electric shocks, and she was suspended naked and upside down on a stick. She eventually suffered a hemorrhage of the uterus, which prevented her from having more children.

Dilma Rousseff is now the first female president of Brazil, having won in a comfortable election in 2010 for the center-left Workers' Party. But her first entry into national political life was as a member of the Palmares Armed Revolutionary Vanguard, a far-left guerrilla group which took up arms to overthrow the military dictators who ran the country from 1964 to 1985. Her predecessor, Luiz Inácio Lula da Silva, was locked up by the military for his political activity against the dictatorship. His predecessor, Fernando Henrique Cardoso, fled to exile in Chile and then France after the military ordered his arrest. The man that both Lula and Dilma defeated to win the presidency, José Serra, was also an exile in Chile. For the last twenty years, Brazil has been run by a generation of leaders who got into political life to oppose the military dictatorship and to fight against the abuses committed against Brazilians by their own government.

Yet, over the last decade, Brazil has been a persistent critic of Western-led efforts at humanitarian intervention in countries where other dictators were conducting grotesque abuses of their populations. Celso Amorim, Lula's foreign minister, once described the idea of the "Responsibility to Protect" as *"droit d'ingérence . . . in new clothes,"* a concept dating back to the seventeenth century about interfering in the affairs of another nation. On the occasions when Brazil has been a rotating member of the UN Security Council, it has often used its votes to express skepticism about U.S.-backed pressure or interventions. In 2004, when international outrage at the violence in Darfur was escalating, Brazil joined China in opposing any resolution on Sudan that smacked of new international sanctions. When China and Russia vetoed a UN Security Council resolution in October 2011 which criticized the violent oppression of opposition in Syria, Brazil was again on the Security Council. This time it abstained.

Just as in China, the defense of state sovereignty has been hard-wired into Brazilian elites for several generations. In the early twentieth century, Brazil was opposed to the use of military interventions to collect on the bad debts of countries that had defaulted on bond payments. (Before the IMF, it was the marines that enforced repayment of debts in developing countries.) Suspicions about the great powers hardened in the 1950s, with the era of decolonization. At the end of the Cold

War, Brazil did not see the West's new enthusiasm for humanitarian interventions as part of a welcome, modern activism in defense of the oppressed; instead, it saw this as the old wine of colonial interference, in new bottles.

Among the elites of many other large developing countries, it is pretty easy to find similar sentiments, especially in nations with a recent colonial past. In that high-profile 2011 vote on Syria during which Brazil abstained, South Africa and India also happened to be on the Security Council at the time. They also abstained. In South Africa, the years of struggle against the apartheid regime left the African National Congress deeply cynical about the motives of Western governments in preaching humanitarian intervention. In the six decades since its independence, India's self-image has been intimately linked to the concepts of the Non-Aligned Movement, making it another natural skeptic of Western motives. Susan Rice, who was the U.S. ambassador at the UN during the first Obama administration, chided Brazil, India, and South Africa for taking positions that "one might not have anticipated, given that each of them came out of strong and proud democratic traditions." Yet, on the face of it, Brazil, India, and South Africa appear to have more in common with China about the basic ground rules of how the international system should work—at least more than they do with Washington.

In many ways, the dispute over intervention and sovereignty is one part of a much broader challenge that the U.S. faces as a result of the big shifts in relative power that are taking place around the world. Even those who deny that America is in decline recognize that economic power is becoming more diffuse as a group of populous, developing nations try to turn strong growth rates into a bigger international presence. China is not the only potential challenger to the international order that the U.S. erected after the Second World War. There is now a new generation of powers, not just India, South Africa, and Brazil, but also Turkey, South Korea, and Indonesia, who are in some ways the floating voters of international politics, new entrants to the top table of global governance who have not yet decided how they want to apply the influence that their economic heft is accruing. If, more often than not, these governments were to side with China and Russia, it would represent a much broader threat to Washington's ability to keep setting the international agenda.

Of course, the U.S. has faced a parallel challenge before, in the 1960s and 1970s, when the dominance it enjoyed after the war was put into question by the rise of Western Europe and of Japan. It seems obvious in retrospect that these countries would make common cause with the U.S. and become part of the unified political entity we now call the Western powers. But at the time it was not so clear—think about the Gaullist efforts to distance France from the U.S., or the period of intense economic rivalry with Japan that lasted well into the 1990s. Washington was able to find ways to integrate these new powers into the institutions and rules that it had established. The U.S. is facing another, similar inflection point. Either it finds a way to embrace some of these newer powers, or it will see its influence over the international community gradually slide. That is true for a range of issues, from trade rules to the membership of international institutions, but it is also very much the case with the values at the heart of the international system. It is hard to argue for the moral legitimacy of the U.S. approach to abusive dictators when several of the biggest democracies in the world are openly opposed. Handing out lectures to these countries about their democratic heritage will not do the trick.

It might seem surprising at first, but one long-term U.S. objective should be to try not to alienate Russia. Of course, in many of the most contested votes at the UN in recent years, Russia and China have been very much on the same side. Indeed, Moscow has often been more of an obstacle than Beijing. Many Russia analysts suspect that Vladimir Putin has taken confidence from the success of Chinese authoritarianism as he has cemented his own control of power in Moscow. Some American neoconservatives warn that the Shanghai Co-operation Organisation, a security group that brings together Russia, China, and several Central Asian countries, is becoming an authoritarian anti-NATO. The antipathy in the U.S. toward Russia is particularly pronounced on the right—and was given voice when presidential candidate Mitt Romney called Russia "without doubt, our number one geopolitical foe." Yet the obsession with Russia among some on the American right is itself something of a Cold War hangover that vastly overstates Moscow's influence. Russian power rises and falls these days with the price of oil, not the potency of its political system or its economy. More to the point, it is a major strategic error to overplay the ideological affinity of the two countries. A China that behaves more and more like an ambitious great power is likely to be seen by Russia as being as much a rival as a partner. Moscow is already worried about the political and economic inroads that Beijing is making into Central Asia, about Chinese migration into eastern Siberia, and about Chinese naval intentions in the northern-Pacific Arctic region. As Chinese power grows in the coming decades, Russian anxieties are only likely to expand, too. During the Cold War, Washington was so intent on opposing communism around the globe that it ignored the emerging split in the Sino-Soviet relationship throughout the 1960s, until Richard Nixon finally exploited the opportunity when he met Mao in 1972. Some conservatives would have America make the same mistake again. Russia will never be a close partner to the U.S., but its own competition with Beijing will afford Washington opportunities to peel Russia away from China on the occasional issue. At the very least, the U.S. should be at pains to avoid pushing the two countries together by treating them as a new authoritarian axis.

When it comes to finding more common ground with the large democracies in the developing world, the prospects are actually much better than their voting record at the UN over the last few years would suggest. Beneath the surface, there has been something of a revolution in political attitudes in the developing world toward human rights and outside interference in crises. Two decades ago, the dominant position in Africa and Latin America was an energetic defense of the Westphalian order and its rigid interpretation of sovereignty. There was little appetite for interference, and strong opposition to collective commitments on human rights. The Cold War had only added to the distaste for being manipulated by great powers. In recent years, however, there has been a gradual but important shift in attitude toward the sorts of ideas the U.S. and Europe would like to see at the heart of the international system— not just toward democracy and the rule of law, but also toward regional agreements on human rights. Many developing countries have come to see the maintenance of stable democracies in their region as a bulwark against instability. In 2000, the African Union rejected the idea of nonintervention in favor of a concept it defined as "non-indifference"— a slightly vague formulation, to be sure, but one that leaves open the possibility of intervening in the event of crimes against humanity. Since 1997, no government that has come to power through a coup has been allowed to participate in an African Union summit. The organization's limitations may have been exposed when it was tasked with running the peacekeeping operation in Darfur. But in terms of the political philosophy, the shift has been marked.

In recent years, the Arab League has also sharply changed its approach to outside intervention, eagerly backing the U.S.-led operation in Libya and working energetically to encourage stronger measures against the Syrian regime in the face of opposition from China and Russia. Turkey, another important new swing state, joined forces with the Arab League in its efforts. Something similar has also been happening in South America, with Brazil in the lead. Mercosur, the regional grouping, has twice threatened coup plotters in Paraguay with expulsion, maintaining that only democracies can be members (although its criteria for democracy have been elastic enough to include Venezuela). In 2004, Brazil sent peacekeepers to Haiti under Chapter VII of the UN Charter, which allows for the use of force. Across the developing world, there has been a steady erosion of support for the idea that national sovereignty should be defended at all costs. A political corner has been turned.

The real issue is not U.S. rhetoric: it is U.S. practice. Developing world democracies are not opposed to the idea of outside interference in human-rights disasters, but they are worried about the potential manipulation of these rules by the U.S. to justify the sort of behavior countries like India and Brazil consider to be bullying. Skepticism about American motives did not begin with the invasion of Iraq. But the way the war was conducted—the attempts to railroad the UN, the manipulated intelligence, the character assassinations of those who stood in its way—confirmed the very worst fears that many governments hold about the U.S. UN diplomats from developing countries still talk about the contempt for the institution that they felt they received from John Bolton, when he was George W. Bush's ambassador to the UN. The Libya conflict in 2011 added to their mistrust. Like China and Russia, some of the governments were dismayed by the way the Libya operation in 2011 developed, when the U.S., U.K., and France quickly transformed UN approval for a humanitarian operation in the east of the country into a military campaign to oust Muammar Qaddafi. "We never said it was OK to go for regime change," one Indian diplomat told me. Many of the new swing powers agree on the need to respond to humanitarian crises, but they are loath to underwrite a new set of rules which could become a blank check for further U.S. unilateralism.

If the West wants to establish legitimacy for its new agenda of humanitarian activism, then it needs to find a way to overcome some of these reservations among the new swing states. As it happens, Brazil is the country that has offered up the most interesting olive branch. In late 2011, Dilma Rousseff's government published a little-noticed document it called "Responsibility While Protecting." The basic idea was to try and find a way to regulate and monitor foreign interventions that are approved by the UN. It would establish clearer rules for what sort of military behavior is permitted, and a monitoring mechanism to review interventions as they are conducted. For some U.S. officials, the Brazilians are more interested in grandstanding than in providing constructive leadership. Rousseff's initiative was dismissed by many as the actions of a "spoiler" government with no interest in working with Washington. But in reality, it was a serious attempt to start a debate about ways to make Western intervention work. Brazil was offering itself as a mediator between the West and other sections of the developing world. This is a conversation the U.S. needs to engage in, for the balance of influence in these global debates will depend heavily on where the new swing states position themselves. If the U.S. cannot build a common understanding with the largest democracies in the world, it will be hard work to retain its position at the center of the conversation.

GREAT POWER BURDENS

For a country like South Sudan, which is the newest in the world and one of the very poorest, it probably helps a little to have a leader who is physically imposing and highly recognizable. At six foot four, with a bushy black beard, Salva Kiir towers over most of the other presidents and prime ministers he meets. He also stands out because of the black cowboy hat he always sports, whether addressing the United Nations or having coffee at the White House. His first ten-gallon Stetson was a present from George W. Bush, who played an important role in South Sudan's independence campaign, and Kiir liked it so much he bought a large collection for himself. It is tempting to speculate what the Chinese made of Kiir when he made his first trip to Beijing in 2007. If they thought of him then as a folkloric figure with his black cowboy hat, they certainly do not now. For Kiir's 2007 visit turned out to be a groundbreaking moment in China's relations with the rest of the world.

The Darfur conflict in the 2000s is not the only war that has torn apart Sudan since it gained independence in 1956: the country also suffered a two-decade-long civil war. In 2005, Kiir took over the leadership of the Sudan People's Liberation Movement, the political group from the south of the country that fought the government in Khartoum, when their leader, John Garang, died in a helicopter crash. In the same year, he became vice president of Sudan after a peace agreement was signed ending the war. It was in this capacity that he visited Beijing two years later. Given its huge oil investments in the country, China was delighted by the end of the civil war, but the relief was short-lived. Around three-quarters of Sudan's oil reserves are in the south of the country, and according to the 2005 peace agreement, the south would be given a chance in 2011 to vote on independence. When he was in Beijing, Kiir met with President Hu Jintao and a series of other senior leaders, and at each appointment he presented his Chinese hosts with two documents. One was a copy of the oil map, showing just how many of the wells China had invested in were in the south of the country. The other was a copy of the peace agreement guaranteeing the south's right to secede. "He placed the two documents on the table and said, 'You figure it out,'" a South Sudanese official later explained. Kiir put China on the spot in a way that had never quite happened before. Support our bid for independence, he suggested, or lose your oil. He was calling Beijing's bluff on its principle of never interfering in the politics of another country.

Noninterference is a luxury that great powers sometimes cannot afford. The policy was a perfect adjunct to Deng Xiaoping's advice about keeping a low profile, but it is running up against the reality of China's global footprint and its expanding overseas interests. China's economy is now fed by iron-ore mines in Peru, copper mines in Congo's Katanga

Province, and oil fields in South Sudan. This web of interests is gradually drawing a reluctant China into the life of countries whose affairs it was once completely unconcerned about, a slow-burning but profound shift in China's global role. In a sense, China is beginning to experience its own split between foreign-policy realists and idealists. Chinese idealists push for a rigid policy of noninterference, but the realists suggest that China would be better off letting principles slide and defending the new interests that it is developing. Over the last decade, China's capacity to stand aloof from important events around the world has been slowly compromised.

One element of these new obligations is the way Beijing has been forced to respond to the growing number of Chinese workers who are now overseas. As a result of China's new network of global interests, there are probably around six million Chinese living abroad now, some in the most dangerous and unstable places in the world. There are forty-five thousand Chinese in Nigeria, around twenty-five thousand in Sudan, and ten thousand in the Democratic Republic of the Congo, as well as another ten thousand in Pakistan. In 2007, seven Chinese oil workers were killed during an attack on a Sinopec facility in Ethiopia. In Pakistan, there have been several kidnappings of Chinese workers, including the 2007 abduction of a group of Chinese women in Lahore, an event that led to the siege of the Red Mosque.

In the space of a decade, Beijing's response to such problems has been revolutionized. In 2000, a long-simmering ethnic conflict in the Solomon Islands erupted in Honiara, the country's capital, when the prime minster was seized by an armed gang. Lawlessness broke out, and mild panic ensued. Honiara has a sizable Chinese population, which began to feel itself under considerable threat. Messages were sent to Beijing asking for help. But the Chinese government had few options at its disposal. It did not even have an embassy in Honiara, because the country recognized Taiwan, not the People's Republic. In the end, Chinese diplomats in Papua New Guinea managed to get through to one of the rebel leaders on the telephone to negotiate safe passage for the Chinese residents who wanted to leave. A commercial ship owned by the state-owned group COSCO picked them up. The navy was asked if it could launch a rescue operation, but it was unable to do so. When

China faced a similar dilemma just over a decade later, in February 2011, when the security situation in Libya was becoming precarious as a civil conflict intensified, the Chinese Foreign Ministry made a staggering announcement. There were, it said, thirty thousand Chinese working in Libya, on construction sites and at oil facilities, making them by far the largest group of overseas residents apart from those from Libya's direct neighbors. As law and order broke down across the country, several of the Chinese facilities in Libya were attacked—which some in Beijing suggested was because the assailants did not fear any comeback from the Chinese authorities. This time there was no prevarication in Beijing. China sent the frigate *Xuzhou* to help evacuate its workers—the first time ever that a Chinese warship has been on active operation in the Mediterranean Sea, and a striking example of China's emerging capacity to project naval power.

As well as protecting vulnerable overseas residents, China now also has to deal with volatile, nationalist reactions to such incidents. When the workers in Ethiopia were killed in 2007, the Internet in China exploded with calls for revenge. Chinese officials privately admit that they now feel considerable public pressure to take more decisive action when Chinese workers are at risk, as they were in Libya. China is still a long way from having the capacity or political desire to intervene militarily in such conflicts on its own, but it is not too hard to imagine that in the future it might launch an armed operation to get its people out of a particularly dangerous situation. At the very least, the perils that Chinese workers are now exposed to are forcing Beijing to be less sanguine about the internal politics of some of the places where it is doing business.

The real baptism by fire, however, has been in Sudan, where Chinese ideas about nonintervention have been steadily undermined by its interests. During the Darfur crisis, Sudan had been Exhibit A for those who believe a powerful China will block efforts at humanitarian intervention and defend a strict interpretation of state sovereignty, undercutting Western ideas for a more active international community. Yet it is precisely Sudan where Beijing has been confronted with the contradictions of its expanding global interests, where its investments have suffered a head-on collision with its political principles. Much to its discomfort,

Beijing has found itself thrust into the unfamiliar role of power broker in a distant land.

When China started to invest in Sudan in the early 1990s, the Darfur conflict was still years away, but the country was mired in the fierce civil war between the government in Khartoum and the south of the country. Whereas the north of the country is largely desert and populated by Muslims, including the groups who dominate the government in Khartoum and who consider themselves Arabs, the south is more lush and is populated by Christians and animists. As many as two million people died in the civil war, which lasted for more than two decades and left the south of the country a wasteland.

China was not even a signatory to the 2005 peace treaty, which the Bush administration helped broker, preferring to keep its distance from the whole process. And on the face of it, the cease-fire was good news for Beijing, reducing the risk of attacks on its facilities and opening the prospect of new business opportunities. Yet, as the biggest investor and biggest customer of Sudan's oil, China was caught right in the middle of a new political dilemma. Around 75 percent of Sudan's oil was in the south of the country, but from there it traveled by a Chinese-built pipeline that traverses the border and goes all the way up to Port Sudan, on the northeastern coast. And as Salva Kiir made clear to his Chinese hosts in 2007, the south would be allowed to hold a referendum four years later on outright independence. Every observer who knew the country predicted overwhelming support for secession.

The situation in Sudan presented a series of different diplomatic nightmares for Beijing. Not only does China like to avoid getting involved in internal politics, but it is particularly allergic to any move that endorses the breakup of multiethnic countries. Beijing fears that such campaigns could encourage similar demands from its own ethnic regions, such as Tibet and the heavily Muslim Uighur population in Xinjiang, as well as encouraging an independence push by Taiwan. When Kosovo declared independence from Serbia in 2008, China refused to recognize the new state. In addition, Beijing was intensely suspicious of the role of the U.S. in the Sudan situation. In its early years, the SPLM had adopted a leftish posture and had received support from Cuba, but gradually it began to win heavy backing from conservative groups in the U.S., many of whom were mobilized by the prospect of a group of Christians being oppressed by Muslims. (Some South Sudanese see themselves as the descendants of the Biblical "Kushites," an identity that is embraced by some of their American sympathizers.)

Some Chinese officials and scholars thought that the U.S. was supporting the referendum as a way of trying to engineer a regime change in Khartoum. Others suggested it was part of a plot to slow Chinese progress in Africa. So at first Beijing stuck with its principle and supported the maintenance of a united Sudan. Yet, as the independence vote approached, Beijing began to realize the trap it was facing. If it opposed the referendum, it could face hostility from an independent government in the south that would see China as the principal backer of its enemy. To the South Sudanese, China had never been a neutral political force in their country—on the contrary, Beijing's heavy oil investments and weapons sales to Khartoum made it a partisan supporter of the government side in Sudan's civil war. For them, China had already taken a side.

Salva Kiir's 2007 visit to Beijing turned out to be the start of a process whereby China quietly but decisively changed its policy 180 degrees—from protecting the sovereignty of Sudan, as it did over Darfur, to endorsing the country's breakup. In 2008, China opened a consulate in Juba, the main city in the south. Before long, officials from both countries were exchanging regular visits. China intervened in 2010, when reports surfaced that the Khartoum government might try to delay the referendum. Liu Guijin, Beijing's special envoy for Africa, insisted the vote go ahead on time and called for international help to make sure the process was credible. China itself donated $500,000 to the Southern Sudan Referendum Commission and sent observers for the vote—in which independence was approved by 97 percent of the people voting. In the past, China might have claimed indifference to the internal problems in Sudan and turned a blind eye if Khartoum had used violence to sabotage the referendum. But in this case, Beijing found itself promoting an orderly vote for independence—and on the same side as the U.S. Whatever its initial reservations, China became one of the midwives for the birth of an independent and democratic Southern Sudan. To defend its oil, Beijing decided to tear up its pledge of noninterference. On July 9, 2011, South Sudan declared independence. Wei Zhixin, China's housing-and-infrastructure minister and a close confidant of President Hu Jintao, traveled to Juba to witness the occassion. The highlight of the seven-hour-long ceremony was the moment when the flag of Sudan was electronically lowered at the same time as South Sudan's new flag was raised. Two Chinese engineers were on hand to make sure the remote-control system worked properly.

———

In some ways, the partition of Sudan was only the start of China's political dilemma in the country. Even once Juba had declared independence, many of the main issues between Sudan and South Sudan remained unresolved—including where the actual borders lie, control of some of the oil wells, and the division of oil wealth between the two governments. China was again caught right in the middle of the new disputes. Beijing's first response was to try and retreat back into its shell. Li Zhiguo, China's ambassador to South Sudan, insisted there was no need for China to get involved in mediation: "The issue is an internal affair of the two brothers of Sudan." Events on the ground, however, swiftly undermined Beijing's policy of studied indifference and sucked it back into the toxic politics of the "two brothers." By November, four months after South Sudan declared independence, negotiations between the two governments were floundering, with Khartoum asking for $36 for each barrel crossing its territory and Juba offering $1 (which was closer to international levels). Khartoum halted all exports of oil from South Sudan until the payment situation was resolved, and impounded several shipments of oil. In effect, China's oil imports were being held hostage.

South Sudan responded to this brinkmanship by trying to put pressure on Beijing. Juba felt that China could do more to restrain Khartoum and tried to use its own leverage to force Beijing's hand. Chinese oil executives in South Sudan were summoned to a meeting in Juba, where they were told once again that if China continued to take Khartoum's side passively in the dispute, it could lose its oil contracts in South Sudan. Unsatisfied with China's response and Khartoum's tactics, Juba upped the ante in January 2012 by shutting down its entire oil industry. And a month later, just to make sure that Beijing understood what Juba believed to be its complicity in the dispute, South Sudan also expelled from the country Liu Yingcai, the president of Petrodar, the China-owned company which dominates the industry. The disputes between the government and Petrodar were long-running and complex, but the principal allegation was that the Chinese company had been siding with Khartoum.

At the same time that the oil dispute was heating up, violence in the border areas intensified, with Chinese interests again stuck in the middle. Two of the border provinces contained large numbers of guerrillas who had fought with the SPLM. Bashir had alleged (probably correctly) that Kiir was giving the rebel groups unofficial support and threatened to "chop off their hands." When South Sudan shuttered the oil industry, Bashir stepped up his military activities, sending warplanes to bomb oil fields in the south. At the same time, rebels linked to South Sudan captured a large oil field in Heglig, on the Sudanese side of the border. To make matters worse for the Chinese, twenty-nine Chinese oil workers in South Kordofan were kidnapped by rebel groups, prompting a huge outcry at home. They were released ten days later.

Finding itself squeezed on all sides, China was forced to get involved in crisis mediation. In April, Foreign Minister Yang Jiechi traveled to Addis Ababa to meet with Salva Kiir, while, at the same time, Jia Qinglin, one of the most senior Communist Party officials, visited Khartoum. Chinese leaders were also feeling pressure at home, where different groups wanted the government to take more decisive steps to try and resolve the standoff. As one official told the International Crisis Group, in a comment that perfectly encapsulates the new dilemma of the reluctant great power: "We are bystanders: we cannot just be bystanders, we need to be a player. Can you imagine how any Western country would engage if they had all these interests?"

When various efforts at mediation failed, the only solution was to go to the United Nations. On May 2, 2012, the UN Security Council unanimously approved Resolution 2046, which called for an immediate halt to fighting between Sudan and South Sudan. The resolution was remarkable for a number of reasons.

First, China approved a measure that not only heavily criticized Sudan, a country which for nearly two decades had been almost a client state, but it also threatened to impose sanctions under Chapter VII of the UN Charter, the sort of meddling punishment that Beijing is usually so reluctant to inflict on other countries. That alone indicates how China's position on outside interference can bend out of all recognition when its own interests are at stake.

But the timing was also interesting. Two months before the Sudan vote, China and Russia had vetoed a resolution that included a much vaguer threat of possible sanctions on the Syrian regime, a position that the U.S. ambassador to the UN described as "disgusting." Two months later, they vetoed a similar resolution on Syria again, prompting Hillary Clinton to denounce Beijing and Moscow as "despicable." The Syrian vetoes garnered all the attention and seemed ample evidence of the emerging authoritarian axis. It was these Syria votes at the UN that prompted Michael Ignatieff to say of China's and Russia's worldview: "This is not your world, they want us to know, and history is not moving in your direction. You will have to reckon with us. We shall indeed." Yet, in between the bitter standoffs over Syria, the UN vote on Sudan was compelling evidence that the historical forces are also pulling China in a different direction from the one Ignatieff imagines, one in which it has little choice but to immerse itself in the messiness, the compromises, and, most of all, the meddling that conflict resolution demands. The dispute between Khartoum and Juba is far from resolved, but in the breakup of Sudan, China has found itself the indispensable outside power in a country whose politics it barely understood but could not escape.

Just like a new president or prime minister taking office, one of the luxuries of being the new great power is the chance to promise a break from the vices of the old order and its addiction to cynical power plays. For several decades after it started to become a global force, America's leaders insisted they could help shape the world without behaving like the old European powers. Fifty years after Rudyard Kipling wrote the poem "White Man's Burden" in reference to the violent American conquest of the Philippines in the 1890s, President Franklin Roosevelt was still castigating Europe for its imperial misbehavior. By the same logic, it will be quite a while before Beijing changes its rhetoric about nonintervention. The policy is just too useful and too central to China's self-image. Yet, over time, China will find itself compelled to get its hands dirty on a more regular basis, to play the local power broker, to pick sides, maybe even to send in its military for more than just peacekeeping operations. None of this means that China and the U.S. will always be on the same side, as they ended up in South Sudan. But China's ideological aversion to outside intervention will start to fade.

ECONOMICS

8

Taking On the Dollar

In 2009, I had lunch in Hong Kong with a lawyer who was describing to me his many professional woes. We were sitting at the bar of an Italian restaurant in Pacific Place, a complex of tinted-glass office towers in the Admiralty District of the city with a cavernous shopping mall down below. Outside the restaurant, wealthy women flitted between the Chanel and Louis Vuitton stores, their high heels echoing on the marble floors. The set lunch of Caprese salad followed by linguine with crab was perfectly executed, but my lunch companion was not enjoying the meal. He launched into a lengthy whinge about how his business was all disappearing to Shanghai, which the Chinese central government wants to turn into the country's main financial center. Companies were listing their shares in Shanghai, instead of Hong Kong, he complained. Multi-nationals were shifting their headquarters to Shanghai, and fund managers were also moving up there. Hong Kong was suffering the gradual erosion of its role as China's conduit to the international financial world. "And another thing," he said, almost without pausing for breath. "Our landlord wants to raise our rent by fifty percent."

I have been traveling to Hong Kong regularly for much of the last decade, and on each visit I hear the same foreboding about the future of the city and the same fears about the lethal competition from Shanghai. It is the second-most-common complaint, after the pollution being blown down from the factories in southern China. Admittedly, Hong Kong did suffer two huge body blows, from the 1997 Asian financial crisis and the SARS outbreak in 2003, which possibly colors some of the grumpiness. Yet the soul-searching always seems out of place, a narrative that is rebuked by the constant bustle and progress. More than most other cities, Hong Kong adapts. To the visitor it always seems to be booming, with new high-rises, new malls, and new slivers of land reclaimed from Hong Kong Harbor. And the rents just keep going up.

The next new business opportunity for Hong Kong is already starting to take shape, and it could be a huge one. Beijing is putting in place an ambitious plan to allow the Chinese currency to play a larger role in the global economy, and Hong Kong is the launchpad. It is the first place where the Chinese currency, the renminbi, can be freely traded by Chinese and non-Chinese companies. There is also now a market in Hong Kong for corporate bonds issued in the Chinese currency, known as "dim sum bonds," which allows people to put some of their savings into securities denominated in renminbi. (One of the first issuers was the McDonald's Corporation, which must now sell Big Macs in China to repay the dim sum.) The financial world is abuzz with talk about the start of a momentous shift. HSBC predicts that by 2015 at least half of China's trade with the developing world will be in renminbi, around $2 trillion. "We could be on the verge of a financial revolution of truly epic proportions," says Qu Hongbin, HSBC's China economist. "The world is slowly, but surely, moving from greenbacks to redbacks." The Washington-based economist Arvind Subramanian predicts that the Chinese renminbi could become "the premier reserve currency by the end of this decade, or early next decade." Hong Kong has found a new role. It could be the international hub for the world's new global currency.

This might sound like arcane business-speak, the kind of thing that is of interest to financial professionals but not to anyone else. Yet, in reality, the question of whether the renminbi will supplant the dollar is one of the central contests that will determine the shift of power from West to East over the course of the next few decades, a delicate combination of high finance and geopolitics. The political influence of the U.S. dollar is the often overlooked anchor of American global influence.

Just as the period of British pre-eminence from around 1850 to 1914 was sustained by the central role of sterling, American global reach in the post–World War II era has been underwritten by the pervasiveness of the U.S. dollar, which is used in 85 percent of cross-border business. The dollar's position as the main reserve currency is both cause and effect of American power, a symbol of confidence in the world's most productive economy and a manifestation of America's position at the center of a series of economic, political, and military relationships at the heart of the international system. American politicians sometimes like to talk about the U.S. as the "indispensable" nation, a phrase that never fails to grate on foreign audiences, but in the case of the dollar it is quite apt. The dollar's role in the world is a reflection of continuing trust in Washington as the guardian of the global order.

Washington is drowning in warnings about the end of the dollar era. Edward Luttwak, a hardheaded scholar of military strategy, downplays the military threat from China, but adds: "The real challenge to American and Western strategy is far more subtle: a slow, not uncomfortable slide into subordination in a China-centred world, with the renminbi as its currency." The National Intelligence Council, which publishes the U.S. government's official intelligence estimate, forecasts that "the fall of the dollar as the global reserve currency . . . would be one of the sharpest indications of a loss of U.S. global economic position, strongly undermining Washington's political influence too." If the dollar does start to lose that position to the renminbi, it would indicate that a real power shift was taking place and that China was assuming a central role in the world's political and economic affairs. Since the financial crisis, there has been a lot of talk about a "currency war," a somewhat faux dispute about U.S. and Chinese efforts to weaken the value of their currencies that was coined by the Brazilian finance minister. The real "currency war" for the next few decades is the contest for the title of global reserve currency.

The privilege of issuing the main reserve currency is more than just symbolism. The advantages are enormous. All governments borrow money, even in the very best-managed economies, and if a country does not have enough savings at home, the Finance Ministry will have to borrow abroad in someone else's currency. When countries face economic problems, these overseas borrowings often become the weak link. If markets start to lose confidence in a government and its policies, it becomes much harder to roll those debts over, or to issue new bonds. The country's currency also starts to weaken sharply as investors get cold feet. The government then faces a double whammy—it loses access to new international funding, and the cost of its existing debt suddenly shoots up, because its currency is now worth less. Imports also become more expensive, putting further pressure on dwindling sources of foreign currency. Many of the economic crises that developing countries have faced in recent decades have followed this pattern.

Yet America has been shielded from such troubles. The U.S. dollar is overwhelmingly the preferred unit for business and financial transactions around the world. Global trade is lubricated by dollars—99 percent of all foreign-exchange transactions in both South Korea and Chile, two big exporting nations, are sales of local currency for dollars. For the world's central banks—the biggest, most conservative, and most influential investors on the planet—the U.S. dollar remains the principal anchor of their foreign-currency reserves. It is the same in the black market economy. When Somali pirates or Mexican drug lords demand payment, it is U.S. dollars they want to receive. Because the dollar is used so widely in commerce and investment, and because it is such a trusted store of value—it is "as good as gold," as the saying goes—foreigners are only too happy to buy bonds from the American government that are issued in its own currency. As a result, the biggest and most liquid bond market in the world by far is the U.S. Treasury bond market. Even if the dollar suddenly gets weaker, this does not affect the American government in the same way it would affect other countries, because the U.S. repays foreign investors in the same currency it collects in tax revenues. That makes the position of the U.S. dollar a hugely powerful tool. It gives an important competitive advantage to American companies and banks, which get to do business in their own currency and avoid the vagaries of foreign-exchange markets. And it allows the U.S. government to live beyond its means without facing the punishment that other governments inevitably suffer. Washington can finance its global power projection with a credit card that has no limit. "Deficits don't matter," as Dick Cheney liked to say.

Except that, eventually, they do. Even for America, there are limits to the sorts of deficits it can run. At some stage, the credibility of the U.S. dollar will be called into question—and with it the underpinnings of America's global position. To be fair, there have been many dollar scares in the past that proved to be unfounded. When I was studying in Washington in the 1990s, my dissertation supervisor was David Calleo, who was one of the leading voices in the school of thought sometimes called "imperial overstretch." He wrote persuasively about the ructions caused by Lyndon Johnson's budget deficits in the 1960s, which were needed to finance the Vietnam War, and the subsequent stresses the dollar came under in the 1970s, when Nixon eventually abandoned the convertibility of the dollar into gold. Yet the dollar's primacy survived the episode. To Europeans who worried about the risk of inflation, then treasury secretary John Connally retorted: "It is our currency and your problem."

The same pressures returned during the Reagan years and the arms race with the Soviet Union. The Soviets eventually blinked first, their economy imploding under the burden of heavy defense spending, but America's finances also came under intense pressure, prompting a new bout of predictions that American dominance and the dollar era that financed it were coming to an end. Paul Kennedy had a massive publishing success at the time with his *Rise and Fall of the Great Powers*, a tome about imperial overstretch over the centuries which captured the prevailing mood. Again, the pessimism proved short-lived. The end of the Cold War and the supreme confidence of the early years of the George W. Bush administration made these sorts of predictions seem alarmist, almost foolish, and in the boom years of the mid-2000s they were brushed aside as a kind of intellectual defeatism. Yet, after a decade of two expensive wars and the biggest financial crisis since the 1930s, which forced the government to run a deficit of $1.1 trillion in 2012, America's outstanding government debt is now almost as large as the economy itself—something that has not happened since the Second World War. The credibility of the dollar is once again being called into doubt, and the idea of "imperial overstretch" is very much back in vogue. In the financial world, some talk about when rather than if there will be a dollar crisis. It is precisely at this moment of uncertainty in the fate of the U.S. currency that China has chosen to start claiming a bigger role for the renminbi in the global economy.

THE DOLLAR TRAP

"How do you deal toughly with your banker?" Hillary Clinton asked, shortly after she became secretary of state. Since the start of the financial crisis, a new phantom has started to loom over U.S.-China relations: the massive amounts of American government debt that are now in China's hands. China has the largest foreign-exchange reserves in the world, at around $3.3 trillion, and overtook Japan in 2008 to be the largest overseas holder of U.S. debt. Although the exact composition of China's reserves is a state secret, analysts who have sifted through the available information estimate that around two-thirds of those reserves are in U.S. dollar assets. The likely result is that China owns around $2 trillion of U.S. government debt. "Never before has the United States relied on a single country's government for so much financing," as economist (and later White House official) Brad Setser put it. "Political might is often linked to financial might and a debtor's capacity to project military power hinges on the support of its creditors."

The handover of global responsibilities from the U.K. to the U.S. was a long and drawn-out process, but the final blow was delivered because Britain owed too much money to Washington. In 1956, when the U.S. wanted to show its displeasure at the British invasion of the Suez Canal, Eisenhower refused to let the IMF issue an emergency loan which Britain needed to defend its currency. Fearing a complete financial collapse, Britain pulled out its soldiers from the Canal Zone. British influence in the world was never the same again. If China could turn this financial power into real political leverage, it would have dramatic consequences for both America's economic policy and its ability to exert influence around the world. It would give Beijing the hold over Washington that the U.S. once held over its own great-power predecessor.

China is well aware of the potential significance. Every now and then, there have been comments from low-level Chinese officials raising the potential threat. In 2007, Xia Bin, who was then a leading economist at a government think tank called the Development Research Center, caused an international fuss when he suggested that China's dollar holdings should be used as a "bargaining chip." When the U.S. announced it would sell more arms to Taiwan in 2010, three senior PLA officers—Major General Zhu Chenghu, Major General Luo Yan, and Senior Colonel Ke Chunqiao—told the Xinhua News Agency that China should retaliate by selling U.S. government debt, which could lead to a sharp rise in U.S. interest rates. According to American diplomats, the threat to sell dollar assets has also occasionally hung over conversations about the Dalai Lama. The more nationalistic sections of the Chinese press call it "the nuclear option"—threatening to dump dollar bonds in order to change American policy. Or, as Gao Xiqing, the head of China's sovereign-wealth fund, told the American journalist James Fallows: "I won't say *kowtow*, but at least be nice to those countries that lend you money."

In the U.S., this potential threat from China has now been a feature in two presidential elections. When he was running for the 2008 presidential nomination, then senator Joe Biden warned, in a Democratic debate, about the risks of having China finance U.S. debt. We need to "make sure that they no longer own the mortgage on our home." Hillary Clinton, also then a senator and a presidential candidate, piped in: "I want to say 'Amen!' to Joe Biden, because he's 100 percent right." In 2012, the theme returned with a vengeance. In May, there was a standoff in Beijing over the blind activist Chen Guangcheng, who, having escaped house arrest and taken refuge in the U.S. Embassy in Beijing, announced that he wanted to leave China for the U.S. Paul Ryan was asked if the U.S. still had any influence over China in such a dispute. The Republican vice-presidential nominee answered: "When you depend on another country like China for the cash flow in your country and for your debt, there is not a lot you can do when you are asked to stand up to them on a principled matter such as this." Ryan somewhat misread the situation: the next day Chen was given permission to move to New York.

———

Paul Ryan was wrong for a reason. The supposed leverage that China derives from its dollar holdings is something of a myth—and China knows it. The curious thing about this discussion is that, although some Americans complain that the debt gives China excessive influence, China is increasingly angry at how little sway it has. In the years since the financial crisis, there has been a growing frustration in China that its U.S. bond holdings give it almost no leverage whatsoever. When the crisis broke, Beijing started to issue a series of warnings about American economic policy and its obligations to do right by China. "I request the U.S. to maintain its good credit, to honor its promises and to guarantee the safety of China's assets," Premier Wen Jiabao told a 2009 press conference. Beijing worried very loudly about the inflationary risks of the monetary expansion the U.S. Federal Reserve launched in response to the crisis. Chinese officials started to push for guarantees about repayment on their U.S. debt, especially in the troubled mortgage agencies Fannie Mae and Freddie Mac. It is possible that Chinese pressure had something to do with the timing of when the two mortgage agencies were brought under government control. But, by and large, China's attempt to strong-arm the U.S. did not work. Beijing did not receive any formal guarantees, and it exerted no influence over American monetary or fiscal policy. The Fed has continued to do as it wishes. The Tea Party has more influence over the Fed than does the Chinese Communist Party.

Larry Summers, the former U.S. Treasury secretary, once described the situation between the two countries as "mutually assured economic destruction." Beijing has come to realize that it is trapped—trapped by the size of its exposure to the U.S., trapped by the reality of financial markets, and trapped by the logic of its own policies. In any month when China exports more than it imports, this leads to an inflow of foreign currency into the country. In order to prevent the value of the renminbi from rising, which would hurt its exports, the Chinese central bank buys up the dollar excess. China's foreign-currency reserves are the direct product of this policy of keeping its currency artificially cheap, in order to boost exports. This was a choice made by China, not by anyone else. Indeed, large parts of the world have called on China to change its approach and to allow its currency to become more expensive. Having built up such a stockpile, China's official money managers are then faced with limited options. The U.S. Treasury market is by far the largest and most liquid in the world. It is also the only one with the size to absorb the sort of volumes of reserves that China has been accumulating. China therefore has little choice but to recycle a large portion of its surpluses into U.S. government bonds.

The harsh reality for China is that it has too much at stake to turn its back completely on U.S. bond markets. Economic interdependence makes it hard for China to rock the boat. At best, China can gradually scale back the rate at which it buys new American debt. But if China were to try and sell a substantial chunk of its U.S. bond holdings, it would send the market into a tailspin, and bond prices—including China's own investments—would plummet. Such action would also force down the value of the U.S. dollar, making China's exports less competitive and threatening hundreds of thousands of factory jobs. It would be a huge self-inflicted wound. This formula does not make sense for a regime whose legitimacy is tightly wound up in delivering economic results. China's holdings give it theoretical leverage over the U.S., but it is leverage that it is technically difficult and politically suicidal to exploit. Beijing knows as much. "We hate you guys . . ." Luo Ping, a senior Chinese banking official, admitted in 2009. "US Treasuries are the safe haven. For everyone, including China, it is the only option." He continued: "Once you start issuing $1 trillion–$2 trillion . . . we know the dollar is going to depreciate, so we hate you guys but there is nothing much we can do."

———

Luo Ping was only half joking. His mock anger was politically important because that sentiment became one of the starting points for the campaign to take the Chinese currency global. Frustrated at its inability to influence American economic policy, Beijing has started to think much more seriously about finding ways to rein in the influence of the dollar and Washington's ability to run endless deficits. Resentment at the "dollar trap" helped launch a much broader Chinese critique about the place of the U.S. dollar in the international economy. If China could not influence the way the U.S. managed its economy, it would try and reshape the international financial system instead, and make the dollar less indispensable. Hu Jintao called in 2008 for a "new international financial order that is fair, just, inclusive and orderly."

The first sign that something was brewing in Beijing came from the governor of the Chinese central bank, Zhou Xiaochuan. Zhou is a chemical engineer by training but is considered one of the Communist Party's intellectual heavyweights in the field of international economics. With his donnish air, he likes to tease journalists with the sort of delphic pronouncements that once made Alan Greenspan a cult figure—before the financial crisis, that is. In March 2009, six months after Lehman Brothers collapsed, the central bank started to put up on its Web site a series of long and detailed speeches and essays by Zhou that called for substantial reforms of the international financial system. Zhou had himself some fun at the expense of the Western investment banks, which had almost felled the global economy. He criticized the "herding phenomenon" among investors and the "inertia and sloppiness" that stopped executives from "asking tough questions." But his broader message was aimed at the role of the U.S. currency. The international financial system, he said, needs a reserve currency "that is disconnected to individual nations and is able to remain stable in the long run, thus removing the inherent deficiencies caused by using credit-based national currencies." In between the technical language of international financial policy, the message was clear: the world needs to become less reliant on the dollar.

Zhou's speech was the starting gun for China's campaign to develop a more international currency. Since then, China has unveiled a steady series of reforms aimed at forging a bigger role for the renminbi. Using Hong Kong as a trial ground, the government in 2009 started to allow the use of the renminbi to settle international trade—the first stage in a plan to turn it into the main currency for trade in Asia and between developing countries. In 2011, it allowed renminbi bonds to be sold in Hong Kong, letting foreign investors buy assets denominated in the Chinese currency. Since then, Beijing has announced a slew of reform measures that will gradually make it easier to trade and invest in the Chinese currency. By the end of 2012, around 15 percent of China's trade was being conducted in renminbi. The final stage would be to turn the renminbi into the sort of international safe haven that attracts the world's central banks to park a substantial share of their reserves in the currency. That would be the real stamp of approval. In what was largely a symbolic gesture, Malaysia has already taken the first step, acquiring some renminbi bonds.

Chinese policy makers usually couch the project in technical terms, pointing out that it will reduce the costs of doing business for Chinese companies and expand the opportunities for Chinese banks. But they also do little to hide their broader political objective of forging a new international system that is not dominated by the U.S. dollar. Li Ruogu, head of the China Export-Import Bank, argues that "the financial crisis . . . let us clearly see how unreasonable the current international monetary system is." Another official told me: "We have the second-biggest economy in the world, so we should have a currency that enjoys many of the privileges that the U.S. also gains." According to Zha Xiao-gang, a researcher at the Shanghai Institutes for International Studies: "The shortcomings of the current international monetary system pose a big threat to China's economy. With more alternatives, the margin for the U.S. would be greatly narrowed, which will certainly weaken the power basis of the U.S." One Chinese academic even goes so far as to say that ending the dominance of the dollar is as important for Beijing's ability to project power as was "China becoming a nuclear power."

Attacking the power of the U.S. dollar is not a new form of geo-political sparring. In the 1960s, General Charles de Gaulle sought to challenge American leadership of the West and to position himself in the middle ground between Washington and Moscow. One of his tactics was to withdraw France from the military arm of NATO. The other was to take aim at the dollar. Throughout the mid-1960s, as America became bogged down in Vietnam and its public finances came under pressure, de Gaulle gave a series of press conferences in which he called for an end to the primacy of the dollar and urged other countries to convert their holdings of U.S. currency into gold. And it was a French finance minister (and later president), Valéry Giscard d'Estaing, who famously complained in the 1970s that the benefits America derived from the dollar were "an exorbitant privilege." "There was no doubting de Gaulle's intention: to promote his drive to reduce US economic, military and cultural influence," *Time* magazine said of his campaign. (As part of his effort to demonstrate independence from Washington, de Gaulle recognized the People's Republic of China in 1964, a full seven years before Nixon and Kissinger made their celebrated opening to Beijing.) China sees a global role for its currency in a similar light to de Gaulle's, as both good business and good power politics. Even though

Beijing knows it will be a long process that could take several decades, some officials see it as a central part of a broader struggle to place limits on American power and to increase China's own room for maneuver. In their minds, it is a rather nerdy, pointy-headed proxy war for influence.

———

When then U.S. treasury secretary Tim Geithner spoke to a group of students at Peking University in 2009, he was asked if China's holdings of U.S. government debt were safe. Of course they are, he responded. The audience laughed. It is not just the Chinese elite who frets about the dollar. One of the surprising aspects of the Chinese reaction to the financial crisis has been the way in which seemingly technical issues about the international financial system have seeped into public debate. The U.S. dollar has become a flashpoint for some of the broader nationalist tensions that have been boiling up within China. In 2012, the car of the U.S. ambassador to China, Gary Locke, was surrounded by an angry mob of around fifty people who had been protesting at the nearby Japanese Embassy. One demonstrator grabbed the flag off the front of the car. Then the crowd shouted: "Give us back our money."

In Song Hongbing, China's currency nationalists have found an unlikely cheerleader. A few years ago, Song was an unknown economist at a Chinese government think tank. But his 2007 book *Currency Wars* turned him into an unlikely star of the publishing world, selling half a million copies, and making him the spokesman for popular resentment at the dollar-based world. The book aims to be a sort of financial history, but it is really a hodgepodge of dubious stories about financial conspiracies down the ages, arguing that the Rothschild banking dynasty has been pulling the strings in the international financial system ever since the nineteenth century, when it made a fortune speculating on the outcome of the Napoleonic wars. He claims the Rothschild family wealth is now a hundred times greater than that of Bill Gates. One of his main targets is the fact that the regional U.S. Federal Reserve banks are technically owned by the private banks rather than the government. But Song also manages to recycle some ugly myths about the prominence of Jews in the financial sector and their alleged role in events ranging from Waterloo to the Asian financial crisis. Such insinuations did not prevent the book from generating buzz in some surprising places—two different sources told me that Premier Wen Jiabao had asked to read a copy of *Currency Wars*.

Song's background does not make him an obvious critic of American financial excess. While he was living in the U.S., he did some work creating financial-risk models for Fannie Mae and Freddie Mac, the two mortgage finance institutions at the center of the housing bubble. But the book seems to have tapped into popular suspicions that international finance is rigged against China and that the U.S. will debase its currency. His timing was impeccable: *Currency Wars* came out just before a massive financial crisis which was caused in part by the arrogance of a U.S.-based international financial elite. That has helped turn Song into an often quoted authority on the links between finance and politics. In the process, he has also helped popularize a certain strain of victim nationalism that sees the dominance of the dollar as one of the tools used to curtail China's rise. "Before my book, people thought currencies were really an academic issue, but now they see it as a political issue, as a struggle for power," Song told me. "The big power is the one who issues the money, who can define what money is. The currency war is a struggle, a fight for who controls the money and who can issue it."

One of the peculiar aspects of Song's writings is that he shares many of his concerns with a section of the right wing in America. He has not only an intense aversion to the investor George Soros, but also a deep suspicion of the powers of the U.S. Federal Reserve. "Congress should have the power to issue money, not the Fed," he told me. "No one audits the books of the Fed." He added: "Ron Paul has very much the same view. Why is money issued by a small group of unelected people?" When I asked him why he was so obsessed about Jews in finance, such as Soros, he smiled a little uncomfortably and attempted the sort of compliment that runs its own risks of stereotyping. "I personally admire the Jews," said Song. "They were prohibited from doing anything else, they could not own land, so money was the only way to succeed."

A bespectacled forty-something in a starched shirt with personalized cuff links, Song was clearly enjoying his success when I met him. He had opened a new consulting business, called the Global Business and Finance Institute, to give advice on international financial issues. A sequel to his book, *Currency Wars 2,* which describes plans by a small group of bankers to launch a new global currency, had been published, and a third volume is in the works. He had also just rented a suite of offices in Beijing near Dongzhimen Avenue, modern China's new power center, which houses the imposing and slick headquarters of many of China's largest state-owned companies. One side of the office was taken up by a new side business: a group of young computer programmers were designing a video game based on *Currency Wars.* Song described to me the outline for the game. The early stages would involve starting your own business and building up capital. If a gamer managed to reach the final stage, he would get to become a big hedge-fund speculator who could launch an attack on the U.S. dollar. "You can become the sort of financial big guy who has the resources to start a currency war," he said. "Someone like George Soros."

JEKYLL ISLAND

In November 1910, a group of the great and the good from America's financial elite assembled after dark in a railway car at a quiet siding in Hoboken, just across the river from Manhattan. They used only their first names in front of the porters. When they reached Brunswick, Georgia, two days later, they took a boat to Jekyll Island and checked in at the private club partly owned by J. P. Morgan. They told people they were going duck hunting, and one of the party even carried a shotgun onto the train to keep up the pretense, although he had never used one in his life. But their real purpose was to draft legislation to completely shake up the country's banking system. In the process, they also revolutionized the role of the U.S. dollar.

The men at the secret meeting on Jekyll Island included Benjamin Strong, head of Bankers Trust; Henry Davison, who was J. P. Morgan's right-hand man; Paul Warburg of Kuhn, Loeb; and Frank Vanderlip, a former journalist who was by then the boss of what became Citibank. They were joined by Senator Nelson Aldrich of Rhode Island, head of the Senate Finance Committee, whose daughter was married to John Rockefeller, son of the richest man in the country, and Abraham Piatt

Andrew, assistant secretary of the Treasury Department. The most famous consequence of the meeting was the bill that created the Federal Reserve, America's central bank. The 1907 financial crisis had exposed the vulnerabilities of the economy to such an extent that the government effectively had to rely on J. P. Morgan to broker a solution—he called leading bankers to his Manhattan town house and would not let them leave until they had devised a rescue plan. As a result of the legislation they wrote, the Federal Reserve System took over that role of regulating and managing credit conditions in the country. Every modern economy in the world now has a central bank that plays the role of lender of last resort. But, given that sections of the American right believe the Fed is an example of excessive government interference, the Jekyll Island meeting is, to this day, viewed by some as an elite conspiracy against the interests of ordinary Americans. In 2010, the libertarian politician Ron Paul was the headline guest at a conference on Jekyll Island about the misdeeds of the Fed. "People are demanding that we not put up with a secretive organization like the Fed that prints all this money and causes all this mischief," the former presidential candidate told the audience.

Establishing the Fed was only one part of the 1910 Jekyll Island plan, however. The legislation they developed also created the legal instruments for the dollar to become an international currency—as it happens, a plan quite similar to the one China is now pursuing. They started by establishing procedures so that trade could be settled using U.S. dollars. Then they created the legal framework for the issuance of international U.S. dollar bonds. The impact was dramatic. According to the financial historian Barry Eichengreen, just one decade after the bill was passed in 1913, the U.S. dollar already accounted for a larger share of central-bank reserves than the British pound. It was also used in more bond issues and exceeded sterling in loans linked to trade by a factor of two to one. Even before the Jekyll Island plan was implemented, the American economy had the scale for the dollar to play a larger role in the global economy, but lacked the legal instruments and market infrastructure. Within just a decade of its approval, the status of the U.S. dollar had been transformed and sterling's diminished.

Just as Americans should not be surprised by China's urge to build a grand navy, they should also not be blindsided by Beijing's ambitious plans to turn the renminbi into a global currency. After all, this is precisely what America did at a similar stage in its development, when it wanted to start turning its economic scale into greater international influence. Whereas America's plan was written by an elite band of Wall Street and Washington figures, China's global-currency push has been orchestrated by a small group of the Communist Party elite. (The party's senior officials also often plot new strategies at its own beachside retreat, Beidaihe, a few hours east of Beijing.) Given America's current troubles and China's inexorable growth, it is tempting to think that something similar might happen again over the coming decade or two, when it is quite likely that China will become the biggest economy in the world. But for history to repeat itself, and for the renminbi to eclipse the dollar, two very substantial conditions will need to be met. China will have to tear up its economic model, and America will need to let it happen. Both are possible, but neither is inevitable.

GRIDLOCK

As to the second condition, there certainly is no shortage of reasons for thinking that the U.S. could be heading for the sort of crisis that would shake the foundations of the dollar era. The litany is a familiar one—high debt levels, chronic budget deficits, political gridlock, spiraling entitlement spending, and crumbling infrastructure. In some ways, the status of the dollar is actually making things worse. The U.S. government's ability to keep borrowing from abroad allows it to put off taking some of the tough decisions that will eventually need to be taken. Some Americans worry that having a reserve currency is the equivalent of a "resource curse," the sort of natural advantage that leads to indulgent, ineffectual government.

Yet, despite all these problems, the fate of the U.S. dollar still lies largely within the control of the U.S. government. Big shifts in the international monetary system take place rarely, and then usually only in response to dramatic events. Once gained, the position of reserve currency is not easily lost. The system is a reflection of the collective confidence and force of habit of millions of economic agents around the world and only changes from one anchor to another when there is little alternative. The loss of influence suffered by the British pound is one example. The decade starting in 1914, which was the period in which the U.S. dollar began to stake its claim at the heart of the international monetary system, was also the decade that included the First World War, an event which all but bankrupted Great Britain. With the value of sterling plummeting from 1915, all of a sudden Brazilian coffee traders started pricing their goods in dollars, and Dutch tulip-bulb farmers wanted export credits to be issued in dollars. The Second World War finished the job on Britain's finances and completed the process of transition from sterling to the dollar. The ascendance of the dollar required not only the decisive plan that was devised on Jekyll Island, but also a collapse of confidence in sterling.

Now, admittedly, it is not completely out of the question that the U.S. will suffer a similar financial convulsion. In the summer of 2011, some members of the U.S. Congress seemed quite happy to use the threat of default as a short-term political tactic. The subsequent downgrading of U.S. government debt by Standard & Poor's was a stark warning about the potential erosion of confidence in the dollar. Ever since then, Washington has been living from one budget crisis to another. Yet even this 2011 mini-crisis served to demonstrate the unique position that America holds in the international financial system. In such moments of nervousness, investors seek a safe haven, and the place they looked to was, ironically, the U.S. Treasury bond market. In the very week when America's credit rating was downgraded, the price of American debt actually rose by near-record levels. There are huge incumbent advantages to being the principal reserve currency that are not easily dismantled. If the U.S. can muddle through its current troubles and present a coherent long-term plan for bringing its debts under control, the U.S. dollar will retain a central role, if for no other reason than inertia. That is politically easier said than done, of course, but the correct response to the Chinese challenge to the dollar is nothing more and nothing less than good housekeeping. The U.S. holds its fate in its own hands.

STATE CAPITALISM

The China model of economic management had its finest moment in November 2008. Lehman Brothers had collapsed two months earlier, sending the Western economic world into the sort of panic not seen since the 1930s. Over the next few weeks, the brutal consequences for China started to mount. In southern and eastern China, the areas where most of the export factories are concentrated, tens of thousands of migrant workers would line up every day at railway stations to return home to their villages, their jobs having disappeared almost overnight. Seeing a potential threat to its legitimacy, the Chinese party-state snapped into action. In November, Beijing announced a massive economic stimulus plan with a headline figure of $586 billion to backstop the collapsing economy. The Chinese government's main planning agency—the National Reform and Development Commission—is based in the northwest of the city, in a neighborhood that has three or four modest hotels. For several weeks after the government announced the stimulus plan, every conference room in these hotels was booked by local government officials from around the country who came to present their best "shovel-ready" projects. From dawn to dusk, planning officials surveyed the plans for construction and infrastructure, giving a quick yes or no. The state-owned banks then provided the initial financing, and work began as quickly as possible. Roads, bridges, airports, and tunnels were built in record time. It was probably the biggest-ever emergency public-works program.

It turns out that China had the perfect "model" to respond to the sort of economic crisis that seems to happen every eighty years. When foreign analysts talk about Chinese "state capitalism," they are usually referring to the presence of state-owned businesses in many areas of the economy. But the real key to the system is the way the financial system works. China was able to respond so quickly to the crisis because of the control the state has over the big four banks, which are responsible for between a third and a half of new credit in the country. The government was able to use its direct influence over the banks to funnel credit quickly to infrastructure projects. In the U.S., when the crisis hit, bank lending all but seized up as uncertainty took hold of economic decisions. In China, bank lending exploded. In 2009, the country's banks issued twice as many new loans as they had written the year before. These banks had spent the previous five years getting stock-exchange listings, attracting foreign shareholders, and publishing ambitious statements about corporate governance. But, for all the talk that they were becoming more independent, when it came to the crunch they took a political order from the top and opened the credit floodgates. As China rebounded much more quickly from the global financial crisis than any other major economy, the normally disciplined Premier Wen Jiabao let slip a somewhat triumphalist note. China's economic model, he said, allowed the government to "make decisions efficiently, to organize effectively, and to concentrate resources to accomplish a large undertaking."

Yet this same brand of state capitalism is also the main obstacle to China's developing a major global currency. The project to take the renminbi global is actually a pivotal moment in modern China, because it presents the leaders with an almost existential choice. For the renminbi to become an internationally accepted currency and a trusted store of value, China will need to make the sort of root-and-branch economic and financial reforms that would transform the way the economy is run. The scale of the changes that China would need to implement to achieve this goal makes the problems facing the U.S. at the moment look modest in comparison.

At the moment, Beijing is trying to square an economic circle. Although China is now the biggest exporter of manufactured goods in the world, the reason few people use the renminbi to settle trade transactions is that Beijing maintains a high wall of capital controls that protect its economy from the fickleness of international financial markets. As a result, it is still very hard to take Chinese currency in and out of the country, and for foreigners to invest money in China's financial markets. This is where Hong Kong comes in—it is a perfect halfway house, an offshore laboratory where Beijing can experiment with allowing its currency to be widely held without the risk of a destabilizing financial blowback. But the offshore market in Hong Kong can only take the renminbi so far, because the volumes will always be limited. To turn the renminbi into a currency that even the world's deeply conservative and cautious central banks would feel comfortable holding, China would need to tear down some of those barriers, allowing money to move freely in and out of the country. In other words, to boost the credibility of its currency, China would need to open itself up to international capital in just the way that New York does. This would not be a simple technical change: it would mean a revolution in how China runs its economic affairs.

Opening the economy to financial flows would put huge strains on the Chinese economic model. Beijing would have to dismantle many of the tools that allow it to funnel huge volumes of cheap credit to its favored investment projects. One reason the state banks have such a stranglehold on the financial system is that Chinese citizens have little choice but to put a large part of their savings into the banks. To a large extent, they are captive bank-depositors. But in a more open financial system, Chinese citizens would have many more options about how and where to invest their money. Banks would have to compete for deposits by offering higher returns, which would slash the profits they made from lending. And in order to retain the confidence of depositors, they would also have to be much more transparent about the risks they were taking with loans to pet government projects.

The Chinese authorities also use the tight control they have over the banking system to effectively set interest rates in the economy— another powerful tool that allows them to shape macroeconomic policy and keep credit cheap. But the power of the banks would be diminished by another necessary change. If foreign investors are going to hold a significant share of their assets in renminbi, they will need access to a large, liquid, and credible Chinese bond market. The global role of the dollar is underpinned by the huge U.S. government bond market, which gives investors an easy way to buy and sell large volumes of securities. It is that liquidity that makes it such a reliable store of value. Yet, in a large and transparent bond market, the price of credit is set by the market, not by government fiat. In essence, the decision to open up the economy to foreign capital would transform the position of the big state-owned banks. They would need to be run on much more stringent commercial principles and could no longer be used as piggy banks for other state-owned companies. And in the process, the Communist Party would lose a vital element of its current political control over the economy.

China would also need to transform the way it manages its exchange rate—another revolution in economic policy making. If China were to allow capital to flow more easily in and out of the country, it would have to adopt a much more flexible exchange rate in order to manage the volatility. China would probably end up floating its currency, at least partially. That means it would become much harder for Beijing to depress the value of its currency artificially to help its exporters—another central element of the economic model of the last few decades.

The implications do not end there. If foreign investors are going to park large sums of money in the Chinese financial system, then China would also need a much more independent legal system. Why invest in a Chinese security if a Communist Party official can tell a court what to decide in any legal disputes that might arise? The system of making economic policy would also need to be much more transparent. At present, it is not clear who actually makes decisions about interest rates in China, let alone why they are made. The central bank almost certainly does not make these decisions. But is it the premier? The Finance and Economics Leading Small Group? The Politburo? Or the Communist Party Standing Committee? If the world's central banks are going to put a large part of their reserves into Chinese government bonds, they will want to know more about the key economic decisions.

Over time, the Chinese renminbi will doubtless increase in importance and is likely to rank alongside the euro, the yen, and the British pound as one of the second-string reserve currencies, accounting for 10 to 20 percent of global reserves. But if it is to supplant the U.S. dollar and establish itself as the principal safe-haven currency, the harsh reality for China is that it has two options. It can keep its particular model of state capitalism. Or it can have a global reserve currency. But it cannot have both.

And that is, of course, the central irony of this whole discussion. The project to make the renminbi into an international force has been dressed up in the geopolitics of dethroning the U.S. dollar, a reflection of both the frustrations of the economic elite and the popular resentment of the U.S. Yet this project requires precisely the economic and political reforms that U.S. leaders have been calling for in China over the last couple of decades. Many of the frictions over economic issues that have built up between the U.S. and China in recent years would disappear if Beijing introduced these policies. The exchange-rate controversy would evaporate as China adopted a more market-based currency policy. And Beijing would be much less able to use its banks to subsidize its own companies with cheap loans—one of the core issues behind the current fears about a new wave of "state capitalism."

Indeed, some believe this has been the hidden agenda all along of Zhou Xiaochuan, the central-bank boss. Along with a group of other reform-minded officials, he has been trying for much of the last decade to get China to gradually open its financial system, which he thinks is essential for improving the efficiency of investment in China and maintaining high growth over the coming decades. But at almost every stage, he has been frustrated by the caution and conservatism of his Communist Party bosses, some of whom have legitimate complaints about financial capitalism, and some of whom fear an American conspiracy to weaken the Chinese economy. The push to take the Chinese currency global could end up as Zhou's Trojan Horse—a policy proposal which appears at first sight to have a nationalist, anti-American agenda but which, if followed through, will actually involve groundbreaking liberalization of the economy, the sort of things that American Treasury secretaries want to see happen. In its bid to end the dominance of the dollar, China could end up taking down its great financial wall much more quickly than Beijing would like. Challenging America's exorbitant economic privileges brings its own very high costs.

9

Post-American Globalization

FOR PETER BOSSHARD, the end of the Cold War was the moment when people finally started to pay attention. A Swiss national with a Ph.D. from Zurich University, Bosshard has spent most of his adult life trying to get foreign banks and engineering companies to rethink their support for large dams in developing countries. He would explain patiently why he thought these projects were white elephants that brought little benefit to the countries in question, other than to the officials who were able to cream off some of the contracts, while causing enormous damage to the surrounding environment. For years, his warnings were suffered in polite silence. Yet, after the fall of the Berlin Wall, development and environmental issues started to move center-stage. This was the era of the big UN conferences in Cairo, Rio, and Beijing on human rights and climate change, and Bosshard saw the mood shift. "People began to return my phone calls," he says.

One of the unexpected consequences of the end of the Cold War was the space it opened for activists. The 1990s became the era of the international NGO—the nongovernmental groups that lobby, campaign, and occasionally harass politicians and companies over issues in the developing world. During the Cold War, many of these NGOs struggled to find any oxygen, given that aid and finance to developing countries were wrapped up in the political expediency of bipolar competition. That started to change when the Wall fell. All of a sudden, clever young graduates wanted to work for Oxfam or ActionAid, instead of McKinsey. Bosshard, who wears wire-rimmed spectacles and Birkenstocks, is a soft-spoken engineer whose fluent English still carries a European accent. Since 2002, he has run International Rivers, an NGO based in a small office in Berkeley, California. "No one could accuse us anymore of doing Moscow's bidding," he says.

Before long, dams became one of the main political battlefields in this new wave of international activism. From the 1960s, large hydropower dams had been pushed as a silver bullet for developing economies. Under the leadership of Robert McNamara, the former U.S. defense secretary who had helped prosecute the Vietnam War, the World Bank put large amounts of resources behind these projects. The dams also became major earners for engineering multinationals such as Switzerland's ABB, one of the biggest companies in the world for much of the 1980s and 1990s. But with the end of the Cold War, activist NGOs started to point loudly to the failures and the high costs attached. As many as eighty million people had been displaced by large dams in the previous three decades, they claimed, many of whom did not manage to find a new livelihood. Bosshard, who fell in love with rivers while walking in the Alps as a child, started to go after the banks backing the projects, accusing them of "environmental money laundering." Under heavy pressure, the World Bank dramatically scaled back its lending to large dams. One senior executive complained in the mid-1990s that dams were "responsible for 95 percent of our headaches." Once the World Bank pulled out, most private banks also stood back. By the end of the 1990s, funding had dwindled so much that companies such as ABB exited the sector. The global approach to dam building had been completely transformed. It was one of the most successful lobbying campaigns by an NGO anywhere in the world. Then along came China.

Bosshard says he first started to take notice of China at the end of 2003, when Beijing agreed to build the Merowe Dam in northern Sudan, on one of the major tributaries of the Nile. The Sudanese government had been pushing the idea since the 1970s, and in the 1990s government delegations from Sudan toured Canada, Europe, and Southeast Asia, looking for financial backers for the project, only to return empty-handed each time. The World Bank also declined to get involved. Not only would the dam end up displacing tens of thousands of farmers who worked fertile Nile Valley land, but many governments were also put off by the Sudanese government's record of human-rights abuses. Yet for China's dam builders Merowe was a perfect chance to start taking their expertise global—expertise they had recently gleaned from the West.

In the 1990s, construction began on the massive and controversial Three Gorges Dam, on the Yangtze, the biggest hydroelectric power station in the world. Given that the market for dams had dried up elsewhere, the competition to get involved in the Three Gorges was intense. In order to get some of the multi-billion-dollar contracts that were on offer, Western groups had to enter joint ventures with Chinese companies, and under the terms of those agreements, they were obliged to hand over some of their technology. A decade later, the Chinese dam-building companies had absorbed these technologies and were ready to export them back overseas. Chinese banks also offered huge financing packages to convince other developing countries to begin construction, forging a powerful partnership with the new generation of dam-building companies. China has single-handedly revived the international market for large dams. By 2010, Chinese companies were involved in 220 dams in fifty different countries around the world and were constructing nineteen of the twenty-four largest hydropower stations ever built. Bosshard did not realize it at the time, but he was one of the first people to understand the potential for Chinese finance and investment to completely reshape globalization. "They are pretty much everywhere now," he says.

———

Mao Zedong was the central figure in the two events that produced the current era of globalization. The first was his 1972 meeting with Richard Nixon, which paved the way for China's re-entry into the international community. The second was his death. Deng Xiaoping was then able to launch the market reforms in the late 1970s that turned China from a centrally planned basket case into an economic juggernaut. During the three decades in which China has been on this reform path, Beijing and Washington have both placed a large strategic bet on economic integration. China felt that it needed access to American consumers and technology if it was to advance its economy; America decided that the global economy would be much stronger with China on the inside rather than outside. What we now call globalization was born.

China and the U.S. are approaching another critical crossroads in their economic relationship, which is as important as the 1972 meeting and will determine the future shape of the global economy. For the last three decades, globalization has been an American project, driven by American values, American capital, and American-led institutions. Peter Bosshard was one of the first witnesses of a new phase, in which Chinese finance and investment will play leading roles. The U.S. and China have to decide whether they now want to double down with a new stage of economic integration and cooperation. Down one road lies even greater interdependence between the two biggest economies on the planet, which will place restraints on their militaries and on other areas of competition. Yet down the other lies the formation of a two-track global economy, with a Western system revolving around the U.S. and a separate China-led economic sphere guided by Beijing's priorities. Will globalization break in half?

China's economic influence is usually thought of as a function of trade, all those T-shirts, widgets, and iPhones it makes for the world. China is now the world's largest exporter of manufactured goods, something that would have seemed preposterous to the officials who accompanied Mao and Nixon. In the process, it has displaced the U.S. as the largest trading partner of a host of countries, from Japan and South Korea to South Africa and Brazil, slowly turning the map of global commerce red. Trade is just the first stage, however. China is also now starting to become a global power in finance and investment. Until now, China has been a receiver rather than a giver of direct investment in factories and equipment. But that axis is shifting, as Chinese companies start to look overseas for investment opportunities and Chinese banks offer generous loans. The process began slowly in the late 1990s, after the government launched a "go out" strategy that led to a trickle of investments in mining and oil, and it is now gathering pace quickly in manufacturing and even services. As with so much else in modern China, the numbers will have an epic scale. Daniel Rosen, a China specialist at the Peterson Institute in Washington, D.C., calculates that if China follows the pattern of other developing economies, over the next decade it will invest overseas between $1 trillion and $2 trillion. This financial muscle will be one of the most important driving forces in the global economy over the coming decades. Corporate China's new export market will be its own money.

China is arriving at the same sort of inflection point that the U.S. economy reached in the 1890s. Before then, few American businessmen had even considered trying to operate abroad, as there was just too much money to be made at home. But eventually the lure of foreign markets started to become powerful. In the early 1890s, Senator Albert Beveridge of Indiana summed up the prevailing mood of a country ready to spread its commercial wings. "American factories are making more than the American people can use; American soil is producing more than they can consume," he said. "Fate has written our policy for us; the trade of the world must and shall be ours." Having reached a certain critical mass at home, many companies began to look for new markets and new investment opportunities overseas, particularly in the Americas. Before long, the United Fruit Company dominated banana production in Honduras, Guatemala, and elsewhere, to the extent that by 1925 it was the biggest employer in Central America. By the 1920s, American companies also owned 60 percent of Cuba's sugar plantations, and dominated the hotel-and-entertainment scene in Havana. And it was in the late 1890s that Washington started to push for an "Open Door" policy in China, which would allow American companies to trade and invest in China, along with the European colonial powers. Before long, Buicks had become the car of choice for the Chinese elite, with the list of proud owners including nationalist leader Sun Yat-sen and Pu Yi, the last Qing emperor.

As it contemplates this new stage in its development, the big strategic question for China is whether the U.S. should be at the forefront of its new investment plans. When Chinese companies survey the potential opportunities overseas, one instinct is to channel a large slice of this investment toward the U.S., which is still by far the largest economy in the world and the most powerful consumer market. America has a strong track record of consistent improvements in productivity, the real long-term guarantee of continued economic growth that companies are looking for when they make investment plans. It is basic business logic to go where the money is. As a result of shale oil and gas, the U.S. could be on the verge of a new energy boom, one of China's key priorities. Yet several Chinese companies that have tried to invest in the U.S. have suffered bruising political battles in Washington over their ties to the Chinese government. In 2006, the Chinese state oil company CNOOC tried to buy an American group called Unocal and put forward an offer bigger than the one already on the table from Chevron, another U.S. group. But after a storm of protest in Congress about Chinese interference in the U.S. energy sector, CNOOC decided to withdraw, feeling completely humiliated in the process by the political drubbing it had taken. Events such as this have left many Chinese companies in a wait-and-see mode, trying to work out whether or not they are really welcome in the U.S.

Even while they are testing the political mood in Washington, the Chinese also have a strong instinct to move in a very different direction, to use China's financial heft to fashion an alternative pattern of globalization that bypasses the U.S. The financial crisis was a profound shock for Beijing, revealing a level of dependence on the U.S. economy that left many in China deeply uncomfortable. Some of the Chinese officials who had supported close ties with the U.S. were dumbstruck to find that the U.S. financial system could have been so badly managed. The idea of trying to decouple China from the U.S. started to become more attractive. At the same time, it is part of the DNA of the aspirant great power to use its economic weight to begin shaping the rules and relationships that are at the heart of the global economy. China's efforts to challenge the role of the U.S. dollar are part of this mindset. There is now a lobby in Beijing that wishes to use the coming wave of investment to generate a new phase of globalization in which all the roads—business, financial, and political—converge on Beijing. Xu Shanda, a Chinese economist, argues for the launch of a Chinese "Marshall Plan" in the developing world, loans and aid that would create their own demand for Chinese goods. Some senior policy makers talk about how China's financial firepower could spark a new cycle of global growth among developing countries, with Beijing in the engine room, winning both new markets for China and new political partners, and all the time bypassing the developed markets of the U.S. and Europe. China is being tempted by the idea of post-American globalization.

To get a sense of what post-American globalization might look like, a good place to start is a small town called Açu, 175 miles north up the Atlantic coast from Rio de Janeiro in Brazil. Until recently, Açu used to be a small seaside village that attracted a modest crowd of weekenders to its long beaches. Now, it is a huge port with a two-mile-long pier and the ambition to be a strategic conduit between the Brazilian and Chinese economies. One of the world's largest dredging ships was used to carve a huge dock from the sand dunes, so that it will be able to house the new generation of Chinamax ships that can carry 400,000 tons of iron ore at a time across the oceans. A Chinese vice minister who came to visit the project described it as "a new highway to China."

The Açu port is the brainchild of Eike Batista, Brazil's most controversial businessman, whose spectacular rise and fall have become a potent symbol of the boom-and-bust cycles that have long scarred Brazilian capitalism. Batista made his first fortune as a gold trader in an area of the Amazon jungle that was undergoing a massive gold rush and which was a lawless place of legendary knife fights between the miners over who owned the precious metal. Over the last decade, he managed to ride the commodities boom that the China boom sparked, especially after he invested in a series of oilfields off the coast of Brazil in 2003. At one stage, his net worth was calculated at $34.5 billion, making him the seventh-richest person in the world. "Eike is a special kind of entrepreneur," Brazil's President Dilma Rousseff said during a visit to the Açu port project. "He comes up with extremely ambitious dreams and then seeks to fulfill them."

Once married to a *Playboy* cover girl and Carnival dancer, Batista once endorsed a new treatment for restoring the hair on his balding head, however, his wealth has demonstrated weaker roots. When Batista's oil wells produced much less oil than he had promised investors, his heavily indebted companies started to face a series of cash calls that have wiped billions off their market value in 2012 and early 2013. Batista could be forced into selling many of his businesses, which also include mining and shipbuilding.

Amid the scandals and schadenfreude that have accompanied the demise of Eike Batista's business fortunes, it is easy to lose sight of the fact that he has been a genuine trailblazer in ways that will have a lasting impact on Brazil. Batista was one of the first businessmen in Brazil to harness demand and finance from China, the country which has emerged over the last decade as Brazil's leading economic partner. "There is an endless market for us on the other side. China has endless pent-up demand," as Batista puts it.

One of the reasons America has maintained its dominant position in the world is that the size of its economy makes it a sort of customer of last resort, a constant source of demand that keeps the global economy ticking along. But China's growing ties with Brazil are one example of the way that it is starting to play the role of economic anchor in important relationships at the heart of the global economy. Brazil is good business and good politics for China. It is a fast-growing market of 200 million people, and China is building ties with a country in the backyard of its potential rival, a subtle intrusion into the Monroe Doctrine. The Brazil connection is part of a series of new economic links that have the potential to shape a different growth axis for the global economy, one that bypasses the West.

Brazil's improved economic performance over the last decade, including the China-style growth rate of 7.5 percent in 2010, was partly the result of demand from China for its natural resources, from iron ore and copper to beef and soybeans. In the process, China has become Brazil's biggest trading partner, overtaking the U.S. Batista was also one of the first in Brazil to understand the next phase, direct investment by Chinese companies. The Chinese group Wuhan Iron and Steel (Wisco) owns a large stake in MMX, the mining group he established. Before his troubles hit, Batista was talking to Wisco about an even bigger investment, a $5 billion steel plant in Açu next door to the port, which would have been the biggest ever Chinese investment in Brazil. Those talks may have floundered, but China has already become the biggest direct investor in Brazil in 2012, again outpacing the U.S. The investors have included car manufacturers and telecom companies, as well as natural resource businesses. "There is an enormous highway developing between Brazil and China," says Batista, who set up a high-end Chinese restaurant in Rio de Janeiro, called Mr. Lam, with two giant terra-cotta warriors flanking the entrance. "The world should start paying attention to it because it is fabulous." Batista might not manage to retain control of the Açu project, but there is a long list of potential investors lining up to finish the project that he started.

Brazil is involved in another interesting example of this new Chinese strategy to move beyond America-led globalization, the plan to create a BRICS bank. "BRICS" was a concept first invented by Jim O'Neill, an economist at Goldman Sachs, who wanted a catchy title to capture the exciting investment opportunities in a diverse group of emerging countries—Brazil, Russia, India, and China (South Africa was added later). Since then, the idea has taken on a geopolitical life of its own. The leaders of the five countries now hold annual summits, and some have high hopes that the BRICS can become an important political voice. Vladimir Putin, the Russian president, believes the group can develop into "a full-scale strategic cooperation mechanism that will allow us to look for solutions to key issues of global politics together." The leaders of the five countries are in detailed discussions to establish their own development bank, which would lend funds to other developing countries, providing a powerful alternative to the World Bank and International Monetary Fund. With China the driving force behind the project, the BRICS countries are discussing an initial capital injection of $50 billion.

It is one of the ironies of the international system the U.S. created after the end of the Second World War that so many of its institutions are deeply unpopular in the U.S. On the American right, the visceral dislike of the United Nations is so intense that the U.S. Senate cannot pass any UN agreement, even if it is something the U.S. initially proposed. In late 2012, the Senate refused to ratify a UN treaty to promote the rights of the disabled that was based on American legislation. The World Bank and the International Monetary Fund are sometimes the butt of the same disdain, criticized on the right for their cushy perks and on the left as bastions of neoliberalism. But the reality is that both the World Bank and the IMF, which are based a couple of blocks away from the White House, have been powerful instruments for pushing an American vision of politics and economics on the developing world. Especially since the end of the Cold War, the World Bank and the IMF have been important conduits for the promotion of privatization and free trade, the policies that have been the international priorities of the U.S. Treasury Department.

Their impact goes well beyond economics. These Washington-based institutions have also used their influence to encourage ideas about governance which have a strongly American flavor: a push for greater transparency, accountability, and respect for the rule of law. That makes the World Bank and the IMF hugely important and often underestimated tools in the global battle for influence. If China's banks really do start to undercut some of the authority of the World Bank, providing an alternative source of financing that comes with far fewer political and economic strings attached, that would have a significant impact on Washington's ability to shape attitudes in the developing world. Beijing does not want to tear up the World Bank or the IMF; indeed, it is lobbying hard for a bigger say in how they are managed. But without any announcement or grand design, it is also quietly setting up an alternative system of global development financing that has the potential to make the Washington institutions less relevant. "I sometimes ask the Chinese why they are making such an effort to be more involved at the World Bank," says a senior Brazilian official who used to work at the bank, "because they are at the same time effectively putting it out of business."

At the heart of most of China's new economic relationships is one institution: China Development Bank. In the space of just a few years, it has become one of the most influential banks in the world. The state owns almost all the main banks in China, but CDB is different. Like the China Export-Import Bank, it is defined as a "policy bank," which means that its objective is to support the overall economic goals of the government. China Development Bank is the sort of hybrid institution that can only really exist in Beijing, a branch of the Chinese state but for a long period it was also the political fiefdom of a very ambitious official from the Communist Party's aristocracy. In the late 1990s, the bank was effectively bankrupt when Chen Yuan, a former vice governor of the Chinese central bank, became its chairman. His father, Chen Yun, was one of the most influential of the first generation of Communist revolutionaries and one of the "Eight Immortals," the group of Deng's contemporaries who acted as a parallel power structure during the 1980s and 1990s, and who pushed for the military to take control of Tiananmen Square in 1989. Under Chen Yuan's leadership, CDB managed to follow a delicate path of supporting government goals while also being hugely profitable. Dragonomics, a Beijing consultancy, calls it "the best-run bank in China."

Chen used his close personal contacts within the Chinese system to create a central role for CDB in Chinese urban development. In the early part of the last decade, the bank used an innovative financing structure to help unleash a surge in infrastructure projects by Chinese local governments—all those new airports, highways, and high-speed trains that have attracted so much attention. Then, from the middle of the last decade, Chen decided to take his bank overseas. He bought a small stake in the U.K.'s Barclays Bank and flirted with a much bigger investment, before pulling out of the deal. Instead, when the financial crisis started, he realized there was a huge opportunity for China in the energy sector. Given the sharp drop in prices, energy-producing countries were "now in a difficult situation because they can't raise capital from the West," he said in 2008. "So they are shifting their focus to China. Therefore, we should grasp this opportunity to do deals." He decided to build up an informal branch network for the bank overseas. Each of the main offices in China was given responsibility for a different region of the world. The Henan branch, in northern China, was told to scout for business in southern Africa; the Chongqing office, from central China, was sent to develop contacts in the Balkans. By the end of 2009, the bank had teams in 141 countries, including almost all the fifty-four countries in Africa. In a book he wrote about his experiences working overseas for CDB, Shi Jiyang recalls sitting in his office in Shenzhen in 2006, looking at a map of the world, and wondering if he would ever get the chance to visit South America; a month later, he was sent there to find new business. "South America is going to be the hotspot for Chinese investment over the next ten years," he writes. "Entrepreneurs who want to 'challenge the blue ocean' should be ready to go to South America." In early 2013, Chen Yuan stepped down from CDB, after more than a decade in charge. His new job is to establish the BRICS development bank.

Ambitious companies, not the Foreign Ministry, are forging many of China's new international relationships. In a short period of time,

CDB started to sign a rapid succession of eye-catching deals. It provided the financing for the $2-billion Burma pipeline, as well as a series of big deals in Russia, Kazakhstan, and Turkmenistan. The bank was also behind a $9-billion development-financing deal that China signed with the government of Ghana. Africa gets most of the attention in China's overseas investments, but CDB has also made a big splash in Latin America. Kevin Gallagher, a development economist at Boston University, calculated the amount of loan commitments that China made to Latin America between 2005 and 2011. The figure he came up with, $75 billion, was more than the entire amount loaned to the region by the World Bank, the Inter-American Development Bank, and the U.S. government. Some of those funds went to countries such as Argentina and Bolivia, which had effectively been cut off from international financial markets. "The key thing is that the Chinese are financing the sorts of projects that Latin American governments actually want, rather than the projects that the Washington financial institutions think that they need for their development," says Gallagher.

The World Bank insists that it does not really compete with CDB and China Eximbank. In the strict sense, that is often correct. The Chinese are not involved in anything similar to many of the projects that the World Bank supports, such as microcredit schemes or health-care initiatives. According to World Bank officials, the Chinese are mostly interested in using their loans to get access to energy and natural resources, which is a different sort of business. But this explanation leaves out a number of things. It ignores the way in which Chinese money can alter the development priorities of governments. Dams are one of the best examples. After the World Bank succumbed to pressure from NGOs and withdrew from backing large dams in the 1990s, their construction ground to a halt. But when Chinese banks entered the fray, developing countries' governments could ignore Washington's advice about the risks of dam building. Whatever China's motives, the money it makes available gives governments new options and reduces the leverage of the Washington-based banks.

The World Bank's argument also ignores the broader political implications of China's overseas lending spurt. The China Development Bank's biggest client is Venezuela, whose firebrand leader, Hugo Chávez, liked nothing better than taking potshots at Washington until his death in 2013. From 2007 to 2012, the bank lent $42.5 billion to the government of Venezuela—roughly a quarter of its overseas loans during that period. Venezuela is one of the world's largest oil producers, and the loans are backed by oil revenues, which gives China some comfort about repayment. As part of the deal, Chinese companies are also getting access to some oil exploration projects which have become available because U.S. oil companies have been expelled. Most of the loans have gone into a development fund run by the Venezuelan government. It is not too much of an exaggeration to say that the Chinese money went a long way to securing Chávez's hold on power. "Venezuela's oil is at the service of China," Chávez once told Xi Jinping. Ecuador, another Latin American country with a left-populist government that enjoys snubbing its nose at Washington, has negotiated a similar oil-for-loans deal with China. The $7.3 billion in loans it has signed are equivalent to around one-third of its annual budget.

Venezuela's experience in recent years demonstrates the potential of Chinese financing to alter some of the dynamics of international politics. When its oil revenues plummeted during previous financial crises, Caracas was often obliged to look to the Washington institutions for support. The price of that help was to adopt some of their advice about how the economy should be run. During the 2009 crisis, Venezuela's finances were under heavy pressure as oil prices fell. But, courtesy of the Chinese money, Chávez was able to carry on as if nothing had happened. Indeed, as a result of Beijing's backing, Chávez went so far as to pull out of the World Bank and IMF formally in 2010. "We will no longer have to go to Washington," Chávez boasted.

Lurking behind the surge in Chinese lending there is also an economic philosophy that puts China at odds with the Washington institutions. When Deng Xiaoping decided to start opening up the Chinese economy, one of the first things the government did was to take out a large loan from Japan in 1978, on terms quite similar to the sorts of deals China has struck over the last five years in Africa and Latin America. China pledged to import $10 billion of Japanese technology and capital equipment, which it repaid with exports of coal and oil. (This was an era when Japan, not China, was the country scouring the world for natural resources to feed its rapid industrialization.) China used the funds to build new ports and roads, to construct power plants, and to build up its telecommunications network—the core industrial foundations it needed to help kick-start the economy. "China was getting a discount on finance the country needed for its modernization," according to Deborah Brautigam, an American academic who has done extensive research on China's links with Africa. China sees its hands-off financing in Africa and Latin America in a similar vein. Little of this is aid: the borrowing countries have to repay the loans, which are at international interest rates. But Chinese officials argue that economic development can only take place if governments are given the freedom to experiment with the sorts of projects that might work in their countries and which are important for their economy. "We had to learn from our own mistakes," as a senior Chinese official explained to me. "We are letting other countries do the same. We cannot tell them what they need or how to run their economy. All we can do is share some of our own recent experiences."

HACKED OFF

In 2004, a security officer at Nortel, a leading maker of telecommunications equipment, noticed something peculiar on the group's computer network. One of Nortel's senior executives appeared to be downloading a large series of sensitive documents about the company's technology and strategy. The executive claimed to know nothing about the downloads, so the company's IT-security staff started to investigate. They eventually followed the intrusion in Nortel's networks all the way back to Internet servers in China.

Over the next few years, Nortel continued to notice signals that hackers were still present in its system. Brian Shields, a longtime Nortel executive who led the company's internal investigation, concluded that the passwords of seven senior company officials, including the chief executive, had been stolen. Every so often, one of the company's computers would send a large packet of electronic data that would end up at one of the Internet addresses in China. The hacking had probably started as far back as 2000, Nortel concluded. "They had plenty of time to get pretty much anything they wanted," says Shields. "This is not the kind of thing that ordinary hackers can do. It has to be something organized by a state."

Nortel is already an also-ran of the fast-moving IT industry. One of the pioneers in making the electronic switches that power mobile-phone networks, the Canadian company filed for bankruptcy in 2009 and has since been sold off in different pieces. The company could never definitively prove that China was behind the hacking of its system, and Beijing has denied it. It is also not clear whether there was any link between the hacking and the company's deteriorating results. But the accusations that Shields has aired have become part of a familiar refrain in recent years, as American companies and politicians have started to accuse China of a staggering campaign of stealing trade secrets. The most detailed case has been compiled by Mandiant, a U.S. Internet-security company, which claims to have traced hacking attacks on 141 companies in the U.S. and fifteen other countries to one particular Chinese military unit based in Shanghai. According to the Mandiant report, a well-known group of hackers named APT1 is actually part of a PLA group called Unit 61398. By tracing a large volume of hacking activity back to telecom networks near the unit's base in a twelve-story building in central Shanghai, Mandiant concluded that the PLA had to be involved. Amid the increasing volume of evidence linking China to hacking, senior U.S. politicians and officials have taken to denouncing Beijing. In Congress, there is a strong move to try and find some sort of payback, to punish the companies that are benefiting from cybertheft. "What has been happening over the course of the last five years is that China—let's call it for what it is—has been hacking its way into every corporation it can find listed in Dun & Bradstreet," says Richard Clarke, former White House counterterrorism officer under Bill Clinton and George W. Bush. "Every corporation in the U.S., every corporation in Asia, every corporation in Germany. And using a vacuum cleaner to suck data out in terabytes and petabytes."

If China is having second thoughts about its close economic links with the U.S., then America is returning the compliment. The business community was once the most important supporter in the U.S. of strong ties with China, but over the last five years many companies have become much more wary. "I am not sure that in the end they want any of us to win, or any of us to be successful," Jeffrey Immelt, chief executive of General Electric, America's biggest manufacturing company, complained in 2010 at a dinner in Rome.

The hacking revelations have only added to the impression that China is stacking the cards against Western multinationals, especially when it comes to actually doing business in China. The country may be the second-largest economy in the world and the biggest market for many industries, but many foreign businesses have had a bruising experience over the last few years, which makes them think that the opportunities available to them in China are gradually being squeezed. They point to a complex web of Chinese industrial policies that affect their ability to compete, including generous financial subsidies for important Chinese state-owned companies, new industrial standards that favor Chinese competitors, and predatory regulations that seek to get foreign companies to hand over important technologies in return for market access. Chinese regulators believe that, because the Chinese market is so large, they can drive a very hard bargain with foreign companies who want to do business in the country. The fear that the Chinese military and security services are helping foreign companies' competitors steal their trade secrets has only added to the sense of disillusionment. "Many U.S. companies believe they are not competing with similar entities," says John Veroneau, a former deputy U.S. trade representative. "They are used to competing with market players, but not against governments. Not only are they up against subsidies, but they are also up against China's intelligence services."

The lightning rod for a lot of these suspicions has been a Chinese company called Huawei, one of the world's biggest makers of telecom equipment. Huawei has become a sort of Rorschach test for views on China: its supporters believe it is a shining example of Chinese innovation, whereas its critics argue it is a secretive, military-friendly corporation that could be a Trojan Horse for a future cyberwar. Along with Ericsson of Sweden and Cisco of the U.S., Huawei is one of the main companies making the essential infrastructure that goes into modern phone systems, including mobile networks. (Nortel used to be a leader in this market.) That is where the cyberwar fears come in. Security experts say that such expertise means that Huawei could leave devices in American phone systems that might be used to listen into telephone conversations, or it could hide corrupted computer code that would allow China to disable a phone network during a conflict.

Huawei has become such a sensitive political issue in part because of its background. The company was founded by Ren Zhengfei in 1987, when he started selling telephone-exchange equipment imported from Hong Kong. For much of the 1970s, however, Ren had served in the People's Liberation Army, latterly in its information-technology research unit. As a result of that PLA connection, Huawei has never been able to shake the impression that it cooperates with the military and China's security services. The suspicion is enhanced by the opaque management structure of the company, which revolves around the mercurial Ren. He has now become chairman of the company, but his idea of stepping back from the business has been to appoint three people to act as chief executive on a rotating basis, a recipe for backseat control.

Every time it has tried to expand in the U.S., Huawei has found itself frustrated. In 2008, its $2.2-billion attempt to buy an American company called 3Com, which makes Internet routers and networking equipment, was blocked on national security grounds. It had the same experience in 2011, when it tried to buy some assets from 3Leaf, another American technology company. The Intelligence Committee of the U.S. House of Representatives effectively fingered Huawei as a threat to national security in 2012 in a report which recommended not only that it be blocked from all U.S. government business, but that American telecom companies should not buy any equipment made by Huawei. "We simply cannot trust such vital systems to companies with known ties to the Chinese state, a country that is the largest perpetrator of cyber-espionage against the U.S.," says Mike Rogers, chairman of the House Intelligence Committee. "You would have to be mad to let that company into our networks."

Not every Western country is quite as hostile to Huawei as is the U.S. In order to do business in the U.K., Huawei, which has invested $2 billion in the country, has established a separate testing center which works closely with British government agencies to ensure that the equipment and software sold by Huawei are reliable. Governments can never know for sure that the equipment they are buying is not compromised, but this British unit is as good a way as any of getting reassurance. There are also some members of the U.S. security establishment who are not opposed to Huawei. One former senior official at the U.S. National Security Agency says that if the Chinese wanted to set traps in U.S. communication networks or in its infrastructure, the last route they would use is equipment made by high-profile Chinese companies, because of the inevitable scrutiny: instead, they would look for ways to plant hidden code in the products of other suppliers. Yet the high-level political opposition to Huawei is so strong in Washington that it is hard to imagine a compromise emerging. One former senior Pentagon official says, "It is simply too dangerous to let a Chinese company near our phone networks, the potential problems are so great."

Perhaps telecom equipment in the twenty-first century is destined to be like the defense industry, a tightly controlled domain that is open only to companies from that nation. But the U.S. also runs a great risk in rejecting companies like Huawei so aggressively. There is bound to be retaliation: China is as afraid of Cisco as the U.S. is of Huawei. Banning major Chinese companies can also easily become a slippery slope. The initial focus has been on telecom equipment, but the U.S. Congress has started introducing restrictions in some areas for all Chinese information-technology products, from computers to smartphones. This sort of action raises the prospect that a core industry in the modern economy will end up being divided into two distinct camps, a group of companies that America politically approves of, and another group of companies that Washington does not trust, mostly from China. Such techno-nationalism can easily become the gateway to a broader outbreak of protectionism. The financial crisis and the great recession that followed did not lead to the flood of protectionist measures that many expected, but the panic over cybertheft of trade secrets might just do so.

———

Of all the China challenges facing Washington in the coming years, in many ways this is perhaps the most complex: how to prevent the political and protectionist pressures that are building up in both countries from splintering the rules and understandings at the heart of the global economy.

The postwar, liberal economic order that America promoted has survived so long because it has been attractive to enough countries that a decisive challenge never emerged. China has been one of the biggest beneficiaries of the existing system, but the clash between its model of state capitalism and America's free-market creed could easily tear it apart. While some in China want to tilt the system more to China's advantage, many in America think Beijing is defying the rules.

Over time, China's economic model will gradually change. Former premier Wen Jiabao described the Chinese economy as "unbalanced, uncoordinated, and unsustainable"—and he liked the phrase so much, he repeated it on several occasions. Among senior Chinese officials, there is a broad consensus on the direction of change toward an economy that depends less on heavy industry and investment and relies more on services and individual consumption. These reforms will inevitably reduce the power and importance in the economy of state-owned companies and banks, softening some of the edges of the system that have aggravated foreign businesses. But such changes will be fiercely resisted and will take a long time to implement, which means the tensions will remain. In the meantime, Washington needs to find new ways to build support for ideas for an open global economy and to steer China away from a major rupture with the system.

One way to do that is to try and establish more areas of common ground with China over the major issues of international economic governance. The last few years have served to demonstrate the big difference in their approaches to financing the developing world, as the China Development Bank has started to challenge the enormous political and economic influence of the World Bank. Yet, over time, this could be an area where the two sides end up with a more similar viewpoint.

For the Washington-based institutions, the obvious first step would be to abandon the charade of awarding the top jobs only to Westerners—the Americans currently get the leadership of the World Bank, while the Europeans have a hold on the post of managing director of the IMF. In order to remain relevant, the Bank and the Fund need to find ways to engage not just China but the other large developing countries, many of whom are deeply ambivalent about them. Opening up the leadership-selection process would be one obvious step. Competition from China will also likely lead to a gradual shift in philosophy. The World Bank and IMF have already been forced over the last decade into a thorough re-examination of some of the more rigid orthodoxies from the 1990s that were so heavily criticized after the Asia crisis. Whereas once they pushed for rapid budget cuts in the event of economic problems, the World Bank has become more sensitive to the importance of maintaining health care and other public goods. But there is still something to be learned from the Chinese emphasis on providing finance for the kinds of projects, including infrastructure, that the borrowing countries actually want to do.

China, too, is likely to find that its approach shifts. In a short space of time, China has issued a large volume of loans, mostly to countries with which it has quite shallow relations and only modest understanding. This lending boom has also taken place during one of the biggest bull markets in commodities the world has ever seen. Many of the Chinese loans are backed by oil, copper, or some other natural resource, which gives the Chinese banks the impression of complete security. But if commodity prices ever start to fall sharply and these economies suffer serious financial difficulties, there is a good chance that China will begin to suffer some defaults on its loans. Chinese bankers will learn the harsh lesson about all those difficult conditions that the World Bank and IMF attach to their loans: these conditions may force governments to adopt the sorts of free-market policies that Washington likes, but they are also partly designed to ensure the banks actually get repaid. If China is hit with a wave of defaults, its banks are likely to start paying a lot more attention to the way their clients are actually governed. The most likely candidate for a showdown could well be Venezuela, a country with incredibly opaque finances and looming economic problems, which is by far China Development Bank's biggest client. Even before the death of Hugo Chávez, CDB had realized it needed to be more hands-on in its approach to Caracas. The former CDB boss Chen Yuan at one stage presented Chávez with a six-hundred-page book of recommendations for how to run its economy. With Chávez no longer around, there is considerable uncertainty about the country's political future. It is possible that a revived opposition in Venezuela could seek to make the loans now owed to China into a political issue, just as the World Bank and IMF have often become political targets in the past in Latin America.

Even the recent explosion in dam building could become a source of compromise. After initially despairing at the way Chinese money had completely neutered the campaign against dams, Peter Bosshard at International Rivers is now trying to find a middle ground between the Chinese and Western approaches. Before the Chinese became so influential, his usual tactic would have been to put pressure on the financial backers of a dam-building project, but neither China Eximbank nor China Development Bank needs to go to international capital markets to get their funds, which meant there were no investors or partner banks he could lean on. With his leverage gone, he decided to engage. Bosshard started to visit China and talk with local NGOs, who he thought could become useful allies. He also tried to meet some of the companies involved in the industry. On his second trip to China, in 2006, he got a call out of the blue from China Eximbank, which was then bankrolling much of China's overseas dam building, asking him to come and meet its chairman, Li Ruogu. It was almost certainly the first-ever meeting between a Western, campaigning NGO and the head of a large state-owned bank.

Li Ruogu, a former deputy governor of the central bank and one of China's leading financial officials, has a reputation as something of a bully. But on the day when Bosshard was due to meet him, Li was suffering from a bad cold and had partly lost his voice, so he opened the meeting by asking Bosshard to outline his concerns. Then Li started to talk. Bosshard assumed he was about to hear the sort of evasions he used to get from Western banks in the 1980s and 1990s, to the effect that environmental and human-rights concerns were not really the responsibility of a bank. Instead, he received a lecture on how China had developed its economy using precisely these types of projects. "Li said that the bank had some responsibility for the social and environmental aspects of the projects it took on, but he also told me that China had needed to first grow out of poverty before it could start to worry about the environment," Bosshard says. "He said that China would not stand in the way of other developing countries that were trying to do the same thing. China was not just lending them money—it was exporting its development experience." At the end of the meeting, Li proposed a sort of informal collaboration. He said he would send a team to investigate problems at the Merowe Dam in Sudan and other cases brought up by Bosshard. But he asked that Bosshard talk to him before making any more public criticisms. Although he was aware that he risked being muzzled, Bosshard agreed. "If we believe that people are listening to us, that is not really a problem," he says, in justification of his acceptance of the deal.

The private dialogue with China Eximbank lasted for about a year. In May 2007, the African Development Bank held its annual meeting in Shanghai, another striking indicator of the new economic symbiosis between China and Africa. Bosshard decided to bring along two activists, one from the Merowe region of Sudan and the other from Mozambique, where Eximbank had signed another controversial dam-building agreement. He tried to organize a chance for them to talk to officials at the bank about their experiences, but after a lot of delaying, Eximbank declined to arrange a meeting. So Bosshard went to the media instead, offering a session with his two African visitors to the Shanghai Foreign Correspondents Club. Eximbank was furious and has not spoken to International Rivers since.

After falling out with China Eximbank, Bosshard began a similar dialogue with Sinohydro, the biggest dam-builder in the world. International Rivers has been discussing with the company a new policy of environmental guidelines. Sinohydro has ordered that all its overseas subsidiaries must use Chinese environmental law if they are working in countries that have weaker regulation, which Bosshard says could be an important step forward. He says they are taking it more slowly this time, after the bust-up with Eximbank, to see what sort of response the NGO gets from the company. But the revealing aspect of Bosshard's attempt to engage with China's hydropower sector is the way it has started to change some of his own views on dams and economic development. Bosshard is now married to a Chinese woman, and when I met him in Beijing, he had just come back from spending Chinese New Year with her family in Benxi, a rough mining town in the northeast. Even there, he said, it was clear how life has improved for the residents as a result of the booming economy. Western NGOs can be so focused on their particular human-rights or environmental issues, he says, that they can sometimes forget that economic growth is also a prerequisite for improving the welfare of ordinary people. He has not altered his views on the need to have much greater social and environmental protections attached to large dams, but he has come to see how major infrastructure projects do not always end up as huge boondoggles that hurt the poor. If well executed, they can have a major impact on the broader economy. "The years we have spent coming to China have definitely persuaded us that things are more complicated than we thought," he admits.

———

Working more with China is one approach. At other times, the U.S. will need to work around Beijing. In a contest for influence, the country that prevails will be the one that manages to draw a larger number of other governments to its side. By building strong coalitions of support on specific issues, Washington can shape Chinese behavior, even in areas where they do not agree.

This approach is already being used in trade policy. As well as the Trans-Pacific Partnership (TPP), the trade agreement that brings together a group of countries from Asia and the Americas, the U.S. is also negotiating a trade agreement with the European Union which would unite into one economic zone 40 percent of the world's GDP. The two negotiations have a powerful theme in common: they are partly designed to take on Chinese state capitalism. The agendas of both agreements cover subjects like intellectual-property protection, generous financial subsidies, protection of foreign investment, and labor rights— precisely the areas that are becoming so contentious because of China's model of doing business. American negotiators see these agreements as a firewall against what they describe as Chinese abuse of trade rules. If Washington can get enough of the most important economies in the world to sign up for this sort of trade agreement, it can effectively set standards for the way international trade is conducted that China would find very hard to overturn.

These trade talks reflect a very different approach to dealing with China. American officials once talked about encouraging China to be a "responsible stakeholder" in the international system, and in the first year of the Obama administration there was a brief flirtation with a sort of G-2, an informal compact to try and solve some of the world's problems together. But by working around China in this way, Washington is almost trying to present China with a fait accompli. If the international consensus is strong enough, China could risk appearing like a pariah if it tried to resist the new rules. On many of these issues of economic governance, the U.S. is likely to find that the EU shares the exact same concerns—from cyberhacking, which is a huge issue for German manufacturing companies, to fears about Chinese subsidies. As China's economic influence grows, the U.S. and Europe are likely to find greater common ground, although Europe will likely remain divided on how to deal with China.

The talks are also the harbinger of a different way of trying to address global issues. The U.S. used to push its ideas through the ambitious global organizations it set up after the Second World War, including the UN, the World Bank, and the World Trade Organization. But whether it is the prolonged deadlock over the Doha round of trade talks or the endless series of climate-change talks that produce little, there is now a pervasive sense of gloom about the idea of big global agreements. TPP and the U.S.-EU trade talks are a reflection of a more modest approach, the idea that the best way to get things done now is through smaller agreements with like-minded governments, diplomatic coalitions of the willing.

The danger in such an approach, of course, is that it alienates China further and gives it more reason to break with the American-led system. Beijing is frank about what it thinks of the new trade talks. "The U.S. is trying to rewrite global trade rules behind our backs," says one senior Chinese official. A strategy based on sticks alone will likely only create a more frustrated China: Washington also needs to devise some carrots.

———

During the decade when he ran China, Hu Jintao rarely looked more relaxed than on the day he visited a Boeing factory in Seattle in 2006. He smiled broadly, donned a baseball cap with the Boeing logo, and gave a factory supervisor a hug. Hu's speech was somewhat leaden, but he still received a loud round of applause from the workers. As the event was coming to an end, the then head of Boeing's aircraft division, Alan Mulally, put one hand on Hu's shoulder, pumped his fist with the other, and shouted: "China rocks!" Such moments have been rare, however.

It has become so common to talk about the interconnectedness of the U.S. and Chinese economies that it is surprising just how shallow the personal links are in China. For all the powerful financial and trade ties that bind China to the U.S., the number of members of the Chinese elite with a direct stake in the U.S. economy is limited. China may own $2 trillion of U.S. assets, but those investments are handled by the small group of bureaucrats who manage the central bank's reserves. Trade offers a similar story. At least half of China's exports of consumer products are manufactured by foreign-owned companies in China. The number of Chinese firms that rely on the U.S. is much smaller than the headline figures would suggest. Investment has been even shallower. Of all the money that Chinese companies have started to invest in other countries in recent years, only 1 percent has come to the U.S. In terms of big-picture economics, China leans heavily on the U.S., but that does not translate into business careers and life experiences.

The coming wave of overseas Chinese investment is a new opportunity for the U.S. to think about what sort of relationship it really wants to have with China. Given the toxic politics over cybersecurity and the suspicions that Chinese companies enjoy unfair financial advantages, it would be easy to see a repeat of the Japan scare that accompanied Japanese investments in the early 1990s. Some politicians might be tempted to indulge in a round of China bashing. Yet that would be a big mistake. At a time when military rivalry between the two countries is accelerating, and when new economic tensions are swirling, one way to persuade China that the U.S. has no plans for containment would be to roll out the red carpet for Chinese investments that do not have clear national security implications. This is one of the tools America has at its disposal as it tries to influence China's long-term calculations.

The U.S. has an opportunity to build up its own lobby of supporters within the Chinese system. The bosses of the large Chinese state-owned companies are among the most important officials in the country, and if they have a personal stake in continued good relations with the U.S., this can only help Washington. Until China started to play hardball with foreign multinationals, the biggest supporter Beijing had in the U.S. was the business lobby. A surge in Chinese investment would also give the U.S. a bigger window to try and shape the behavior of large

Chinese companies as they become important global players. CNOOC, the oil group which was humiliated in its 2006 effort to buy Unocal, has since then acquired a group of smaller assets in the U.S. One upshot is that CNOOC and the rest of the Chinese oil industry have been relatively cooperative with the U.S. over the issue of Iran sanctions. Chinese companies have not progressed with the large investment deals they had signed in Iran and, under pressure from Washington, they have scaled back imports of oil from Iran. Encouraging Chinese state-owned groups to operate in the U.S. is one way of acquiring a little more leverage over them and the senior party officials who manage the companies.

America, it should be said, also needs the money. There is an odd disconnect between the way some in Washington see Chinese investment and the response in the rest of the country. In 2011, when Hu Jintao visited the U.S., the White House put on a grand state dinner in his honor, yet that evening the leaders of Congress—the speaker and the Senate minority and majority leaders—realized that they had somewhere else they would rather be. Not one wanted to be seen having dinner with the Chinese leader. The next day, Hu went to Chicago, which put on a lavish reception for him in the hope that China would send some investment its way. Richard M. Daley, the mayor and heir to his family's political dynasty in the town, called Hu a "man of vision."

During the 2012 election campaign, Barack Obama and Mitt Romney crisscrossed Ohio, slamming "Chinese cheaters" who were taking American jobs. On the same September day when both candidates were in Toledo, the city's mayor, Michael Bell, was hosting a conference for a group of 150 Chinese businessmen he had invited to try and attract investments. "I have to say, the campaign is really hindering us," Bell told me, referring to both candidates' China bashing. "The Chinese people we invited here are asking, 'Why are you picking on us?' or 'Why are we suddenly the big issue?'" Bell had made three trips to China in the previous two years to solicit investments. (His business card has his name in Chinese on the back.) In turn, he has received thirty different delegations of potential Chinese investors, many of whom have been treated to private performances of the Toledo Symphony.

Toledo is the vision of a rundown Midwestern city. The downtown area has plenty of old warehouses whose windows are boarded up or broken. Nearby, along the river, is a plot of unused land that the City Council has been trying to develop for a decade, only to see two deals with local developers fall through. In 2011, however, two Chinese investors bought the sixty-nine-acre stretch of land for $3.8 million in cash and have announced a $200-million retail-and-residential project on the riverfront plot, which is known as the Marina District. "We are planning on building it into an international city," said Yuan Xiaohong, one of the Chinese investors. Exactly how the project will develop is still not clear, but Mayor Bell thinks the reality is obvious. "There is a difference between the political rhetoric and what is actually happening in the country," says Bell, whose city faces a large budget deficit. "All we are trying to do is to get people to invest in our city."

The tidal wave of Chinese investment is coming. The only question is whether a significant slice of it is directed toward the U.S., or whether China ends up channeling more of its investment toward places like India or Brazil, in a bid to decouple from the U.S. and curry political favor elsewhere. This is a pivotal test for the U.S. It gives the U.S. an opportunity to deepen the links between the two countries, placing new restraints on China's more hawkish elements, and to build up its own vested interest within China. At the same time, if Washington routinely blocks Chinese companies from coming to the U.S., alleging national security and the excessive influence of the Chinese state, it would deeply antagonize Beijing, where large parts of the Chinese establishment would see this as concrete evidence that America is out to curtail its rise and weaken its economy. The rest of the world would interpret a Closed Door policy in America as a major failure of leadership, a sign that Washington was backing away from its basic commitments. America wants to cement its position as the leading power in a new age, and it aspires to continue setting the international agenda. To do so, the U.S. will need to remain open for business, including from China.

Conclusion

WHOSE PROBLEMS would you rather have?

On November 6, 2012, Barack Obama won what was in the end a comfortable re-election, but it followed a dispiriting campaign that rarely lifted above the resentful. Even before his second term began, Obama seemed mired in a never-ending series of budget crises and at the start of an era of grinding cuts. The following week, a new generation of leaders was unveiled in Beijing, the group of seven men who will run the country for the next decade. With the new party boss Xi Jinping at the head of the line, they filed onto a stage in the Great Hall of the People, a row of begonias and ferns separating them from the cameras. Standing in the center of the group, the new leader did not take any questions. Instead, he gave a brief speech laced with a few populist hints, which contrasted with his wooden predecessor but gave away little about his governing philosophy.

There have been three new Chinese leaders since the Tiananmen Square crackdown, and each one has assumed office amid the same sniping prediction in the West that only drastic action can fend off a looming crisis. Yet there does seem to be something different this time, a powerful sensation that China is approaching the end of a road. Chinese officials, scholars, and acquaintances almost universally acknowledge that the economic and political structures that have got them this far so fast are breaking down.

In domestic politics, the party's rigid control on power is being tested by a growing middle class that wants more rule of law and less corruption, by the irreverent irony and indignation of the Internet, and by Beijing's choking pollution. On the economic side, the growth model that relies on funneling cheap bank loans to investment projects is running out of steam and needs to be replaced by more emphasis on consumers. Most of the goals that China has set itself for the coming decades, whether it is encouraging more innovation or winning cultural recognition, are rooted in the initiative of private citizens. The next Chinese era will be less about the state and much more about the individual. Xi's challenge is to chart a series of reforms that start to address these demands without provoking a backlash from the party's many and powerful vested interests. Even in his very careful speech, Xi almost admitted as much. "We are not complacent . . ." he said. "Under the new conditions, our party faces many severe challenges, and there are also many pressing problems within the party that need to be resolved."

The bewildering series of domestic problems may grab all the attention, but this same reform agenda is also the key to unlocking Chinese influence abroad. To win a bigger role in the world, it is not enough to be wealthy; a country also needs to secure trust. Without a political system that embraces a greater degree of pluralism, allows more dissent, and is rooted in the rule of law, China will struggle to get the respect it needs to turn its economic weight into power and influence.

The link between domestic politics and soft power is the most obvious: China will not be truly admired abroad while it shows such disrespect to some of its more impressive citizens. But China's role in global economic affairs is also tied to its politics. The status of reserve currency is ultimately a question of trust and credibility. Having the biggest economy is an important but not sufficient condition. For the world's central banks to invest heavily in a currency, they must have a high level of confidence about why and how important decisions are made, a comfort that China does not yet provide.

The same goes for the PLA. China's military buildup was always bound to arouse intense suspicion in its Asian backyard, but the closed, opaque nature of the Chinese political system only adds to these tensions. The lack of transparency about its military spending, the absence of real discussion about China's long-term, strategic objectives, and the

PLA's ambiguous status within the country all make suspicion inevitable. Given such uncertainties, neighbors are forced to respond to China's rapidly expanding capabilities, not its intentions, which remain unclear. Over the last few years, China has contented itself by winning small tactical victories that advance its territorial claims, but in the process has sown even greater mistrust.

Ultimately, China's brittle domestic politics, with its squalls of nationalist anger, undermine its ability to forge the sorts of relationships with the peoples of other nations that are the route to enduring influence. The real way to alter the balance of power in Asia at the expense of the U.S. is not for China to bully its neighbors over small islands, but to win the lasting confidence of their populations. Instead, China has been doing the opposite.

The U.S. is also entering a critical period in which its economic problems are starting to undermine its role in the world. If the American economy remains sluggish and unemployment stays high, both allies and rivals will question its ability to meet future commitments. Indeed, the contest for influence that is emerging between the U.S. and China will be partly answered by the way both governments respond to the sense of malaise they both face. I am probably not the only person who has two mental lists about America's economic future, unsure on any given day which is correct. On the pessimistic list, there is a familiar litany of problems, including rising debt and health-care costs, stagnant wages, inequality, crumbling infrastructure, failing schools, and a pervasive sense that Washington politics will prevent any real solutions from emerging. On the other side of the ledger is the potential energy boom, the universities that attract the world's best and brightest, the unique ability to commercialize innovations, a cheaper currency, and the potential that the U.S., in the words of Australian Foreign Minister Bob Carr, is "only one budget deal away" from ending all the talk of decline. The single most important thing the U.S. can do to enhance its influence overseas is to get its domestic house in order.

The management of the domestic economy is so important because one of the central priorities for the U.S. in Asia is to demonstrate a sense of staying power. A large number of the tensions with China in recent years are rooted in the Chinese perception that the U.S. is in decline—

a view that was almost uniform in 2008 and which is still strong today. The best way to sway Chinese behavior and to deter adventurism is to demonstrate that the U.S. is not going anywhere. That means maintaining a robust military presence in the region, although without the sort of rapid buildup that would provoke China. It also means constructing a convincing long-term economic agenda that ties the U.S. to Asia.

A second priority is the patient, long-term task of fostering new partners in Asia and elsewhere who will support a U.S.-led order. The core ideas that the U.S. has promoted since the end of the Second World War—free trade, freedom of navigation, and open government— remain popular. But in a world where American dominance is being replaced by a more uncertain balance of power, the careful diplomacy of building different coalitions of support will become the deciding factor. The U.S. will sometimes have to take a backseat as other countries pick up the baton, an approach that some might even be inclined to call leading from behind. In Asia, China's belligerence over the past few years has done a lot of America's diplomatic work for it, allowing it to shore up alliances and strengthen other friendships. But even in Asia, managing these alliances will require skillful diplomacy that persuades other countries to do more to defend themselves.

Over time, the U.S. and China will eventually have to find a way to live together in the western Pacific, to establish a middle ground that respects each other's security interests. Before then, there is likely to be a lot of tension, and potentially some brinkmanship. But if Washington is successful in demonstrating staying power and in finding new sources of support, it will be in a much stronger position to influence China's choices and to steer Beijing away from a broader confrontation.

ACKNOWLEDGMENTS

First-time authors always underestimate the amount of effort and time that goes into writing a book, and I was no exception. But along the way, I had the immense good fortune to receive the help of some of the best professionals in the industry. Sarah Chalfant at the Wylie Agency was extremely generous with her time and indispensable with her advice: without her, my initial ideas would never have made it into print. Her colleague James Pullen was also endlessly helpful.

Through Sarah, I was lucky enough to meet Andrew Miller at Knopf, an incisive and perceptive editor, who provided just the right combination of support and pressure that any writer needs. I also owe huge thanks to his colleague Mark Chiusano for all his assistance and comments.

I would like to thank Lionel Barber, the editor of the *Financial Times,* for his indulgence during the writing of the book. I also received enormous help from a number of other colleagues at the *FT,* including Richard McGregor, Demetri Sevastopulo, David Pilling, Jamil Anderlini, and Kathrin Hille. During my years in China, I was fortunate to work closely with a number of Chinese journalists, without whom I really would have been lost and to whom I owe a special thanks—Helena Yu, Zhang Chenhao, Yang Jie, and Zhao Xue.

During the course of my research, I have benefited from the advice and wisdom of countless people, including good friends with whom I have talked regularly and occasional acquaintances whose insights I value highly. They include, in no particular order, Arthur Kroeber, Shi Yinhong, Joerg Wuttke, Jeff Wasserstrom, David Shambaugh, Shen Dingli, Stephanie Kleine-Ahlbrandt, Geoff Wade, Jim Holmes, Zhu

Feng, Bonnie Glaser, Chu Shulong, Chip Gregson, Michael Auslin, Jin Canrong, Mark Leonard, Andrew Small, Mike Green, Zha Daojiong, Paul Haenle, Chris Nelson, and Yan Xuetong.

Finally, I would like to thank my parents, Iain and Anne, for all their help in the early stages and my wife, Angelica, for her love and support. Without her, I really would never have made it through.

NOTES

INTRODUCTION

4 "remarkable symbols of China's defense muscle": http://news.xinhuanet.com/english/2009–10/01/content _ 12146098.htm.

5 the spontaneous greeting was restaged and edited: Geremie Barmé, "Chinese Military Parades," *East Asia Forum*, Oct. 31, 2009.

8 "No nation has ever experienced": Henry Kissinger, *Diplomacy* (New York: Simon & Schuster, 1995), p. 37.

10 "The veneration of an abstract idea": Fareed Zakaria, *The Post-American World* (New York: W. W. Norton, 2008), p. 125.

14 "Wall Street's crack-up": David Roche, "Another Empire Bites the Dust," *Far Eastern Economic Review*, Oct. 2008.

1 CHINA TAKES TO THE NEAR SEAS

21 "This is the most important communication": Walter Isaacson, *Kissinger* (New York: Simon & Schuster, 1992), p. 333.

24 "the great revitalization of the Chinese nation": quoted in Toshi Yoshihara and James R. Holmes, *Red Star over the Pacific* (Annapolis, Md.: Naval Institute Press, 2010), p. 64.

24 "When we look at history": Luo Yuan, "Call from Blue Sea to Protect the Development Interests of the Country," *Liaowang*, Feb. 9, 2009.

25 "Ignoring the oceans": quoted in Robert S. Ross, "China's Naval Nationalism," *International Security*, vol. 34, no. 2 (Fall 2009), pp. 46–81.

25 "Restricting China to the shallow seas": Zhang Wenmu, "Back to Yalta: A Roadmap for Sino-US Relations," *China Security*, issue no. 19, 2012.

28 "I am . . . devouring Captain Mahan's book": quoted in Robert K. Massie, *Dreadnought* (New York: Random House, 1991), p. 75.

28 "really responsible for the German Navy": *New York Times*, Dec. 2, 1914 (accessed at http://www.nytimes.com/learning/general/onthisday/bday/0927.html).

28 "Mahan was one of the causes": quoted in *Makers of Modern Strategy from Machiavelli to the Nuclear Age*, ed. Peter Paret with collaboration of Gordon A. Craig and Felix Gilbert (Princeton, N.J.: Princeton University Press, 1986), p. 474.

28   "A big country that builds": quoted in Yoshihara and Holmes, *Red Star over the Pacific,* p. 20.

29   "His sea power philosophy remains hypnotic": ibid., p. 18.

30   "China is knowingly, operationally and incrementally": transcript available at http://www.china-business-intelligence.com/content/transcript-remarks-capt -james-fanell-pacfleet.

32   "You, the US, take Hawaii East": quoted in Manu Pubby, "China Proposed Division of Pacific, Indian Ocean Regions, We Declined: US Admiral," *The Indian Express,* May 15, 2009.

33   "The commerce and command of the Pacific": quoted in Bruce Cumings, *Dominion from Sea to Sea* (New Haven, Conn.: Yale University Press, 2009), p. 138.

33   "U.S. does not hold its ground in the Pacific": *Lee Kuan Yew: Grand Master's Insights on China, the United States and the World,* interviews and selections by Graham Allison and Robert D. Blackwill (Cambridge, Mass.: MIT Press, 2012), p. 35.

37   "The navy of any great power": Mure Dickie and Kathrin Hille, "Chinese Army Turns on Charm," *Financial Times,* Nov. 16, 2008.

41   "If the U.S. can light a fire": Chris Buckley, "China PLA Officer Urges Challenging U.S. Dominance," *Reuters,* Feb. 28, 2010.

42   "the fundamental anti-Chinese force": Lyle Goldstein, "Chinese Naval Strategy in the South China Sea: An Abundance of Noise and Smoke, but Little Fire," *Contemporary Southeast Asia,* vol. 33, no. 3, p. 330.

45   "Deng had to explain": Ezra F. Vogel, *Deng Xiaoping and the Transformation of China* (Cambridge, Mass.: Harvard University Press, 2011), p. 578.

47   a Chinese "anti-navy": Andrew S. Erickson, U.S. Naval War College, "Are China's Near Seas 'Anti-Navy' Capabilities Aimed Directly at the United States?" June 14, 2012 article (http://www.informationdissemination.net/2012/06/are-chinas -near-seas-anti-navy.html).

48   "We want to spoof them": Spencer Ackerman, "How to Kill China's Carrier-Killer Missile": *Wired,* March 16, 2012.

2   THE LURE OF THE INDIAN OCEAN

52   The Battle of Ramree Island is better known: *Guinness Book of World Records,* 2012.

55   "No great power that has become a strong power": quoted in Robert S. Ross, "China's Naval Nationalism: Sources, Prospects, and the U.S. Response," *International Security,* vol. 34, no. 2 (Fall 2009), p. 69.

56   the same sort of "naval nationalism": ibid., pp. 46–81.

58   formed a "String of Pearls": "China Builds Up Strategic Sea Lanes," *Washington Times,* Jan. 17, 2005.

60   the government had asked China: "Pakistan Turns to China for Naval Base," *Financial Times,* May 22, 2011.

60   A peacetime naval strategy: Alfred Thayer Mahan, *The Influence of Sea Power upon History, 1660–1783* (Boston: Little, Brown, and Company, 1898), p. 22.

60   Secretary of State Hamilton Fish described Hawaii: quoted in Niall Ferguson, *Colossus: The Price of America's Empire* (New York: Penguin, 2004), p. 46.

65   "Rivalry has been a defining element": for more on India's looming naval rivalry with China, see C. Raja Mohan, *Samudra Manthan: Sino-Indian Rivalry in the*

Indo-Pacific (Washington, D.C.: Carnegie Endowment for International Peace, 2012).

3 THE ASIAN BACKLASH

71 **It settled the outstanding land-border disputes:** see M. Taylor Fravel, *Strong Borders, Secure Nation* (Princeton, N.J.: Princeton University Press, 2008).

72 **The mood toward China shifted:** see Joshua Kurlantzick, *Charm Offensive* (New Haven, Conn.: Yale University Press, 2007).

73 **"sometimes looked like a French bedroom farce":** Walter Russell Mead, *Via Meadia,* Sept. 26, 2010 (http://blogs.the-american-interest.com/wrm/2010/09/26/in-the-footsteps-of-the-kaiser-china-boosts-us-power-in-asia).

76 **Zheng He's fifteenth-century armadas:** Louise Levathes, *When China Ruled the Seas* (New York: Simon & Schuster, 1994), p. 20.

78 **"China's neighbors recognized the preponderance":** David C. Kang, *China Rising* (New York: Columbia University Press, 2007), p. 50.

78 **"Creating a community is easy":** Parag Khanna, *The Second World* (New York: Random House, 2008), p. 262.

79 **exercise in "shock and awe":** Geoffrey Wade, "The Zheng He Voyages: A Reassessment," Asian Research Institute working paper no. 31, National University of Singapore, Oct. 2004.

83 **"Japan and China now stand at ground zero":** Yoichi Funabashi, letter, *East Asia Forum,* Oct. 20, 2010.

90 **brings together oil, fish, and the potent nationalism:** see International Crisis Group, "Stirring Up the South China Sea (II)," Asia report no. 229, July 24, 2012.

91 **"China is not the maker of these problems":** Jane Perlez, "Political Worries in U.S. and China Color Obama Aide's Beijing Visit," *New York Times,* July 25, 2012.

91 **"There is no arable land here":** Patrick Boehler, "South China Sea City 'Could Become Chinese Business Hub,'" *Asian Correspondent,* March 10, 2013.

92 **government bureaucracies have overlapping:** see International Crisis Group, "Stirring Up the South China Sea (I)," Asia report no. 223, April 23, 2012.

93 **"Grab what you can on the sea":** ibid.

94 **"China's . . . 'blue-colored land'":** Peng Guangqian, "China's Maritime Rights and Interests," in *Military Activities in the EEZ,* ed. Peter Dutton (Newport, R.I.: U.S. Naval War College, 2010), p. 15.

95 **"core interest":** "Chinese Military Seeks to Extend Its Naval Power," *New York Times,* April 23, 2010.

97 **publicly declare himself a "Monroista":** Tereza Maria Spyer Dulci, "O pan-americanismo em Joaquim Nabuco e Olivera Lima," *Anais Eletrônicos do VII Encontro Internacional da ANPHLAC,* 2006.

100 **a role somewhat similar to France's:** David Uren, "Shifting Sands of Diplomacy," *Australian,* June 2, 2012.

100 **"while also preparing to deploy force":** "US Embassy Cables: Hillary Clinton Ponders US Relationship with Its Chinese 'Banker,'" *Guardian,* Dec. 4, 2010.

101 **"we are just an independent arts organisation":** "Chinese Hack Film Festival Site," *BBC News,* July 26, 2009 (news.bbc.co.uk/2/hi/8169123.stm).

101 **"America faces a choice of Euclidian clarity":** Hugh White, "Power Shift: Australia's Future Between Washington and Beijing," *Quarterly Essay,* issue no. 39, Sept. 2010.

102 **"the single, stupidest strategic document"**: Greg Sheridan, "Distorted Vision of Future US-China Relations," *Australian*, Sept. 11, 2010.

103 **A caption at the Shaanxi History Museum**: Ross Terrill, *The New Chinese Empire* (New York: Basic Books, 2003), p. 45.

105 **Hanoi had been "too soft" on China**: "Patriotic Personalities Make Proposals on Defense and Development," *Vietnamnet*, July 16, 2011.

4 AMERICA'S CHOICE

115 **cover story for *The Atlantic***: Robert Kaplan, "How We Would Fight China," *Atlantic*, June 1, 2005.

116 **"we own the sea"**: CNO's Sailing Directions, Sept. 27, 2011.

117 **"blinding campaign"**: AirSea Battle: A Point-of-Departure Operational Concept, Center for Strategic and Budgetary Assessments, May 2010.

117 **in the event of a conflict**: "Joint Operational Access Concept," Department of Defense, Jan. 17, 2012.

118 **"preposterously expensive"**: Greg Jaffe, "U.S. Model for a Future War Fans Tensions with China and Inside Pentagon, *Washington Post*, August 1, 2012.

120 **"war limited by contingent"**: Toshi Yoshihara and James R. Holmes, "Asymmetric Warfare, American Style," *U.S. Naval Institute Proceedings Magazine*, vol. 138, no. 4 (April 2012), p. 1310.

120 **In the event of a broader conflict**: see T. X. Hammes, "Offshore Control: A Proposed Strategy for an Unlikely Conflict," strategic forum no. 278, National Defense University, June 28, 2012.

122 **"big, expensive, vulnerable"**: Henry Hendrix, "At What Cost a Carrier?" Center for a New American Security Disruptive Defense Papers, March 2013.

133 **"I informed the government"**: "Eleven CEO: Amazing Changes in Myanmar," *Nation* (Thailand), May 14, 2012.

134 **"an explicit American project"**: Henry Kissinger, *On China* (New York: Penguin, 2011), p. 526.

135 **U.S. military has reopened links**: Joshua Kurlantzick, "The Moral and Strategic Blindspot in Obama's Pivot to Asia," *New Republic*, Nov. 20, 2012.

136 **he visited Washington at the invitation of the Johnson administration**: Thant Myint-U, *Where China Meets India: Burma and the New Crossroads of Asia* (New York: Farrar, Straus and Giroux, 2011).

5 CHINA'S BRITTLE NATIONALISM

142 **China's pre-Olympics burst of learning English**: Evan Osnos, "Crazy English," *The New Yorker*, Apr. 28, 2008.

142 **posted pictures on the Internet**: "American Woman Gives Domestic Abuse a Face, and Voice, in China," NPR, Feb. 7, 2013.

144 **"The West is central to the construction"**: Peter Hays Gries, *China's New Nationalism: Pride, Politics, and Diplomacy* (Berkeley: University of California Press, 2004), p. 35.

146 **Elgin had been dispatched to China**: Elgin's time in China is particularly well told in Stephen R. Platt, *Autumn in the Heavenly Kingdom* (New York: Alfred A. Knopf, 2012), pp. 25–32, 164–68.

147 **"We have often acted towards the Chinese"**: ibid., p. 29.

149 "I am familiar with the history of foreign aggression": quoted in Suzanne Xiao Yang, *China in the UN Security Council Decision-Making on Iraq* (New York: Routledge, 2013), p. 218.

150 To mark the 150th anniversary: William A. Callahan, *China: The Pessoptimist Nation* (Oxford, U.K.: Oxford University Press, 2010), p. 38.

151 "It is 1999, not 1899": Han Zhongkun, "China, Not in 1899," *People's Daily*, May 12, 1999.

152 blind nationalism and anti-foreigner sentiment: Yuan Weishi, "Modernization and History Textbooks," *Freezing Point*, Jan. 11, 2006 (trans. available at http://www.zonaeuropa.com/20060126 _ 1.htm).

153 "It would not be an exaggeration": Callahan, *China*, p. 28.

154 "youth, internationalism, and violence": Rana Mitter, *A Bitter Revolution: China's Struggle with the Modern World* (New York: Oxford University Press, 2005), p. 11.

155 the State Department classified its copy: Jonathan Fenby, *Generalissimo: Chiang Kai-Shek and the China He Lost* (New York: Free Press, 2003), p. 401.

155 "as familiar to Chinese schoolchildren": Paul Cohen, *Speaking to History: The Story of King Goujian in Twentieth-Century China* (Berkeley: University of California Press, 2009), p. xix.

163 "The humiliations of the past": Ian Buruma, "Why They Hate Japan," *New York Review of Books*, Sept. 21, 2006.

164 "How could Japanese imperialism dare": Kirk A. Denton, "Heroic Resistance and Victims of Atrocity: Negotiating the Memory of Japanese Imperialism in Chinese Museums," *Japan Focus*, Oct. 17, 2007.

165 "It was an extraordinary outpouring": Interview with James Miles (http://www.cnn.com/2008/WORLD/asiapcf/03/20/tibet.miles.interview/index.html).

166 "The question that now faces China's leaders": Robert Barnett, "Thunder from Tibet," *New York Review of Books*, May 29, 2008.

172 "simultaneous superficiality and depth": quoted in Paul A. Cohen, *China Unbound: Evolving Perspectives on the Chinese Past* (London: Routledge Curzon, 2003), p. 164.

6 SOFT POWER

176 "While our media empires are melting away": David Barboza, "China Puts Best Face Forward in New English-Language Channel," *New York Times*, July 2, 2010.

177 "lost the whole game due to a flaw in its soft power": quoted in *Chinese Soft Power and Its Implications for the United States*, ed. Carola McGiffert (Washington, D.C.: CSIS, 2009), p. 13.

179 what he calls "humane authority": Yan Xuetong, *Ancient Chinese Thought, Modern Chinese Power*, ed. Daniel Bell and Sun Zhe (Princeton, N.J.: Princeton University Press, 2011), chaps. 1–3.

179 "battle for the hearts and minds": Yan Xuetong, "How China Can Defeat America," *New York Times*, Nov. 20, 2011.

180 "The Chinese have always prided themselves": Wang Gungwu, "China Rises Again," *YaleGlobal*, March 25, 2009.

181 Zhao Tingyang is more oblique: see Zhao Tingyang, "A Political World Philosophy in Terms of All-Under-Heaven (Tian-Xia)," *Diogenes*, vol. 221 (2009), pp. 5–18.

182   **"to love China, to long for China"**: Interview with Zhang Jigang, trans. *China Digital Times* from *PLA Times*, Aug. 1, 2008 (http://chinadigitaltimes.net/2008/08/interview-with-zhang-jigang-deputy-director-of-the-beijing-olympics-opening-ceremony/).

184   **"If Westerners feel dazed and confused"**: Nicolai Ouroussoff, "In Changing Face of Beijing, a Look at the New China," *New York Times*, July 13, 2008.

184   **"the most serious challenge"**: Ian Buruma, "China's Dark Triumph," *Los Angeles Times*, Jan. 13, 2008.

188   **"What we are left with"**: Robert Bridge, "America: Drugged Up, Dumbed Down and Crazy Dangerous," *Russia Today*, June 21, 2012.

193   **"Right now, foreigners are awarding Liu Xiaobo"**: Barbara Demick, "Chinese Dissident in U.S. Tells of Harassment, Torture," *Los Angeles Times*, Jan. 18, 2012.

196   **"a cause of a psychological disorder"**: Julia Lovell, *The Politics of Cultural Capital: China's Quest for a Nobel Prize in Literature* (Honolulu: University of Hawai'i Press, 2006), p. 4.

197   **"'Mo Yan is a state writer'"**: quoted in Didi Kirsten Tatlow, "The Writer, the State and the Nobel," *International Herald Tribune*, Oct. 12, 2012.

7 "WE ARE NOT THE WORLD'S SAVIOR"

201   **If the twentieth century saw fierce ideological battles:** see James Traub, "The World According to China," *New York Times*, Sept. 3, 2006.

202   **"an intense desire among humiliated peoples"**: Pankaj Mishra, "America's Inevitable Retreat from the Middle East," *New York Times*, Sept. 23, 2012.

204   **"the most significant adjustment to national sovereignty"**: quoted in Lloyd Axworthy and Allan Rock, "The Unfulfilled Promise of UN Protection," *Globe and Mail*, Sept. 15, 2010.

208   **"Syria tells us that the era of humanitarian intervention"**: Michael Ignatieff, "How Syria Divided the World," *New York Review of Books*, July 11, 2012.

208   **she was known as Estela:** Simon Romero, "Leader's Torture in the '70s Stirs Ghosts in Brazil," *New York Times*, Aug. 4, 2012.

215   **he presented his Chinese hosts with two documents:** first told in International Crisis Group, "China's New Courtship in South Sudan," Africa report no. 186, April 4, 2012.

220   **Two Chinese engineers were on hand:** Jon Lee Anderson, "A History of Violence," *New Yorker*, July 23, 2012.

220   **the partition of Sudan was only the start:** see ICG, "China's New Courtship in South Sudan."

221   **"We are bystanders"**: ibid.

8 TAKING ON THE DOLLAR

228   **"We could be on the verge of a financial revolution"**: Robert Cookson and Geoff Dyer, "Currencies: Yuan Direction," *Financial Times*, Dec. 13, 2010.

228   **"the premier reserve currency"**: Arvind Subramanian, "Renminbi Rules: The Conditional Imminence of the Reserve Currency Transition," Peterson Institute for International Economics, working paper 11-14, Sept. 2011.

229   **"The real challenge to American and Western strategy"**: Edward Luttwak, "National Strategy: The Turning Point," Sept. 8, 2010 (http://www.abc.net.au/unleashed/29746.html).

229 **"the fall of the dollar as the global reserve currency"**: National Intelligence Council, "Global Trends 2030: Alternative Worlds." Dec. 10, 2012.

232 **"How do you deal toughly with your banker?"**: Ewen MacAskill, "WikiLeaks: Hillary Clinton's Question: How Can We Stand Up to Beijing?" *Guardian,* Dec. 4, 2010.

232 **"Never before has the United States"**: Brad Setser, "China's $1.5 Trillion Bet," Council on Foreign Relations working paper, May 2009.

233 **"bargaining chip"**: Michael Pettis, "The 'Nuclear Threat' of Chinese Reserves," Aug. 8, 2007 (http://www.mpettis.com/2007/08/08/the-nuclear-threat-of-chinese-reserves/).

233 **"I won't say *kowtow*"**: James Fallows, "Be Nice to the Countries That Lend you Money," *The Atlantic Monthly,* Dec. 1, 2008.

235 **The harsh reality for China:** see Daniel W. Drezner, "Bad Debts: Assessing China's Financial Influence in Great Power Politics," vol. 34, no. 2 (Fall 2009) *International Security,* pp. 7–45.

236 **"disconnected to individual nations"**: Zhou Xiaochuan: "Reform the International Monetary System: Essay by Dr. Zhou Xiaochuan, Governor of the People's Bank of China," March 23, 2009 (http://www.bis.org/review/r090402c.pdf).

237 **"the financial crisis . . . let us clearly see"**: Geoff Dyer, David Pilling, and Henny Sender, "A Strategy to Straddle the Planet," *Financial Times,* Jan. 17, 2011.

237 **"The shortcomings of the current"**: quoted in Alan Wheatley, "China's Currency Foray Augurs Geopolitical Strains," Reuters, Oct. 3, 2012.

237 **"China becoming a nuclear power"**: quoted in "Redbacks for Greenbacks: Internationalising the Renminbi," European Council on Foreign Relations (http://ecfr.eu/content/entry/redbacks_for_greenbacks_the_internationalision_of_the_renminbi).

241 **just one decade after the bill was passed:** Barry Eichengreen, *Exorbitant Privilege* (New York: Oxford University Press, 2011), chap. 2.

243 **With the value of sterling plummeting:** ibid., p. 29.

9 POST-AMERICAN GLOBALIZATION

253 **"Fate has written our policy for us"**: quoted in Howard Zinn, *The Twentieth Century: A People's History* (New York: HarperCollins, 1980), p. 4.

256 **"There is an enormous highway developing"**: interview with Charlie Rose, Feb. 8, 2010 (http://www.charlierose.com/download/transcript/10851).

259 **he realized there was a huge opportunity for China:** see Erica Downs, *Inside China Inc* (Washington, D.C.: Brookings Institution, 2011).

262 **"China was getting a discount on finance the country needed":** see also Deborah Brautigam, *The Dragon's Gift: The Real Story of China in Africa* (Oxford, U.K.: Oxford University Press, 2011).

262 **one of the company's computers would send a large packet:** the Nortel hacking case was first detailed in Siobhan Gorman, "Chinese Hackers Suspected in Long-Term Nortel Breach," *Wall Street Journal,* Feb. 14, 2012.

263 **"What has been happening"**: Michael Riley and John Walcott, "China-Based Hacking of 760 Companies Shows Cyber Cold War," Bloomberg, Dec. 14, 2011.

268 **presented Chávez with a six-hundred-page book:** Henry Sanderson and Michael Forsythe, "Hugo's Banker," *Foreign Policy,* March 7, 2013.

CONCLUSION

277   **"We are not complacent"**: "China Unveils New Leadership Team with Xi at the Helm," *Agence Presse France*, Nov. 15, 2012.

278   **"only one budget deal away"**: Maggie Haberman, "With Bob Carr's Permission," *Politico*, July 22, 2012.

BIBLIOGRAPHIC ESSAY

There is a rich literature that provides the background for the impact of China on Asia's politics and military balance. The expansion of China's influence during the period from the Asia crisis of the 1990s to the 2008 financial crisis is described in different and interesting ways in David Shambaugh, *China Goes Global: The Partial Power* (New York: Oxford University Press, 2013); David C. Kang, *China Rising* (New York: Columbia University Press, 2007); and Joshua Kurlantzick, *Charm Offensive* (New Haven, Conn.: Yale University Press, 2007). Ross Terrill's *The New Chinese Empire* (New York: Basic Books, 2003) provides rich insights into China's historical legacy in the region. Hugh White's essay "Power Shift" (*Quarterly Essay,* issue no. 39, Sept. 2010), which lays out many of the strategic issues now facing the region in a lucid manner, has been published in book form as *The China Choice* (Collingwood, Australia: Black Inc., 2012).

The growing strategic importance of the Indian Ocean is beautifully told in Robert D. Kaplan, *Monsoon: The Indian Ocean and the Future of American Power* (New York: Random House, 2010). China's complex links with Burma are outlined by Thant Myint-U in *Where China Meets India: Burma and the New Crossroads of Asia* (New York: Farrar, Straus and Giroux, 2011). The single best source for information on maritime disputes involving China is the reports of the International Crisis Group, notably "Stirring Up the South China Sea" (pt. I, Asia report no. 223, April 2012; pt. II, Asia report no. 229, July 2012).

The US Naval War College's James R. Holmes and Toshi Yoshihara have produced a series of writings over the last decade that lift the lid on China's growing naval fascination, including *Red Star over the Pacific* (Annapolis, Md.: Naval Institute Press, 2010). Their colleague at the Naval War College Andrew S. Erickson is another source of great insight into the capabilities of the Chinese military (his writings are collected at www.andrewerickson.com).

China's revival of "national humiliation" education is well told by both William A. Callahan in *The Pessoptimist Nation* (Oxford: Oxford University Press, 2010) and Zheng Wang in *Never Forget National Humiliation* (New York: Columbia University Press, 2012). For the growth in nationalism over the last two decades, see also Peter Hays Gries, *China's New Nationalism* (Berkeley: University of California Press, 2004), and Christopher R. Hughes, *Chinese Nationalism in the Global Era* (New York: Routledge, 2004). For the debates at the UN over Sudan and the "Responsibility to Protect," see James Traub, *The Best Intentions: Kofi Annan and the UN in the Era of American World Power* (New York: Farrar, Straus and Giroux, 2006).

The risk of imperial overstretch has been widely chronicled over the last few decades, from Paul Kennedy's *The Rise and Fall of the Great Powers* (New York: Random House, 1987) to David P. Calleo's *The Imperious Economy* (Cambridge, Mass.: Harvard University Press, 1982). But the best introduction to the contemporary dilemmas facing the U.S. dollar and the Chinese renminbi is Barry Eichengreen's *Exorbitant Privilege* (New York: Oxford University Press, 2011).

INDEX

Page numbers beginning with 283 refer to endnotes.

"axis of evil" rhetoric of, 84
Iraq War and, 190

Cairo, 190, 249
Tahrir Square in, 188
Calcutta, 51, 146
California software and design industries, 21
Callahan, William, 153–4
Calleo, David, 231
Cambodia, 124, 135, 203
Cam Ranh naval base, 109
Canada, 110, 250, 263
Canberra, 98–100, 102
Cao Rulin, 154
capitalism, 201, 248, 255
Cardoso, Fernando Henrique, 209
Caribbean Sea, 28, 45, 60
Carr, Bob, 278
Carrefour, 168–9
CCTV America, 185, 187–91
Center for Strategic and Budgetary
Assessments, 117, 119
Central Military Commission (China), 41, 45
Chan, Melissa, 191
Chang, Iris, 163
Charter 08 pro-democracy petition, 192
Chávez, Hugo, 200, 260–1, 268
Cheney, Dick, 231
Chengdu, 34–5, 189
Cheng Li, 36
Chen Guangcheng, 233
Chen Shaokuan, 55
Chen Yonglin, 100
Chen Yuan, 258–9, 268
Chen Yun, 258
Cheonan, 85–8
Chevron, 254
Chiang Kai-shek, 89, 154–5
Chiang Kai-shek, Madame (Soong Meiling), 155
Chicago, Ill., 145, 274
Chile, 27, 97, 104, 127, 209, 230
China, Imperial, 74–81, 162
Ming dynasty of, 75, 77, 79–80, 103, 146, 150, 153
Qing dynasty of, 4, 146–8, 150, 152–3
Warring States period of, 155–6
Western exploitation and humiliation of, 25, 36, 145–56, 161, 167–8, 205, 253
China, People's Republic of, 3–15
ancient ethical and moral traditions of, 179–82
Anhui Province in, 158
authoritarianism of, 9, 211
censorship in, 35, 152, 195
Communist revolution and 1949 victory of, 150, 155, 161, 178, 195
conspiratorial view of, 61, 90–1, 194, 248
continental size of, 20, 94
creativity suppressed in, 14–15

cultural and intellectual influence of, 77–8, 79, 107–98
Cultural Revolution in, 148, 149, 152, 171, 178–81, 192
cyberwar capabilities of, 38, 48–9, 117, 262–6, 273, 289
decades of inward focus and restraint of, 6, 9, 10, 11–12, 73, 179
defense spending of, 4, 9, 11, 23, 44–8, 53–8, 277
demonizing and exoticizing of, 11
domestic violence in, 142–3
economic blackmail in foreign disputes by, 31
economic reforms in, 7, 11, 144, 161, 236, 245, 247–8, 251, 267
education in, 141–5, 150–3, 155–6, 170–3, 179
energy needs of, 10, 26, 51–3, 61–3, 121
English speaking in, 141–5, 170
entrepreneurism in, 40, 259
era of economic isolation in, 90
exchange rate controversy in, 247–8
expanding overseas interests of, 215–23
film industry of, 101
"first island chain" barrier around, 25, 28, 60, 120
fishing industry of, 90
focus on economic development of, 6, 9–10, 11, 12
foreign criticism of, 6, 11, 43, 127, 204, 207–8
foreign-currency reserves of, 234, 277, 289
foreign development and investments of, 13, 51–3, 61–4, 252–62, 273–5
foreign exports of, 22, 31, 90, 234, 245, 252–3, 273
foreign imports of, 10, 21, 22, 26, 31, 52, 201, 234
foreign policy of, 6–7, 9–10, 11, 36, 39, 63–6, 69–109, 179, 182, 199–223
founding of, 3
fragmentation of power in, 9, 36, 92
global ambitions of, 9, 10, 11, 14–15, 30–1, 55, 67, 176–7, 179
gross domestic product (GDP) of, 61–2, 176
Guangsi Province in, 104
Heilongjiang Province in, 178
human rights offenses in, 11, 13
insecurity and paranoia in, 3–4, 10–11, 25–6, 28, 170
intelligence services of, 264
isolationist rhetoric in, 64–5
Jiangxi Province in, 20, 113
local government in, 36, 61, 63, 92
manufacturing in, 21, 22, 31, 39
Maoist era in, 19, 36, 71, 85–7, 90, 149, 161
map of, viii–ix
middle class in, 9, 36, 142, 154

A NOTE ABOUT THE AUTHOR

GEOFF DYER is a journalist for the *Financial Times* and has been a correspondent in China, the U.S., and Brazil. He is the recipient of a Fulbright award and of several journalism awards, including one Society of Publishers in Asia award for a series of 2010 opinion pieces about China's role in the world. He studied at Cambridge University and the Johns Hopkins School of Advanced International Studies. He lives with his family in Washington, D.C.